2016
SUN SIGN
BOOK

Forecasts by

Kim Rogers-Gallagher

Cover Design by Kevin R. Brown
Editing by Andrea Neff
Background with Sunflower: iStockphoto.com/26602837/© Cobalt88
Sunflower: iStockphoto.com/nick73
Interior Zodiac Icons: iStockphoto.com/Trillingstudio

Copyright 2015 Llewellyn Publications
ISBN: 978-0-7387-3403-3
A Division of Llewellyn Worldwide Ltd., www.llewellyn.com
Llewellyn is a registered trademark of Llewellyn Worldwide Ltd.
2143 Wooddale Drive, Woodbury, MN 55125
Printed in the USA

Contents

2015

SEPTEMBER
S	M	T	W	T	F	S
		1	2	3	4	5
6	7	8	9	10	11	12
13	14	15	16	17	18	19
20	21	22	23	24	25	26
27	28	29	30			

OCTOBER
S	M	T	W	T	F	S
				1	2	3
4	5	6	7	8	9	10
11	12	13	14	15	16	17
18	19	20	21	22	23	24
25	26	27	28	29	30	31

NOVEMBER
S	M	T	W	T	F	S
1	2	3	4	5	6	7
8	9	10	11	12	13	14
15	16	17	18	19	20	21
22	23	24	25	26	27	28
29	30					

DECEMBER
S	M	T	W	T	F	S
		1	2	3	4	5
6	7	8	9	10	11	12
13	14	15	16	17	18	19
20	21	22	23	24	25	26
27	28	29	30	31		

2016

JANUARY
S	M	T	W	T	F	S
					1	2
3	4	5	6	7	8	9
10	11	12	13	14	15	16
17	18	19	20	21	22	23
24	25	26	27	28	29	30
31						

FEBRUARY
S	M	T	W	T	F	S
	1	2	3	4	5	6
7	8	9	10	11	12	13
14	15	16	17	18	19	20
21	22	23	24	25	26	27
28	29					

MARCH
S	M	T	W	T	F	S
		1	2	3	4	5
6	7	8	9	10	11	12
13	14	15	16	17	18	19
20	21	22	23	24	25	26
27	28	29	30	31		

APRIL
S	M	T	W	T	F	S
					1	2
3	4	5	6	7	8	9
10	11	12	13	14	15	16
17	18	19	20	21	22	23
24	25	26	27	28	29	30

MAY
S	M	T	W	T	F	S
1	2	3	4	5	6	7
8	9	10	11	12	13	14
15	16	17	18	19	20	21
22	23	24	25	26	27	28
29	30	31				

JUNE
S	M	T	W	T	F	S
			1	2	3	4
5	6	7	8	9	10	11
12	13	14	15	16	17	18
19	20	21	22	23	24	25
26	27	28	29	30		

JULY
S	M	T	W	T	F	S
					1	2
3	4	5	6	7	8	9
10	11	12	13	14	15	16
17	18	19	20	21	22	23
24	25	26	27	28	29	30
31						

AUGUST
S	M	T	W	T	F	S
	1	2	3	4	5	6
7	8	9	10	11	12	13
14	15	16	17	18	19	20
21	22	23	24	25	26	27
28	29	30	31			

SEPTEMBER
S	M	T	W	T	F	S
				1	2	3
4	5	6	7	8	9	10
11	12	13	14	15	16	17
18	19	20	21	22	23	24
25	26	27	28	29	30	

OCTOBER
S	M	T	W	T	F	S
						1
2	3	4	5	6	7	8
9	10	11	12	13	14	15
16	17	18	19	20	21	22
23	24	25	26	27	28	29
30	31					

NOVEMBER
S	M	T	W	T	F	S
		1	2	3	4	5
6	7	8	9	10	11	12
13	14	15	16	17	18	19
20	21	22	23	24	25	26
27	28	29	30			

DECEMBER
S	M	T	W	T	F	S
				1	2	3
4	5	6	7	8	9	10
11	12	13	14	15	16	17
18	19	20	21	22	23	24
25	26	27	28	29	30	31

2017

JANUARY
S	M	T	W	T	F	S
1	2	3	4	5	6	7
8	9	10	11	12	13	14
15	16	17	18	19	20	21
22	23	24	25	26	27	28
29	30	31				

FEBRUARY
S	M	T	W	T	F	S
			1	2	3	4
5	6	7	8	9	10	11
12	13	14	15	16	17	18
19	20	21	22	23	24	25
26	27	28				

MARCH
S	M	T	W	T	F	S
			1	2	3	4
5	6	7	8	9	10	11
12	13	14	15	16	17	18
19	20	21	22	23	24	25
26	27	28	29	30	31	

APRIL
S	M	T	W	T	F	S
						1
2	3	4	5	6	7	8
9	10	11	12	13	14	15
16	17	18	19	20	21	22
23	24	25	26	27	28	29
30						

MAY
S	M	T	W	T	F	S
	1	2	3	4	5	6
7	8	9	10	11	12	13
14	15	16	17	18	19	20
21	22	23	24	25	26	27
28	29	30	31			

JUNE
S	M	T	W	T	F	S
				1	2	3
4	5	6	7	8	9	10
11	12	13	14	15	16	17
18	19	20	21	22	23	24
25	26	27	28	29	30	

JULY
S	M	T	W	T	F	S
						1
2	3	4	5	6	7	8
9	10	11	12	13	14	15
16	17	18	19	20	21	22
23	24	25	26	27	28	29
30	31					

AUGUST
S	M	T	W	T	F	S
		1	2	3	4	5
6	7	8	9	10	11	12
13	14	15	16	17	18	19
20	21	22	23	24	25	26
27	28	29	30	31		

Meet Kim Rogers-Gallagher

Kim fell in love with astrology in grade school and began her formal education close to thirty years ago. She's written hundreds of articles and columns for magazines and online publications, contributed to several astrological anthologies, and has two books of her own to her credit, *Astrology for the Light Side of the Brain* and *Astrology for the Light Side of the Future*, both available from ACS/Starcrafts Publishing. Kim is the author of daily e-mail horoscopes for astrology.com, and her work appears in the introductory sections of *Llewellyn's Astrology Calendar*, *Llewellyn's Witches' Datebook*, and *Llewellyn's Witches' Calendar*.

At the moment, Kim is having great fun on her Facebook page, facebook.com/KRGFenix, where she turns daily transits into fun celestial adventures. She's a well-known speaker who's been part of the UAC (United Astrology Conference) faculty since 1996 and has lectured at many other international conferences.

An avid animal lover, Kim occasionally receives permission from her seriously spoiled fur-kids (and her computer) to leave home for a while and indulge her ninth-house Sagg Sun by traveling for "work"— that is, talking to groups about astrology (which really isn't work at all). In typical Sagg style, Kim loves to laugh, but she also loves to chat, which comes in handy when she does private phone consultations.

She is a twenty-year "citizen" of Pennsic, an annual medieval event, where she gets to dress up in funny clothes, live in a tent, and pretend she's back in the 1300s for two weeks every year—which, oddly enough, is her idea of a good time.

Kim can be contacted at KRGPhoenix313@yahoo.com for fees regarding readings, classes, and lectures.

New Concepts for Zodiac Signs

The signs of the zodiac represent characteristics and traits that indicate how energy operates within our lives. The signs tell the story of human evolution and development, and all are necessary to form the continuum of whole-life experience. In fact, all twelve signs are represented within your astrological chart.

Although the traditional metaphors for the twelve signs (such as Aries, the Ram) are always functional, these alternative concepts for each of the twelve signs also describe the gradual unfolding of the human spirit.

Aries: The Initiator is the first sign of the zodiac and encompasses the primary concept of getting things started. This fiery ignition and bright beginning can prove to be the thrust necessary for new life, but the Initiator also can appear before a situation is ready for change and create disruption.

Taurus: The Maintainer sustains what Aries has begun and brings stability and focus into the picture, yet there also can be a tendency to try to maintain something in its current state without allowing for new growth.

Gemini: The Questioner seeks to determine whether alternatives are possible and offers diversity to the processes Taurus has brought into stability. Yet questioning can also lead to distraction, subsequently scattering energy and diffusing focus.

Cancer: The Nurturer provides the qualities necessary for growth and security, and encourages a deepening awareness of emotional needs. Yet this same nurturing can stifle individuation if it becomes too smothering.

Leo: The Loyalist directs and centralizes the experiences Cancer feeds. This quality is powerfully targeted toward self-awareness, but can be shortsighted. Hence, the Loyalist can hold steadfastly to viewpoints or feelings that inhibit new experiences.

Virgo: The Modifier analyzes the situations Leo brings to light and determines possibilities for change. Even though this change may be in the name of improvement, it can lead to dissatisfaction with the self if not directed in harmony with higher needs.

Libra: The Judge is constantly comparing everything to be sure that a certain level of rightness and perfection is presented. However, the Judge can also present possibilities that are harsh and seem to be cold or without feeling.

Scorpio: The Catalyst steps into the play of life to provide the quality of alchemical transformation. The Catalyst can stir the brew just enough to create a healing potion, or may get things going to such a powerful extent that they boil out of control.

Sagittarius: The Adventurer moves away from Scorpio's dimension to seek what lies beyond the horizon. The Adventurer continually looks for possibilities that answer the ultimate questions, but may forget the pathway back home.

Capricorn: The Pragmatist attempts to put everything into its rightful place and find ways to make life work out right. The Pragmatist can teach lessons of practicality and determination, but can become highly self-righteous when shortsighted.

Aquarius: The Reformer looks for ways to take what Capricorn has built and bring it up to date. Yet there is also a tendency to scrap the original in favor of a new plan that may not have the stable foundation necessary to operate effectively.

Pisces: The Visionary brings mysticism and imagination, and challenges the soul to move beyond the physical plane, into the realm of what might be. The Visionary can pierce the veil, returning enlightened to the physical world. The challenge is to avoid getting lost within the illusion of an alternate reality.

Astrology Basics

Astrology is an ancient and continually evolving system used to clarify your identity and your needs. An astrological chart—which is calculated using the date, time, and place of birth—contains many factors that symbolically represent the needs, expressions, and experiences that make up the whole person. A professional astrologer interprets this symbolic picture, offering you an accurate portrait of your personality.

The chart itself—the horoscope—is a portrait of an individual. Generally, a natal (or birth) horoscope is drawn on a circular wheel. The wheel is divided into twelve segments, called houses. Each of the twelve houses represents a different aspect of the individual, much like the facets of a brilliantly cut stone. The houses depict different environments, such as home, school, and work. The houses also represent roles and relationships: parents, friends, lovers, children, partners. In each environment, individuals show a different side of their personality. At home, you may represent yourself quite differently than you do on the job. Additionally, in each relationship you will project a different image of yourself. For example, your parents may rarely see the side you show to intimate friends.

Symbols for the planets, the Sun, and the Moon are drawn inside the houses. Each planet represents a separate kind of energy. You experience and express each energy in specific ways. The way you use each of these energies is up to you. The planets in your chart do not make you do anything!

Signs of the Zodiac

The twelve signs of the zodiac indicate characteristics and traits that further define your personality. Each sign can be expressed in positive and negative ways. What's more, you have all twelve signs somewhere in your chart. Signs that are strongly emphasized by the planets have greater force. The Sun, Moon, and planets are placed on the chart according to their position at the time of birth. The qualities of a sign, combined with the energy of a planet, indicate how you might be most likely to use that energy and the best ways to develop that energy. The signs add color, emphasis, and dimension to the personality.

The Twelve Signs

Aries	♈	The Initiator
Taurus	♉	The Maintainer
Gemini	♊	The Questioner
Cancer	♋	The Nurturer
Leo	♌	The Loyalist
Virgo	♍	The Modifier
Libra	♎	The Judge
Scorpio	♏	The Catalyst
Sagittarius	♐	The Adventurer
Capricorn	♑	The Pragmatist
Aquarius	♒	The Reformer
Pisces	♓	The Visionary

Signs are also placed at the cusps, or dividing lines, of each of the houses. The influence of the signs on the houses is much the same as their influence on the Sun, Moon, and planets. Each house is shaped by the sign on its cusp.

When you view a horoscope, you will notice that there appear to be four distinct angles dividing the wheel of the chart. The line that divides the chart into a top and bottom half represents the horizon. In most cases, the left side of the horizon is called the Ascendant. The zodiac sign on the Ascendant is your rising sign. The Ascendant indicates the way others are likely to view you.

The Sun, Moon, or a planet can be compared to an actor in a play. The sign shows how the energy works, like the role the actor plays in a drama. The house indicates where the energy operates, like the setting of a play. On a psychological level, the Sun represents who you think you are. The Ascendant describes who others think you are, and the Moon reflects your emotional self.

Astrologers also study the geometric relationships between the Sun, Moon, and planets. These geometric angles are called aspects. Aspects further define the strengths, weaknesses, and challenges within your physical, mental, emotional, and spiritual selves. Sometimes patterns also appear in an astrological chart. These patterns have meaning.

To understand cycles for any given point in time, astrologers study several factors. Many use transits, which refer to the movement and positions of the planets. When astrologers compare those positions to the birth horoscope, the transits indicate activity in particular areas of the chart. The *Sun Sign Book* uses transits.

As you can see, your Sun sign is just one of many factors that describe who you are—but it is a powerful one! As the symbol of the ego, the Sun in your chart reflects your drive to be noticed. Most people can easily relate to the concepts associated with their Sun sign, since it is tied to their sense of personal identity.

Meanings of the Planets

The Sun

The Sun indicates the psychological bias that will dominate your actions. What you see, and why, is told in the reading for your Sun. The Sun also shows the basic energy patterns of your body and psyche. In many ways, the Sun is the dominant force in your horoscope and your life. Other influences, especially that of the Moon, may modify the Sun's influence, but nothing will cause you to depart very far from the basic solar pattern. Always keep in mind the basic influence of the Sun and remember all other influences must be interpreted in terms of it, especially insofar as they play a visible role in your life. You may think, dream, imagine, and hope a thousand things, according to your Moon and your other planets, but the Sun is what you are. To be your best self in terms of your Sun is to cause your energies to work along the path in which they will have maximum help from planetary vibrations.

The Moon

The Moon tells the desire of your life. When you know what you mean but can't verbalize it, it is your Moon that knows it and your Sun that can't say it. The wordless ecstasy, the mute sorrow, the secret dream, the esoteric picture of yourself that you can't get across to the world, or that the world doesn't comprehend or value—these are the products of the Moon. When you are misunderstood, it is your Moon nature, expressed imperfectly through the Sun sign, that feels betrayed. Things you know without thought—intuitions, hunches,

The Planets

Sun	☉	The ego, self, willpower
Moon	☽	The subconscious self, habits
Mercury	☿	Communication, the intellect
Venus	♀	Emotional expression, love, appreciation, artistry
Mars	♂	Physical drive, assertiveness, anger
Jupiter	♃	Philosophy, ethics, generosity
Saturn	♄	Discipline, focus, responsibility
Uranus	♅	Individuality, rebelliousness
Neptune	♆	Imagination, sensitivity, compassion
Pluto	♇	Transformation, healing, regeneration

instincts—are the products of the Moon. Modes of expression that you feel truly reflect your deepest self belong to the Moon: art, letters, creative work of any kind; sometimes love; sometimes business. Whatever you feel to be most deeply yourself is the product of your Moon and of the sign your Moon occupies at birth.

Mercury

Mercury is the sensory antenna of your horoscope. Its position by sign indicates your reactions to sights, sounds, odors, tastes, and touch impressions, affording a key to the attitude you have toward the physical world around you. Mercury is the messenger through which your physical body and brain (ruled by the Sun) and your inner nature (ruled by the Moon) are kept in contact with the outer world, which will appear to you according to the index of Mercury's position by sign in the horoscope. Mercury rules your rational mind.

Venus

Venus is the emotional antenna of your horoscope. Through Venus, impressions come to you from the outer world. The position of Venus by sign at the time of your birth determines your attitude toward these experiences. As Mercury is the messenger linking sense impressions (sight, smell, etc.) to the basic nature of your Sun and Moon, so Venus is the messenger linking emotional impressions. If Venus is found in the same sign as the Sun, emotions gain importance in your life and have a direct bearing on your actions. If Venus is in the same sign as the Moon, emotions bear directly on your inner nature, add self-confidence, make you sensitive to emotional impressions, and frequently indicate that you have more love in your heart than you are able to express. If Venus is in the same sign as Mercury, emotional impressions and sense impressions work together; you tend to idealize the world of the senses and sensualize the world of the emotions to interpret what you see and hear.

Mars

Mars is the energy principle in the horoscope. Its position indicates the channels into which energy will most easily be directed. It is the planet through which the activities of the Sun and the desires of the Moon express themselves in action. In the same sign as the Sun, Mars gives abundant energy, sometimes misdirected in temper, temperament, and quarrels. In the same sign as the Moon, it gives a great capacity to make use of the innermost aims, and to make the inner desires articulate and practical. In the same sign as Venus, it quickens emotional reactions and causes you to act on them, makes for ardor and passion in love, and fosters an earthly awareness of emotional realities.

Jupiter

Jupiter is the feeler for opportunity that you have out in the world. It passes along chances of a lifetime for consideration according to the basic nature of your Sun and Moon. Jupiter's sign position indicates the places you will look for opportunity, the uses to which you wish to put it, and the capacity you have to react and profit by it. Jupiter is ordinarily and erroneously called the planet of luck. It is "luck" insofar as it is the index of opportunity, but your luck depends less on what comes to you than on what you do with what comes to you. In the same sign as the Sun or Moon, Jupiter gives a direct and generally effective response to opportunity and is likely to show forth at its "luckiest." If Jupiter is in the same sign as Mercury, sense impressions are interpreted opportunistically. If Jupiter is in the same sign as Venus, you interpret emotions in such a way as to turn them to your advantage; your feelings work harmoniously with the chances for progress that the world has to offer. If Jupiter is in the same sign as Mars, you follow opportunity with energy, dash, enthusiasm, and courage; take big chances; and play your cards wide open.

Saturn

Saturn indicates the direction that will be taken in life by the self-preserving principle that, in its highest manifestation, ceases to be purely defensive and becomes ambitious and aspiring. Your defense or attack against the world is shown by the sign position of Saturn in the horoscope of birth. If Saturn is in the same sign as the Sun or Moon, defense predominates, and there is danger of introversion. The farther Saturn is from the Sun, Moon, and Ascendant, the better for objectivity and extroversion. If Saturn is in the same sign as Mercury, there is a profound and serious reaction to sensory impressions; this position generally accompanies a deep and efficient mind. If Saturn is in the same sign as Venus, a defensive attitude toward emotional experience makes for apparent coolness in love and difficulty with the emotions and human relations. If Saturn is in the same sign as Mars, confusion between defensive and aggressive urges can make a person indecisive. On the other hand, if the Sun and Moon are strong and the total personality well developed, a balanced, peaceful, and calm individual of sober judgment and moderate actions may be indicated. If Saturn is in the same sign as Jupiter, the reaction to opportunity is sober and balanced.

Uranus

Uranus in a general way relates to creativity, originality, or individuality, and its position by sign in the horoscope tells the direction in which you will seek to express yourself. In the same sign as Mercury or the Moon, Uranus suggests acute awareness, a quick reaction to sense impressions and experiences, or a hair-trigger mind. In the same sign as the Sun, it points to great nervous activity, a high-strung nature, and an original, creative, or eccentric personality. In the same sign as Mars, Uranus indicates high-speed activity, love of swift motion, and perhaps love of danger. In the same sign as Venus, it suggests an unusual reaction to emotional experience, idealism, sensuality, and original ideas about love and human relations. In the same sign as Saturn, Uranus points to good sense; this can be a practical, creative position, but more often than not it sets up a destructive conflict between practicality and originality that can result in a stalemate. In the same sign as Jupiter, Uranus makes opportunity, creates wealth and the means of getting it, and is conducive to the inventive, executive, and daring.

Neptune

Neptune relates to the deep subconscious, inherited mentality, and spirituality, indicating what you take for granted in life. Neptune in the same sign as the Sun or Moon indicates that intuitions and hunches—or delusions—dominate; there is a need to rigidly hold to reality. In the same sign as Mercury, Neptune indicates sharp sensory perceptions, a sensitive and perhaps creative mind, and a quivering intensity of reaction to sensory experience. In the same sign as Venus, it reveals idealistic and romantic (or sentimental) reactions to emotional experience, as well as the danger of sensationalism and a love of strange pleasures. In the same sign as Mars, Neptune indicates energy and intuition that work together to make mastery of life—one of the signs of having angels (or devils) on your side. When in the same sign as Jupiter, Neptune describes an intuitive response to opportunity along practical and money-making lines. In the same sign as Saturn, Neptune indicates intuitive defense and attack on the world, which is generally successful unless Saturn is polarized on the negative side; then there is danger of unhappiness.

Pluto

Pluto is a planet of extremes, from the lowest criminal and violent level of our society to the heights people can attain when they realize their significance in the collectivity of humanity. Pluto also rules three important mysteries of life—sex, death, and rebirth—and links them to each other. One level of death symbolized by Pluto is the physical death of an individual, which occurs so that a person can be reborn into another body to further his or her spiritual development. On another level, individuals can experience a "death" of their old self when they realize the deeper significance of life; thus they become one of the "second born." In a natal horoscope, Pluto signifies our perspective on the world, our conscious and subconscious. Since so many of Pluto's qualities are centered on the deeper mysteries of life, the house position of Pluto, and aspects to it, can show you how to attain a deeper understanding of the importance of the spiritual in your life.

Astrological Glossary

Air: One of the four basic elements. The air signs are Gemini, Libra, and Aquarius.

Angles: The four points of the chart that divide it into quadrants. The angles are sensitive areas that lend emphasis to planets located near them. These points are located on the cusps of the first, fourth, seventh, and tenth houses in a chart.

Ascendant: Rising sign. The degree of the zodiac on the eastern horizon at the time and place for which the horoscope is calculated. It can indicate the image or physical appearance you project to the world. The cusp of the first house.

Aspect: The angular relationship between planets, sensitive points, or house cusps in a horoscope. Lines drawn between the two points and the center of the chart, representing the earth, form the angle of the aspect. Astrological aspects include the conjunction (two points that are 0 degrees apart), opposition (two points, 180 degrees apart), square (two points, 90 degrees apart), sextile (two points, 60 degrees apart), and trine (two points, 120 degrees apart). Aspects can indicate harmony or challenge.

Cardinal Sign: One of the three qualities, or categories, that describe how a sign expresses itself. Aries, Cancer, Libra, and Capricorn are the cardinal signs, believed to initiate activity.

Chiron: Chiron is a comet traveling in orbit between Saturn and Uranus. It is believed to represent a key or doorway, healing, ecology, and a bridge between traditional and modern methods.

Conjunction: An aspect or angle between two points in a chart where the two points are close enough so that the energies join. Can be considered either harmonious or challenging, depending on the planets involved and their placement.

Cusp: A dividing line between signs or houses in a chart.

Degree: Degree of arc. One of 360 divisions of a circle. The circle of the zodiac is divided into twelve astrological signs of 30 degrees each. Each degree is made up of 60 minutes, and each minute is made up of 60 seconds of zodiacal longitude.

Earth: One of the four basic elements. The earth signs are Taurus, Virgo, and Capricorn.

Eclipse: A Solar Eclipse is the full or partial covering of the Sun by the Moon (as viewed from the earth), and a Lunar Eclipse is the full or partial covering of the Moon by the earth's own shadow.

Ecliptic: The Sun's apparent path around the earth, which is actually the plane of the earth's orbit extended out into space. The ecliptic forms the center of the zodiac.

Electional Astrology: A branch of astrology concerned with choosing the best time to initiate an activity.

Elements: The signs of the zodiac are divided into four groups of three zodiacal signs, each symbolized by one of the four elements of the ancients: fire, earth, air, and water. The element of a sign is said to express its essential nature.

Ephemeris: A listing of the Sun, Moon, and planets' positions and related information for astrological purposes.

Equinox: Equal night. The point in the earth's orbit around the Sun at which the day and night are equal in length.

Feminine Signs: Each zodiac sign is either "masculine" or "feminine." Earth signs (Taurus, Virgo, and Capricorn) and water signs (Cancer, Scorpio, and Pisces) are feminine.

Fire: One of the four basic elements. The fire signs are Aries, Leo, and Sagittarius.

Fixed Signs: Fixed is one of the three qualities, or categories, that describe how a sign expresses itself. The fixed signs are Taurus, Leo, Scorpio, and Aquarius. Fixed signs are said to be predisposed to existing patterns and somewhat resistant to change.

Hard Aspects: Hard aspects are those aspects in a chart that astrologers believe to represent difficulty or challenges. Among the hard aspects are the square, the opposition, and the conjunction (depending on which planets are conjunct).

Horizon: The word *horizon* is used in astrology in a manner similar to its common usage, except that only the eastern and western horizons are considered useful. The eastern horizon at the point of birth is the

Ascendant, or first house cusp, of a natal chart, and the western horizon at the point of birth is the Descendant, or seventh house cusp.

Houses: Division of the horoscope into twelve segments, beginning with the Ascendant. The dividing line between two houses is called a house cusp. Each house corresponds to certain aspects of daily living, and is ruled by the astrological sign that governs the cusp, or dividing line between the house and the one previous.

Ingress: The point of entry of a planet into a sign.

Lagna: A term used in Hindu or Vedic astrology for Ascendant, the degree of the zodiac on the eastern horizon at the time of birth.

Masculine Signs: Each of the twelve signs of the zodiac is either "masculine" or "feminine." The fire signs (Aries, Leo, and Sagittarius) and the air signs (Gemini, Libra, and Aquarius) are masculine.

Midheaven: The highest point on the ecliptic, where it intersects the meridian that passes directly above the place for which the horoscope is cast; the southern point of the horoscope.

Midpoint: A point equally distant to two planets or house cusps. Midpoints are considered by some astrologers to be sensitive points in a person's chart.

Mundane Astrology: Mundane astrology is the branch of astrology generally concerned with political and economic events, and the nations involved in these events.

Mutable Signs: Mutable is one of the three qualities, or categories, that describe how a sign expresses itself. Mutable signs are Gemini, Virgo, Sagittarius, and Pisces. Mutable signs are said to be very adaptable and sometimes changeable.

Natal Chart: A person's birth chart. A natal chart is essentially a "snapshot" showing the placement of each of the planets at the exact time of a person's birth.

Node: The point where the planets cross the ecliptic, or the earth's apparent path around the Sun. The North Node is the point where a planet moves northward, from the earth's perspective, as it crosses the ecliptic; the South Node is where it moves south.

Opposition: Two points in a chart that are 180 degrees apart.

Orb: A small degree of margin used when calculating aspects in a chart. For example, although 180 degrees form an exact opposition, an astrologer might consider an aspect within 3 or 4 degrees on either side of 180 degrees to be an opposition, as the impact of the aspect can still be felt within this range. The less orb on an aspect, the stronger the aspect. Astrologers' opinions vary on how many degrees of orb to allow for each aspect.

Outer Planet: Uranus, Neptune, and Pluto are known as the outer planets. Because of their distance from the Sun, they take a long time to complete a single rotation. Everyone born within a few years on either side of a given date will have similar placements of these planets.

Planet: The planets used in astrology are Mercury, Venus, Mars, Jupiter, Saturn, Uranus, Neptune, and Pluto. For astrological purposes, the Sun and Moon are also considered planets. A natal chart, or birth chart, lists planetary placements at the moment of birth.

Planetary Rulership: The sign in which a planet is most harmoniously placed. Examples are the Sun in Leo, Jupiter in Sagittarius, and the Moon in Cancer.

Precession of Equinoxes: The gradual movement of the point of the spring equinox, located at 0 degrees Aries. This point marks the beginning of the tropical zodiac. The point moves slowly backward through the constellations of the zodiac, so that about every 2,000 years the equinox begins in an earlier constellation.

Qualities: In addition to categorizing the signs by element, astrologers place the twelve signs of the zodiac into three additional categories, or qualities: cardinal, mutable, or fixed. Each sign is considered to be a combination of its element and quality. Where the element of a sign describes its basic nature, the quality describes its mode of expression.

Retrograde Motion: The apparent backward motion of a planet. This is an illusion caused by the relative motion of the earth and other planets in their elliptical orbits.

Sextile: Two points in a chart that are 60 degrees apart.

Sidereal Zodiac: Generally used by Hindu or Vedic astrologers. The sidereal zodiac is located where the constellations are actually positioned in the sky.

Soft Aspects: Soft aspects indicate good fortune or an easy relationship in the chart. Among the soft aspects are the trine, the sextile, and the conjunction (depending on which planets are conjunct each other).

Square: Two points in a chart that are 90 degrees apart.

Sun Sign: The sign of the zodiac in which the Sun is located at any given time.

Synodic Cycle: The time between conjunctions of two planets.

Trine: Two points in a chart that are 120 degrees apart.

Tropical Zodiac: The tropical zodiac begins at 0 degrees Aries, where the Sun is located during the spring equinox. This system is used by most Western astrologers and throughout this book.

Void-of-Course: A planet is void-of-course after it has made its last aspect within a sign but before it has entered a new sign.

Water: One of the four basic elements. The water signs are Cancer, Scorpio, and Pisces.

Using This Book

This book contains what is called Sun sign astrology; that is, astrology based on the sign that your Sun was in at the time of your birth. The technique has its foundation in ancient Greek astrology, in which the Sun was one of five points in the chart that were used as focal points for delineation.

The most effective way to use astrology, however, is through one-on-one work with a professional astrologer, who can integrate the eight or so other astrological bodies into the interpretation to provide you with guidance. There are factors related to the year and time of day you were born that are highly significant in the way you approach life and vital to making wise choices. In addition, there are ways of using astrology that aren't addressed here, such as compatibility between two specific individuals, discovering family patterns, or picking a day for a wedding or grand opening.

To best use the information in the monthly forecasts, you'll want to determine your Ascendant, or rising sign. If you don't know your Ascendant, the tables following this description will help you determine your rising sign. They are most accurate for those born in the continental United States. They provide only an approximation, but can be used as a good rule of thumb. Your exact Ascendant may vary from the tables according to your time and place of birth. Once you've approximated your ascending sign using the tables or determined your Ascendant by having your chart calculated, you'll know two significant factors in your chart. Read the monthly forecast sections for both your Sun and Ascendant to gain the most useful information. In addition, you can read the section about the sign your Moon is in. The Sun is the true, inner you; the Ascendant is your shell or appearance and the person you are becoming; the Moon is the person you were—or still are based on habits and memories.

Also included in the monthly forecasts is information about the planets' retrogrades. Most people have heard of "Mercury retrograde." In fact, all the planets except the Sun and Moon appear to travel backward (retrograde) in their path periodically. This appears to happen only because we on the earth are not seeing the other planets from the middle of the solar system. Rather, we are watching them from our own moving object. We are like a train that moves past cars on the freeway that are going at a slower speed. To us on the train, the cars look like they're going backward. Mercury turns retrograde about every four months for three weeks; Venus every eighteen months for six weeks; Mars every two years for two to three months. The rest of the planets each retrograde once a year for four to five months. During each retrograde, we have the opportunity to try something new, something we conceived of at the beginning of the planet's yearly cycle. The times when the planets change direction are significant, as are the beginning and midpoint (peak or culmination) of each cycle. These are noted in your forecast each month.

The "Rewarding Days" and "Challenging Days" sections indicate times when you'll feel either more centered or more out of balance. The rewarding days are not the only times you can perform well, but the times you're likely to feel better integrated! During challenging days, take extra time to center yourself by meditating or using other techniques that help you feel more objective.

The Action Table found at the end of each sign's section offers general guidelines for the best times to take particular actions. Please note, however, that your whole chart will provide more accurate guidelines for the best time to do something. Therefore, use this table with a grain of salt, and never let it stop you from taking an action you feel compelled to take.

You can use this information to gain an objective awareness about the way the current cycles are affecting you. Realize that the power of astrology is even more useful when you have a complete chart and professional guidance.

Ascendant Table

Your Sun Sign	Your Time of Birth					
	6–8 am	8–10 am	10 am–Noon	Noon–2 pm	2–4 pm	4–6 pm
Aries	Taurus	Gemini	Cancer	Leo	Virgo	Libra
Taurus	Gemini	Cancer	Leo	Virgo	Libra	Scorpio
Gemini	Cancer	Leo	Virgo	Libra	Scorpio	Sagittarius
Cancer	Leo	Virgo	Libra	Scorpio	Sagittarius	Capricorn
Leo	Virgo	Libra	Scorpio	Sagittarius	Capricorn	Aquarius
Virgo	Libra	Scorpio	Sagittarius	Capricorn	Aquarius	Pisces
Libra	Scorpio	Sagittarius	Capricorn	Aquarius	Pisces	Aries
Scorpio	Sagittarius	Capricorn	Aquarius	Pisces	Aries	Taurus
Sagittarius	Capricorn	Aquarius	Pisces	Aries	Taurus	Gemini
Capricorn	Aquarius	Pisces	Aries	Taurus	Gemini	Cancer
Aquarius	Pisces	Aries	Taurus	Gemini	Cancer	Leo
Pisces	Aries	Taurus	Gemini	Cancer	Leo	Virgo

	Your Time of Birth					
Your Sun Sign	6–8 pm	8–10 pm	10 pm–Midnight	Midnight–2 am	2–4 am	4–6 am
Aries	Scorpio	Sagittarius	Capricorn	Aquarius	Pisces	Aries
Taurus	Sagittarius	Capricorn	Aquarius	Pisces	Aries	Taurus
Gemini	Capricorn	Aquarius	Pisces	Aries	Taurus	Gemini
Cancer	Aquarius	Pisces	Aries	Taurus	Gemini	Cancer
Leo	Pisces	Aries	Taurus	Gemini	Cancer	Leo
Virgo	Aries	Taurus	Gemini	Cancer	Leo	Virgo
Libra	Taurus	Gemini	Cancer	Leo	Virgo	Libra
Scorpio	Gemini	Cancer	Leo	Virgo	Libra	Scorpio
Sagittarius	Cancer	Leo	Virgo	Libra	Scorpio	Sagittarius
Capricorn	Leo	Virgo	Libra	Scorpio	Sagittarius	Capricorn
Aquarius	Virgo	Libra	Scorpio	Sagittarius	Capricorn	Aquarius
Pisces	Libra	Scorpio	Sagittarius	Capricorn	Aquarius	Pisces

How to use this table: 1. Find your Sun sign in the left column.

2. Find your approximate birth time in a vertical column.

3. Line up your Sun sign and birth time to find your Ascendant.

This table will give you an approximation of your Ascendant. If you feel that the sign listed as your Ascendant is incorrect, try the one either before or after the listed sign. It is difficult to determine your exact Ascendant without a complete natal chart.

2016 at a Glance

Saturn will continue his march through Sagittarius all year, putting this "just-the-facts-ma'am" energy in the mood for a laugh. More and more, we'll tend to get our news from humorists and political satirists who don't pull any punches, à la Sagittarius, a sign that's nothing if not blunt. In this expansive sign, Saturn will also draw our attention to news of a global nature. This no-nonsense planet will call on leaders in the fields of religion, politics, education, and international finance to account for their actions, and since Sagittarius doesn't keep secrets well, anyone who hasn't been forthright will be called to task. This planet/sign combination will also come in handy as we continue to revamp our laws and societal traditions to better fit the people we are today, as opposed to who we were when those laws were written.

And speaking of calling to task, intense, perceptive Pluto will continue to dig up the facts from his position in Capricorn, the sign that's the personal property of Saturn. With Pluto in Saturn's sign, unearthing and exposing the untruths told to us en masse will continue to go on throughout the year. Our collective awareness will be running on high, and we'll want serious answers to serious questions—global warming in particular.

Now, startling Uranus is technically no longer in a square aspect to Pluto, but that doesn't mean the tension between them has gone away. This square has been going on for years, pitting Uranus—who wants change and wants it now—against Pluto—who's a big fan of change, but only when you know everything you need to make a sound decision. The good news is that in this action-oriented aspect, genius and perceptivity go hand in hand. Uranus is a whiz with electronics, computers, and the like, so we can expect to see more remarkable inventions of a futuristic nature—many of which will be downright unbelievable. Our quest for adventure on other planets will pick up speed, and as always, when Uranus is in the neighborhood wearing a sign as impulsive and spontaneous as Aries, surprising finds are probable rather than just possible.

Neptune will continue on her path through her very own sign of Pisces, inspiring inventions of a wireless nature. Neptune dissolves boundaries and rules all things ethereal, by the way—like "the Cloud," for example. Now, this planet also rules water, so droughts and water shortages may still concern us, especially since factual Saturn will spend several months squaring off with her. The good news is that Neptune's real mission is to pull us all together under a common cause, and although she doesn't move fast, she doesn't fool around. Anything that threatens our ability to connect with one another will gradually disappear.

2016 SUN SIGN BOOK

Forecasts by

Kim Rogers-Gallagher

Aries

The Ram
March 20 to April 19

♈

Element: Fire	Glyph: Ram's head
Quality: Cardinal	Anatomy: Head, face, throat
Polarity: Yang/masculine	Colors: Red, white
Planetary Ruler: Mars	Animal: Ram
Meditation: I build upon my strengths	Myths/Legends: Artemis, Jason and the Golden Fleece
Gemstone: Diamond	House: First
Power Stones: Bloodstone, carnelian, ruby	Opposite Sign: Libra
Key Phrase: I am	Flower: Geranium
	Keyword: Initiative

The Aries Personality

Your Strengths and Challenges

You, Aries, are the first sign of the zodiac, which means you're basically the infant of the zodiac—and that certainly does explain a lot. After all, when infants don't have what they need, they create quite a fuss until the situation is remedied. So while you might not throw temper tantrums on a daily basis, you are most certainly an expert at getting the attention you need to obtain just about anything you want. That doesn't mean you're not totally charming and endearing—after all, what's not to love about someone who is totally honest and upfront about their feelings at all times? The thing is, deceit takes time and planning, and you, Aries, have no patience for that sort of thing. It's a waste of time and energy, and you cherish both too much to waste them.

Your modus operandi is simple: point A to point B. Period. The end. Roadblocks will not be tolerated, and any type of obstacle will be plowed through immediately. The thing is, your ruling planet is Mars, the ancient God of War, an extremely assertive, aggressive, and often quite angry fellow, and you're named after Ares, his Greek counterpart. Needless to say, when you're riled up, you're quite intimidating. When you're not, however, you're also pretty darn intimidating. You're famous for being impatient, and the longer you're made to wait—regardless of why—the more others can feel the emotional steam you're putting out. The good news is that all you really need to do to get over the whole situation is to vent—but it's got to be a big-time vent. You'll yell or at the very least speak quite sternly, but once you know your point has been made, you're done being angry. For all these reasons, it's easy to see why your energy has often been likened to a bullet. You move in a straight line, you have no time to waste, and once it's over, it's over. You crave adrenaline, so exciting experiences are your forte and impulsive playmates are a must. Your mission is to slow down long enough to consider your target and aim before you fire.

Your Relationships

You tend to be pretty darn choosy when it comes to selecting a primary other, Aries, mostly because you're not just looking for a lover. When you consider taking on a partner, it's not just because they appeal to you physically (although that's a good part of it). It's mostly because they've proven themselves to be a friend and a confidant—and, most importantly, a worthy opponent. You're the child of Mars, so it's in your nature to be a warrior, and anyone who can't deal with a few fireworks every now and then simply won't qualify for the position. Truth be told, you enjoy sparring with your sweetheart. If it ever turns physical, however, that's your warning sign. Fiery is fun, but volatile is dangerous. You need to avoid anyone who pushes your buttons in the wrong way—and you know exactly what that means.

You're feisty, but you're also worth the effort, because you have no choice but to be honest with those you're involved with. Deceit is too time-consuming for your impulsive nature, so you're generally quite trustworthy. Besides, in your opinion, if you have to lie to someone to make them happy, it's just not right between the two of you, and the situation should be ended, posthaste. It's not that you don't care, but only that you can see things right away that most of us might miss.

In partnerships, you tend to do best with someone who is fiery and impulsive but also sensible—not easy qualities to come by in one neat package. For that reason, the other three fire signs will often catch your fancy, because they share your love of adventure and new experiences. In the long run, you might begin to think of Leo as high-maintenance, and you do enjoy the spotlight yourself every now and then; so if you're signing up with a lion, be sure they're willing to share the applause of the crowd. Sagittarians make great playmates and lovers, and the air signs (Gemini, Libra, and Aquarius) are always fun and quite appealing. Their curiosity and willingness to try anything once are two qualities you absolutely must have in a long-term companion.

Your Career and Money

Fire is your element, Aries, so occupations that involve dealing with it are well suited to your nature. Firefighting is a natural match. After all, who other than you and your fire-sign cousins would run toward a fire rather than away from it? Welding is also a good match. The thing is, you feel entirely comfortable around the element of fire. You understand it, so it's only natural that you'd make your living dealing with it. Fire also rules the spiritual side of life, however, so if you're not happy and fulfilled wherever you're working, your time there will feel like a jail sentence. Life is too short for that, Aries, as you well know. Fortunately, if you've had it with your current occupation, unpredictable Uranus will see to it this year that you are presented with opportunities to free yourself up and head off for greener, more exciting pastures.

Your sign also rules tools made of iron and steel, so surgery is often your calling—but if the sight of blood makes you queasy, remember that florists wield knives every day as well, as do hair stylists. Whatever you do, your only mission is to be sure that you can exert your energy in a positive way. Your sign rules the muscles in the physical body, so working as an exercise trainer or coach would also suit you just fine.

Your Lighter Side

What's fun, Aries? Well, how about riding your motorcycle—standing up, on one leg—en route to your weekly skydiving lesson? If you're not of a certain age, danger might appeal to you, but if you've been there, done that, and tossed the t-shirt, then an action movie will do the trick—provided there are car chases, explosions, and nonstop thrills. Truth be told, anything that allows you to exert energy—from hiking to exercising to...well, more tender activities—will allow your feisty spirit to come alive, again and again. Not that you'd want this secret to be made public, but you also enjoy a good, old-fashioned argument every now and again—followed by a good, old-fashioned making-up session.

Affirmation
I believe in myself and acknowledge my strengths.

The Year Ahead for Aries

Your ruling planet, fiery Mars, will spend an unusually long time this year in Sagittarius, a fire-sign cousin of yours that you've always gotten on well with. Sagittarius energy blends nicely with your own, since this sign is always game for a new adventure and always ready to take off with you at a moment's notice. That said, from March 5 through May 27 and again from August 2 through September 27, Mars will be storming through your solar ninth house, where long-distance travel, new adventures, and educational experiences are handled. Needless to say, your thirst for adrenaline might just take you to some distant shores—and you'll love every minute of it. With career-minded Saturn also on duty in this house and this sign, you might even be able to mix business with pleasure. From March 25 through August 13, Saturn will be moving retrograde, which signals that it's time to review, redo, and return, so you might be taking a trip back home or to one of your old stomping grounds. You might also return to school to brush up on your skills or amp up your resumé.

Now, from May 27 through August 2, Mars will retrace his steps through intense Scorpio and your solar eighth house of joint resources, finances, and intimate partnerships. You might feel as if you're reliving the events of late February, so a loan may need to be paid back, an inheritance might need your attention—or an old lover might resurface. If that's the case, be careful. Don't go back unless you know you have new solutions to old problems. On the other hand, since this house also indicates how we deal with loss, something you lost and thought was gone forever could be returned to you—and wouldn't that be nice!

Jupiter will spend most of the year in your solar sixth house of work and health, all done up in meticulous Virgo. Jupiter expands the qualities of the sign he inhabits, so your attention to detail on the job will probably surprise even you. This is a terrific year to begin a new health regime, if you haven't already, and since Jupiter will also do the retrograde dance from January through May, getting back to the gym or possibly even returning to an old job might also be on the agenda.

On September 9, the fun begins, when Jupiter sets off for charming, personable Libra and your solar seventh house of one-to-one relationships. If you're already attached at that time, you two will probably begin a very, very good year together—during which, more than once, you'll congratulate yourself on your good taste in partners. If you're single, prepare yourself for a veritable parade of admirers interested in capturing your heart.

What This Year's Eclipses Mean for You

Eclipses occur every six months, ordinarily in pairs, and this year is no exception. In March, the cycle will begin for 2016, featuring a Solar Eclipse on the 8th in ultrasensitive and highly intuitive Pisces, which will directly affect your solar twelfth house of secrets and subconscious thoughts. If you're hiding anything, it will stay hidden for a while, but not forever. Plan on bringing the issue to the surface by September 16, when a Lunar Eclipse will shine its light on this very private area, exposing what was previously hidden. The good news is that if you have been trying to gain information about a certain someone, all that digging you're doing now will bring you results by mid-September. As per usual for you, waiting won't be easy, but it will be well worth it. Sit tight.

The first Lunar Eclipse of the year will arrive on March 23, illuminating partner-oriented Libra and your solar seventh house of one-to-one relationships. If you were born during the first few days of your sign, you will feel this eclipse most intensely, especially if you have been dealing with a relationship issue that seems to be unsolvable. The good news is that it isn't. The tough part will be committing to a decision that has long-lasting effects. The best news is that if you can actually compromise, you two might be able to work things out. The key is to be totally honest.

The second series of eclipses will begin on September 1 as the Solar Eclipse in health-oriented Virgo sets up shop in your solar sixth house of health and work-oriented relationships. This powerful meeting of the Sun and the Moon will prompt you to consider new beginnings, so if you aren't happy with your physical self or your diet, and your exercise habits are not to your liking, it's time to fix things. Get busy and make some serious changes, ASAP. If you're already on a good diet and exercise plan and you'd simply like to step up your game, this is the time to do it. Virgo energy is all about getting healthy—or healthier—and getting things in order, and with expansive, generous Jupiter willing to pass out some blessings from his spot in this same sign, just a bit of physical effort will earn you some wonderful results and inspire you to invest a lot more time and energy in the project.

The final eclipse of the year will be a supercharged Full Moon, set to arrive on September 16, all done up in woozy, dreamy Pisces. Now, Lunar Eclipses illuminate matters that were previously hidden, without much warning and quickly, too. Since this is your solar twelfth house of Privacy, Please, while you might actually want to keep just a bit of your personal life to yourself—especially if you've been enjoying the romantic fantasy—you should keep in mind that Full Moons don't allow us that privilege. If you want to keep something quiet, keep away from it for a few weeks. No, it won't be easy, but other than breaking the news to the world, it's your best bet.

Saturn

Saturn moved into Sagittarius and your solar ninth house of long-distance relationships back in 2015, Aries, and while you're ordinarily quite fond of Sagittarius energy, Saturn is a tough customer and pretty darn hard to please. That said, if you're planning on indulging in ninth-house activities, such as travel or education, you should be prepared to pay your dues before you're allowed to pass Go and collect your 200 dollars. Unlike generous Jupiter, Saturn gives us what we deserve—nothing more and nothing less—so whatever comes your way now will be exactly what you've earned. The good news is that whatever Saturn bestows is permanent, so you won't need to worry about the carpet being pulled out from under you down the road. His gifts are long-lasting, so raises, promotions, and the ability to further yourself in your chosen field via fortunate connections are all possibilities.

Of course, since Saturn also has a lot to do with geography and geographical roadblocks, it might be that scheduling a trip or vacation has been tough, to say the least. Still, if you're determined, serious Saturn will be only too happy to help you make plans to be with someone you love—although in typical Saturnian style, it will not happen overnight and you may have to jump through a few hoops. Think about it, though. Anything worth having really is worth working for.

Uranus

This startling, unpredictable guy has been on duty in your sign and your solar first house of personality and appearance for years now, Aries, and since he's impulsive and you're impulsive, you've definitely raised some eyebrows over that period—and you'll raise some more this year. The thing is, Uranus enjoys shocking and amazing the masses by going against the status quo and rebelling, and so do you, so with this energy added to your own, it's not hard to imagine you suddenly deciding on a Saturday afternoon that you'd like to live on a beach in Bali—and sitting on that beach by Monday morning. Before you hop on that plane, or quit your day job, or dash off to Vegas to get married, you might want to consider the effect of what you're doing over the long haul. Yes, Vegas and Bali are delightful, and yes, those adventures would be fun to talk about, but please do consider the consequences of your actions—just this once—before you do anything too drastic. No one is saying you can't exercise your right to be free and enjoy life any way you see fit, but planning for at least five years down the road wouldn't be a bad idea. You might even find a happy balance between staying put and taking off for destinations unknown. Put your things in storage and consider this phase an extended vacation.

Neptune

Neptune reminds me of Glinda, the Good Witch, from *The Wizard of Oz*. She arrives in a pink bubble, waves her wand, and promises to make everything perfect for Dorothy and the Munchkins. And then she disappears. So when Neptune arrives by transit, you can count on feeling a whole lot like Dorothy—not to mention Toto—because you'll feel as if you're protected, but whoever or whatever is protecting you will be tough to pin down. That said, since Neptune is in Pisces, the sign right next door to your own, her influence by semisextile won't be all that potent unless you were born between March 27 and April 4. In that case, you'll most definitely have the feeling that you're not in Kansas anymore—or wherever you were when you started this journey. Much like Dorothy, however, you're going to learn a lot in the process, through symbolism and "coincidental" encounters with others. Your mission is to be kind to whoever or whatever you meet along the way home. You'll feel as if you've been gone for a bit when this transit is over, but when you wake up, you'll realize that you were right there in your room the whole time—and that guardian angels were by your side every step of the way. In the meantime, avoid the tendency to escape from the harsher side of life via Neptunian escape hatches like drugs or alcohol, and if you feel a bit blue, talk to a professional.

Pluto

Just as he has for the past eight years, Pluto will spend the year in Capricorn and your solar tenth house of career matters, reputation, and dealings with authority figures. If you were born between April 3 and 8, this powerful planet will form a square with your Sun—which can be a very tricky aspect. Squares are irritating. They push us into action to relieve tension and settle matters that call for closure. In your case, a power struggle that's been going on behind the scenes for some time might actually rear its testy little head, and this time around, you won't be able to ignore it or pretend you're imagining things. Pluto asks us to take control of our lives, and from his spot in this professionally minded house, you might have a bit of trouble with a higher-up or superior who seems to have it in for you. This applies to other authority figures as well, by the way. If you finally decide that your buttons have been pushed one too many times, you might decide to walk away, and it will probably be shortly before Halloween. Your mission is to resist the urge to burn your bridges before you cross them. Make sure you have a plan B—then let 'em have it! This is the time to consider becoming your own boss but not necessarily quitting your day job right away. Investigate your options.

Aries | January

Relaxation and Recreation

Venus will spend most of the month in your solar ninth house of travel, education, and new experiences, Aries, all done up in Sagittarius—one of your favorite signs because it's always game for an adventure. Your new experience might just include a lovely new admirer with a terrific accent, so if you're single, keep an ear out!

Lovers and Friends

Mercury will stop in his tracks on January 5 to turn retrograde and bring an old friend back into your life, probably under unusual or surprising circumstances—and you two will feel as if only a day has passed, regardless of how long it's been. The Sun will set off for this sign and house on January 20, too, so group activities will be at the top of your priority list.

Money and Success

January 29 could mark a turning point in your career and professional life, Aries, thanks to a powerful conjunction between Mercury and Pluto. Keep in mind that when these two planets come together, they play for keeps, so if you're at all doubtful about your plans, wait a while and be sure you've considered absolutely everything.

Tricky Transits

Venus and Jupiter will get into an exciting square on January 17, Aries, linking the Queen of Comfort with the King of Excess. You could be on the receiving end of an outpouring of love and attention from a long-distance dear one—but you might end up partying with them and end up over-indulging in at least one department. Ah, well. Every now and then...

Rewarding Days

1, 6, 8, 12, 14, 17, 30

Challenging Days

3, 5, 18, 20, 25, 31

Aries | February

Relaxation and Recreation

If you feel lucky around February 9, a lottery ticket or a few hours at a casino might be fun. The thing is, Venus and Jupiter will form an easy trine in earth signs, so luck will be in the air. Just don't get crazy and lose the mortgage money. Take a limited amount of cash along and hand over the plastic to someone who won't give it back.

Lovers and Friends

Just in time for a delightful Valentine's Day, generous, expansive Jupiter will form a comfy trine with the emotional Moon in sensual Taurus, the sign that most loves creature comforts. We'll all be in the mood to snuggle up and be sweet, but in your case, Aries, you might also be thinking of doing a bit of shopping for your Valentine. Careful! You know how generous Jupiter can be!

Money and Success

Venus and Saturn will come together on February 29 to bring you some wonderful career news. The potential is there for a new job, a new position within your current place of employment, or the chance to learn an entirely new skill. You'll be in the mood to strike out on your own, and with Saturn on board and in a good mood, all the lights are green.

Tricky Transits

A mixed bag of energies on February 6 could be a tad confusing, Aries, and a long-distance missive might be the reason. A sudden change in a financial or romantic situation is on the agenda, too—but not to worry. You'll be initiating that change, and with an easy trine between chatty Mercury and optimistic Jupiter, communicating will be a breeze. Just be gentle.

Rewarding Days
3, 4, 6, 25, 26, 29

Challenging Days
5, 7, 27

Aries | March

Relaxation and Recreation

Allow yourself a long weekend on March 10, when several planets in Pisces will lull even ultra-active you into sitting still—and maybe even taking a nap or two! You'll need the rest, because by the end of the month the Sun and Mercury will join electric Uranus in your sign, and once again the chase for adrenaline will be on.

Lovers and Friends

With charming Venus passing through your solar eleventh house of friendships and group activities, Aries, there is really no way you can avoid meeting some wonderful new kindred spirits—provided, of course, that you get yourself to the places where they gather. On March 7, the Moon and Venus will join forces in that same spot to help you connect with a new BFF.

Money and Success

Venus and Neptune will be in woozy, dreamy Pisces when they collide on March 20, Aries, and since Venus rules money and Neptune isn't too keen on details, you'll need to keep a vigilant eye on your money situation. That goes for cash—which you should be careful not to misplace or lose—as well as your plastic and checkbook. Check your balances before you head out to shop.

Tricky Transits

The Lunar Eclipse on March 23 will occur in your solar seventh house of one-to-one relationships, Aries, all done up in partner-oriented Libra. Now, this lunation means business, so even if serious Saturn weren't standing still with his arms folded, facing off with Jupiter, you still might feel the need to make your point—forcefully, and for the very last time.

Rewarding Days
2, 6, 16, 19, 21, 26

Challenging Days
3, 4, 13, 14, 23, 25

Aries | April

Relaxation and Recreation

Just in time to inspire you to be a trickster, playful Mercury will collide with startling Uranus—both of them in your impulsive, fiery sign and your solar first house of appearance and personality. Needless to say, you'll be in the mood to pull some April Fools' jokes on someone close to you—and heaven knows you're quite inventive. Go easy, now!

Lovers and Friends

The weekend of April 1 looks like great fun, Aries—and not just because it's April Fools' Day. It seems that the Moon will spend her time in your solar eleventh house of friendships and group affiliations, all done up in impetuous Aquarius and set to make contact with no less than five planets. The usual suspects will be on hand, but expect some interesting newcomers, too.

Money and Success

If you've been trying to find the perfect time to chat with a higher-up who can advance your career, Aries, try to schedule it around April 5. Talkative Mercury will be in Taurus, the sign of the money magnet, and Venus will have just moved into your sign. Oh, and the Sun, also in your sign, will hook up with Saturn, from whence all professional boons come. Any questions?

Tricky Transits

Forget about April 1. It's April 9 when you should expect surprises, Aries. The Sun will collide with shocking Uranus in your sign, just two days after the New Moon plants a seed in that same spot. If it's your birthday, fasten your seat belt. If it's not, fasten it anyway. One never knows what Uranus will cook up, but it won't be boring.

Rewarding Days

2, 3, 9, 12, 14, 18, 30

Challenging Days

4, 6, 10, 15, 16, 19, 27

Aries | May

Relaxation and Recreation
You're a huge fan of adrenaline, Aries, but whether you're willing to admit it or not, every now and then, you truly enjoy it when a relaxing day comes along. Well, get ready for a relaxing month, because up until the Full Moon on May 21, a pack of planets in solid earth signs is going to keep things nice and quiet. Enjoy!

Lovers and Friends
Speaking of relaxing, Aries, look to May 10, 11, and 12 for some really lovely opportunities to lounge around, sleep in, and cuddle up with your sweetheart. Oh, and here's a hint: with all these touch-loving earth energies on duty, getting a room with a hot tub wouldn't be a bad idea. Why not indulge while the Universe is pumping out feel-great energies?

Money and Success
The Sun, Venus, and Mercury will all spend some time in your solar second house of personal finances and other money matters this month, Aries, and they'll be all dolled up in earthy, fertile Taurus, the sign that's most often referred to as a money magnet. If you need to get your financial paperwork together to work out a deal, look to May 12, 13, and 30.

Tricky Transits
Your ruling planet is passionate, assertive Mars, and after spending the month in peace-loving, cooperative Libra, he'll shift gears on May 27 and head off into intense Scorpio—the sign that never, ever forgets an offense and always, always finishes battles that others are foolish enough to start. If you were a tad bored last month because things were going so smoothly, just wait a while.

Rewarding Days
1, 2, 7, 10, 12, 30

Challenging Days
4, 5, 14, 22, 24, 25

Aries | June

Relaxation and Recreation

A pack of planets moving through lighthearted and extremely amusing Gemini this month will activate your usual gift of gab—gab of the assertive kind, mind you. In short, making your point and being confident in your verbal abilities could cause you to forget the feelings of others in favor of winning your arguments. Don't do that. Be a good sport. It's ever so much more satisfying.

Lovers and Friends

A sky full of chatty, friendly, fast-moving Gemini energies will keep you happily occupied this month, Aries, and might even bring along a new admirer, courtesy of a sibling or neighbor, right around the New Moon on June 4. No matter what happened last time, you really should allow them to arrange an introduction. Be brave! Have coffee or lunch.

Money and Success

If you've ever had the urge to teach, this would be a terrific time to investigate what it would take for you to do it. On June 2 and 3, Saturn will get together with the Sun and Venus from his spot in your solar ninth house of education, urging you to either learn something new or pass on what you've learned to others.

Tricky Transits

Someone you've never trusted may reappear, Aries, and even if they seem to be fine now, go with your gut. Some things never change, and some people never change. If your antennae are telling you that the story might be nice but the ending will probably turn out exactly the way it did the last time, don't feel bad about passing. It's called self-protection.

Rewarding Days

8, 11, 13, 26, 27, 29, 30

Challenging Days

2, 3, 4, 9, 17, 20, 22

Aries | July

Relaxation and Recreation

Several planets will pass through your solar fourth house of home, family, and domestic matters, Aries, encouraging you to spend some time at your place with loved ones. Look to July 5 and 6 for the chance to make a dream come true, possibly with regard to owning your own home or redoing your current nest.

Lovers and Friends

What a great month to be you, Aries! Lovely Venus sets off for Leo on July 4, followed by Mercury on July 13, followed by the Sun on July 22—and with all these fiery, fun-loving, and extremely entertaining energies on duty in your playful solar fifth house of lovers and recreation, there's no doubt you're going to be a tired but happy little ram. Enjoy!

Money and Success

Arguments about money matters toward the end of the month will come up quickly, Aries, but they may not be solvable right away. In fact, you may need to do a lot of plotting and planning to ensure the matters go your way. Of course, with your ruler, Mars, all done up in intense, perceptive Scorpio, plotting won't be a problem.

Tricky Transits

On July 7 and 10, Venus and Mercury in family-oriented Cancer will square off with unpredictable Uranus, currently on duty in your sign and your solar first house of personality and appearance. This rebellious fellow has been urging you to rebel, too, so heaven help you if a family member issues a dare. Talk about irresistible!

Rewarding Days

9, 10, 11, 18, 20, 26, 31

Challenging Days

2, 4, 7, 19, 21, 29

Aries | August

Relaxation and Recreation

Your innate urge for adventure will be running on high as of August 2, Aries, thanks to the arrival of your ruler, Mars, into fiery Sagittarius. Now, Sagg planets aren't usually timid—to say the least—and Mars will spend the next couple of months in your solar ninth house of travel and new experiences, so there will be plenty of spontaneous escapades on the agenda.

Lovers and Friends

Bright and early on August 1, the Sun in Leo and your solar fifth house of lovers will contact reliable, dutiful Saturn in Sagittarius. Now, Leo planets love to be in love, but Saturn loves permanence and predictability. Ordinarily, this might sound a bit boring, but as you well know, planets in Sagittarius most definitely aren't boring. Consider taking this thing with your current playmate to the next level.

Money and Success

Oh, boy. Right around August 5 and 6, arguments over money could be on the agenda, Aries, and it looks as if they will be work-related. If you're not being paid what you're worth—and more importantly, what you're supposed to be paid—it's time to let the powers that be know that you're not up for that any longer. Let 'em have it!

Tricky Transits

Your trickiest transit of the month involves your very own ruling planet, Mars, who will collide with serious Saturn on August 24, Aries. Now, this can be a great thing or a troublesome thing, depending on how you handle it. If you're unprepared for a major project, get prepared—and know that if you do your homework, you'll have the stamina and determination to finish up.

Rewarding Days
1, 2, 18, 24, 29

Challenging Days
3, 6, 7, 13, 25, 26

Aries | September

Relaxation and Recreation

With planets making their way through your solar sixth house of work all done up in diligent Virgo, there won't be much time for rest, Aries, and playtime will be tough to come by, too. As of September 22, however, when charming Venus sets off for sociable Libra—well, the party will be on! Tend to your duties and take your vitamins.

Lovers and Friends

On September 10, loving Venus in Libra and your solar seventh house of relationships will get into a testy square with intense, relentless Pluto. Now, this could mean that someone close to you is trying to manipulate you, and as per usual, you won't take kindly to it. You may even be so irritated by it that you decide enough is enough and you want your freedom.

Money and Success

If you're after a raise, bonus, or promotion and it doesn't look like it's going to happen on September 1, sit tight for a few days. Around September 6, an easy trine between the Sun in hardworking Virgo and your solar sixth house of work and powerful Pluto in your solar tenth house of authority figures might just prove you wrong.

Tricky Transits

Venus will face off with startling Uranus on September 18, Aries, creating a celestial tug of war between your need for freedom and your urge to keep a steady partnership running smoothly. The good news is that even if the two of you disagree, you'll get your point across calmly and patiently. Let your partner know that you're not going anywhere. You just need a bit of time with friends.

Rewarding Days
5, 6, 7, 19, 20, 23

Challenging Days
1, 2, 3, 11, 12, 13

Aries | October

Relaxation and Recreation

With so much partner-oriented Libra energy circulating in the heavens above you, Aries—not to mention a Full Moon on October 15 that will activate your solar relationship axis—you really should plan on doing just about everything with your current partner or your very best friend. Of course, if you're single, you should also plan on meeting someone delightful when you least expect it. Yum!

Lovers and Friends

Loving Venus and thoughtful Mercury will team up on October 1, directly opposite confusing Neptune, so if someone seems to be blowing you off, don't take it personally and don't write them off until you know exactly what's going on. Neptune travels with a kit of pink smoke and fairy dust, specially designed to make reality go away. Hang tough until you know for sure.

Money and Success

Venus rules money as well as love, Aries, and Mercury rules our thought processes, so you shouldn't get too involved in worrying about partnerships on October 1, but you should definitely be vigilant when it comes to your personal finances. In fact, with Neptune involved, you should be careful not to lose your money, be taken advantage of, or talked into something you really don't want to buy.

Tricky Transits

Venus, the Goddess of Love, will collide with Saturn on October 29, and when these two get together, a couple of things generally come about. For starters, since Saturn loves permanence and Venus loves love, commitments are often made. On the other hand, since both planets are in freedom-loving Sagittarius, if someone tries once again to restrict you—well, that just won't ever happen again.

Rewarding Days
4, 6, 10, 11, 14, 26

Challenging Days
2, 7, 12, 13, 15, 22, 23

Aries | November

Relaxation and Recreation

Relaxing? Nope. Fun? Oh, yeah. Venus, the Sun, and Mercury will pass through fun-loving Sagittarius, a fire-sign cousin of yours who never fails to delight and surprise. Oh, and they'll all take turns forming fun, spontaneous trines with unpredictable Uranus in your very own sign. Yep. It will definitely be fun. What kind of fun? Hey, with Uranus, one never knows. Enjoy the anticipation.

Lovers and Friends

Right around November 4 or 5, someone you adore whom you haven't seen in far too long may be along for a surprise visit, Aries, brought to you courtesy of Venus in Sagg and your solar ninth house of far-off loved ones. Then again, you might run into an extremely sexy new-comer to your circle—with an awesome accent—who catches not just your attention but also your fancy.

Money and Success

What might seem like a stroke of bad luck on November 4, financially speaking, might just turn into the best thing that's happened to your bank account in a while. Venus in Sagg will square off with confusing Neptune on November 4, and mixed signals from an authority figure could be on the agenda. The very next day, however, Uranus in your sign will bring about a most welcome U-turn.

Tricky Transits

On November 24, outgoing Jupiter in partner-oriented Libra will square off with intense, demanding Pluto in your solar tenth house of authority figures and career responsibilities. Sounds like your significant other won't be all that happy with the number of hours you've been working. Remind them that the holidays are coming, and if they're patient, Santa might be especially generous.

Rewarding Days

1, 2, 12, 14, 15, 22

Challenging Days

4, 17, 18, 24, 25

Aries | December

Relaxation and Recreation

You usually enjoy this time of year with your whole heart, Aries—after all, what's not to love? It's the holiday season and the heavens are full of fire and air energies, specially designed to create fun-filled, interesting times with loved ones. December 24 and 25 will be especially wonderful days, full of love, luck, and lollipops.

Lovers and Friends

Your ruler, Mars, is on duty in unpredictable, startling Aquarius and is making his way through your solar eleventh house of friendships and group activities. Since it's the holiday season, you should probably expect some long-lost loved ones to drop in for cameo appearances. Of course, with surprising Uranus in your sign, you might be making an unexpected appearance yourself.

Money and Success

Once Venus heads off into impulsive Aquarius on December 7, Aries, you'll probably have the urge to go crazy with your plastic and spoil someone—just because you can, and because you want to see a delighted smile on their sweet face. Great idea—and after all, 'tis the season, right? Do exercise just a bit of restraint if at all possible. Plastic turns to paper bills in roughly one month.

Tricky Transits

On New Year's Eve, your ruler, Mars, will collide with Neptune, who tends to be in the neighborhood when we dive into an escape hatch— say, drugs or alcohol—to get away from the harshness of reality, and Mars has been known to be around when accidents happen. This is Amateur Night, so you really ought to think about staying home if you're going to indulge. Have friends bring sleeping bags.

Rewarding Days
1, 3, 6, 9, 11, 24, 25

Challenging Days
19, 29, 31

Aries Action Table

These dates reflect the best—but not the only—times for success and ease in these activities, according to your Sun sign.

	JAN	FEB	MAR	APR	MAY	JUN	JUL	AUG	SEP	OCT	NOV	DEC
Move			20, 21			29, 30		12, 13				
Start a class	3		15, 16, 17, 18						5, 6			
Join a club		8, 9					21, 22	18, 19		8, 9	9, 10	
Ask for a raise	7, 8	29		17, 18		3, 4, 12, 13			1, 2, 27, 28			14, 15
Look for work	10, 11			1, 7, 8			18, 19				24	
Get pro advice		15	24, 25						5, 6			
Get a loan			23		26		30	13, 15				
See a doctor	8	22							16			
Start a diet				15	21, 22		4, 5, 12, 13			16, 17		
End relationship		5		17		13		13, 14, 15	23		29, 30	19, 20
Buy clothes			9									
Get a makeover	25		8		22, 23			18				
New romance		22	23		6, 7				9, 22			
Vacation	1, 2		20, 21			10, 11, 12				18, 19, 20, 21, 22,		

Taurus

The Bull
April 19 to May 20

♉

Element: Earth

Quality: Fixed

Polarity: Yin/feminine

Planetary Ruler: Venus

Meditation: I trust myself
and others

Gemstone: Emerald

Power Stones: Diamond, blue
lace agate, rose quartz

Key Phrase: I have

Glyph: Bull's head

Anatomy: Throat, neck

Color: Green

Animal: Cattle

Myths/Legends: Isis and Osiris,
Ceridwen, Bull of Minos

House: Second

Opposite Sign: Scorpio

Flower: Violet

Keyword: Conservation

The Taurus Personality

Your Strengths and Challenges

Your sign is fixed earth, Taurus. Your symbol is the Bull, and it's a good fit, too. You're just as tough to toss off course as that single-minded creature and just as impossible to move when you've planted those hooves and taken a stance. That said, let's deal with this whole "stubborn" thing first. You're probably tired of reading that in every astrological description, especially since you don't see yourself that way—but tell me you're not. Ever look up synonyms for "stubborn"? Words like "stalwart," "tenacious," and "persevering" are listed there—and what's wrong with owning those qualities? After all, being thorough and sticking with a project to the very end isn't a bad thing, is it? Well, no, it's not. In fact, your diligence and determination will get you through just about anything, straight to the very end. The thing is, you often tend to stick around past the very end, especially with regard to relationships, most especially if you've invested years of your life in them. The thing is, in typical earth-sign style, when things go wrong, your first impulse is to fix them. Some things just can't be fixed, however, and hanging on to them is far more trouble than it's worth. So one of your missions this time around is to learn to let go of anyone or anything that's not affecting you in a positive way.

Now, let's talk about your love of creature comforts, physical pleasures, and quality versus quantity. Of course, quality costs, so your sign is necessarily very fond of money and not afraid to work hard to have it. You're the ultimate pleasure machine, Taurus, an unparalleled expert at finding the very best of everything—and you'll wait patiently until you find it. Speaking of patience, you have an endless supply, which certainly does come in handy when you're working on a tough project. If you really want to help someone understand what you're all about, step outside with them after a good spring rain. That good, rich earth smell is Taurus. It's better than perfume, in your book. You'd bottle it if you could!

Your Relationships

You play for keeps, Taurus, in all your relationships—so it often takes you some time to settle down. You observe potential friends and lovers for a good long while, until you're confident you know what makes them tick and you like what you see. At that point, you'll begin investing your time, energy, and affection into keeping them around, and once you sign up as friend, lover, or spouse, that's that. You're in it for the long haul. You place such high regard on quality that being cared for by you is a tremendous compliment—and it comes with substantial perks. Since you folks are nothing if not pleasure-oriented, you keep all your dear ones well fed, spoiled, and oh so contented. Creature comforts are at the very top of your priority list, which makes you simply delightful to play with. You automatically gravitate toward pleasurable experiences, and you love sharing them. A sunset. A mountain view. Dinner and drinks at a five-star restaurant. You'll do whatever it takes to make as many of your lucky companion's senses happy at the same time. Now, speaking of the senses, one of the words that's always used to describe you is "sensual"—and that, too, is a good fit. It's absolutely impossible to find anyone else with your innate knowledge of what feels good—and once others have had a taste of you, they won't bother to look any further. You're simply the best.

The other earth signs—Virgo and Capricorn—are as tried and true as you are, so you stay in each other's lives forever. Either of those signs would make a terrific playmate or lover, along with home-loving Cancer, who loves to settle down just as much as you do. Your nonstop sensuality often attracts Scorpio lovers, who, of course, are famous in their own right for being quite fond of physical touch—of the sexual kind. If it's good between you, neither of you will be going anywhere in a hurry.

Your Career and Money

You do love luxury, Taurus, and when it comes to choosing between quality and quantity, quality always wins out. You'd rather have one expensive, premium item than a roomful of cheap substitutes. You don't mind paying more, and you're not afraid to work hard to have the best that life has to offer.

Now, because you take your time in all things, including and especially shopping for major items, you know what you want and you know how much it will cost, so putting money aside for it is an absolute must. That might mean that you can't pick up the tab like you usually do when you're out with friends, but hey—it's probably high time someone else took a turn, anyway.

When it comes to choosing a career, your earthy, practical sign often does well handling money. This includes anything from being a cashier to the CFO of a major corporation. You people are money magnets, so others just love putting you in charge of their financial affairs. Many of you are also drawn to professions in the real estate field—which only makes sense. You are a big believer in your home being your castle, and you know how important it is to feel grounded and stable in it—so what you're really doing is helping others to find that one patch of earth that suits them best. How rewarding!

Your Lighter Side

If it looks good, tastes good, or smells good, you're in, Taurus. If it makes all of your senses happy, you'll want to own it. That goes for delicious others who are as attractive as they are confident, as well as new recipes, recordings of truly talented musicians, and a cutting-edge phone with so many features you might even be able to train it to drop off your dry cleaning. Of course, touching is also fun, and you'll never have a problem finding a suitable playmate in that department. Cooking makes you happy—especially if it's for your lover—and there's just something about the feel of cash in your hand...kinda makes you want to purr, yes?

Affirmation
I am blessed and have everything I need.

The Year Ahead for Taurus

What's not to love, Taurus? Generous, excessive, and oh-so-playful Jupiter will spend the year in your solar fifth house of lovers, play-mates, and dealings with children, all of which will bring you joy and warm your happy heart. Your kids may have some wonderful news to share at the beginning of May—possibly about a new arrival. If you're single, keep in mind that Jupiter always goes above and beyond the call of duty, so a veritable parade of applicants for the position of lover and/or spouse will be along shortly—and the parade won't be a short one, either. Remember, above all else, that you can afford to be picky now—and with Jupiter in Virgo, that goes double! Take your time. Don't be distracted by beauty alone—which, of course, is easier said than done by you, since you're such a fan of beautiful things. It's time to dig deep, so exercise that famous patience. Wait for the connection. You'll be glad you did.

Now, the fifth house also relates to your creative side and what you consider fun, so if you've mastered a craft, you'll be happily surprised at how little effort it takes to get your name and your skills known to others. You might think about making a side business out of your hobby, and with Jupiter's love of expansion, that business could turn into a career in no time flat.

Of course, Jupiter also loves to travel—internationally, if at all possible—so that may be on your agenda, too. The good news is that Jupiter is in Virgo, a practical, well-organized earth sign like your own, so the plans you make will hold up quite nicely—provided you do your best to avoid trekking around while Mercury is retrograde. This year, Mercury's three reversals will occur from January 5 to 25, April 28 to May 22, and August 30 to September 22. If you absolutely can't get around it and you really need to take your vacation time during one of these three cycles, not to worry. The best way to deal with Mercury retrograde when you know you'll be traveling is to troubleshoot. Troubleshoot absolutely everything, and think Murphy's Law—that is, if something can go wrong, it will, at the worst possible time in the worst possible way. Brainstorm with your traveling companions and have plan B in place for all situations. If you're delayed or stalled, it won't be all that terrible, anyway, since you always travel first-class, which affords you privileges and help at the ready.

Mars will retrograde through Scorpio and your solar seventh house of one-to-one relationships, so don't be surprised if an old lover turns up, anxious for a second shot at the title. The physical attraction between you will still be there, but consider what will happen once you leave the boudoir and begin living daily life together again. If you can honestly say you have new solutions for the old problems that drove you apart, then by all means, give it another try. If you can't, think long and hard about what you'll be allowing back into your life.

What This Year's Eclipses Mean for You

Eclipses arrive in pairs, Taurus. Every six months, a Solar and a Lunar Eclipse occur within two weeks, and when they show up—well, let's just say that life becomes "interesting." This year, the first eclipse will be of the solar variety, and will occur on March 8, all done up in ultra-sensitive and highly intuitive Pisces. Basically, this is a supercharged

New Moon, tailor-made for new beginnings that aren't just attractive but also necessary. Since the eclipse will occur in your solar eleventh house of groups and friendships, you might suddenly decide to seek out a spiritual or religious group of like-minded others. Just be sure they really are who and what they say they are. Neptune and her sign, Pisces, tend to be around when others attempt to misrepresent themselves.

The first Lunar Eclipse of 2016—an ultra-potent Full Moon—will arrive on March 23, wearing partner-oriented Libra and illuminating your solar sixth house of work and work-oriented relationships. If you've been thinking of making a career change or of striking out on your own and going into business with a partner, this is definitely the time to do it—or at least do a detailed study that will tell you exactly what you need to do to get a self-employed career on the road. If you've been trading glances with a charming coworker lately, this lunation will prompt you to put your money where your mouth is and make your feelings known. With your reputation for sensuality preceding you, who could ever resist you—and why would they want to?

The second Solar Eclipse of the year on September 1 will plant a fast-growing seed in your solar fifth house of kids, playmates, and casual relationships, Taurus. If you're single, since this eclipse will be in meticulous, well-organized Virgo, your detail-oriented earth-sign cousin, it would not be surprising to find you doing a bit of "interviewing" for the position of lover. Like Gemini, Virgo is ruled by fast-moving Mercury, who knows what he wants and what he doesn't want just about immediately—so you might consider "speed dating," if it's available in your area. The thing is, you like to take your time getting to know someone once you're interested, so a five-minute mini-conversation might not do it. Lunch would be better—and to be honest, coffee might be your best option.

The last eclipse of the year will be a Lunar Eclipse, on September 16, and this time around, it will put the emotional Moon in ultra-sensitive Pisces and your solar eleventh house of groups, teams, and kindred spirits. If you've been thinking about investigating a metaphysical, religious, or spiritual gathering, trying it out would be a terrific idea for you now. You might not find the right circle on the first shot, but after a bit of trial and error, you're sure to connect with like-minded others. Neptune also rules fiction and fantasy, so if your taste for sci-fi books or movies is suddenly running on high, you'll know why.

Saturn

This strict taskmaster will spend yet another year in Sagittarius, a sign that tends to make him just a bit less rigid—and far more sarcastic. Since he'll spend this time in your solar eighth house of intimate relationships, you might want to watch what you say and how you say it. Your no-nonsense attitude in this tender department could offend someone you love or badly hurt their feelings. The thing is, you might not even realize that what you said or did was hurtful in any way. Saturn will form an uncomfortable inconjunct aspect to your Sun this year, and planets in this aspect have a seriously tough time communicating. Likewise, since Saturn rules authority figures, you might also have a tough time getting your point across to them. The good news is that intense Pluto in authoritative Capricorn will take most of the sting out of this aspect and provide you with myriad alternative ways to express yourself. Just pay attention to your antennae. Joint financial issues could be troublesome, so if you're not happy with how a partnership is going, you might need to make some serious changes. Matter of fact, you'll know instinctively that any relationship that's no longer productive has to end—and that you'll need to end it, because they won't. Well, now is the time. Just be sure you're sure. Saturn plays for keeps, so this will be your final answer.

Uranus

This unpredictable planet has been making his way through your solar twelfth house of secrets and subconscious habits and desires for years now, Taurus, so chances are good that a whole lot of memories from your distant past have been unearthed—possibly thanks to a therapist or other psychological professional you've wisely decided to consult. Some memories have probably been to your liking, while others may have caused you a good amount of pain to relive. Either way, you will have yet another year of this fiery, spontaneous energy on duty in this dimly lit place, so expect even more secrets to come to the surface. If there are any questions in your mind about details from your early upbringing, tend to them now, while those who can answer your questions are available to help. Of course, Uranus is ultra-rebellious and won't stand for freedom even to be threatened, much less stifled, so anyone who tries to do that, especially if they're trying to be manipulative, won't stand a chance. You'll put your hands on those fixed Taurus hips, stop them mid-sentence, and explain that you know exactly where they're coming from—and you're not buying what they're selling. So there. Then give them that look, dust off your hands, and relax. Your work there is done. Oh, and by the way, if you were born between May 6 and 16, all this goes double.

Neptune

For centuries, Neptune has been astrologically regarded as a masculine energy—which, in a career full of scams, illusions, and disguises, may have been her greatest work. Recently, however, we've noticed that this planet is nothing if not intuitive and receptive—both feminine qualities. Now, she has been working her magic on you from her spot in your solar eleventh house of groups and friendships for years and years, and she's quite magnetic, so you've probably been attracting all kinds of energies into your life—for better or worse. This year, however, she has something really special in mind. To start with, if you were born between April 26 and May 5, you've probably just about had it with people who misrepresent themselves. The earlier in your sign you were born, the more familiar (and experienced) you are with the concept of fraud and deceit—often at the hands of those you love best. If you're in the middle of a relationship with someone your antennae are telling you isn't to be trusted, listen up. The good news is that once Neptune is done with her work on your Sun, the end result is always spiritual illumination. It might take a few rough starts to come by it, but your eyes will be opened wide. The best part is that this certainly is a romantic energy, so if you're involved, you two will be impossible to separate.

Pluto

Pluto is a tough energy to deal with, Taurus, since one of the major items in his job description includes the concept of death, decay, and degeneration. It's tough to get past all that and read on, but eventually, if you do, you'll end up learning about regeneration, recycling, and renewal. Of course, Pluto has been forming an easy trine with your sign for years now, so any major changes he's brought along have probably happened acceptably, if not quite pleasantly. There are more changes of that easy nature scheduled for all of you this year, but if you were born between May 5 and 9, you will be quite aware that you are in the midst of evolving. Jot down a few thoughts about this process and read them over in another three years. Bet you won't recognize yourself. Bet you'll also be quite happy with the person you've evolved into.

In the meantime, since Pluto is in your solar ninth house of travel, education, and all mind-opening experiences, sit tight, look around you, and realize that there is a lesson in everything and a purpose for every encounter. It's your job to choose the positive ones.

Taurus | January

Relaxation and Recreation

On January 12, loving Venus will form an easy trine with unpredictable Uranus, and an invitation for an adventure could arrive, quite out of the blue. And since Venus is in fiery, restless Sagittarius, chances are good you are about to be treated to an experience you will never forget. Don't even think about refusing.

Lovers and Friends

Now that generous Jupiter is on duty in your solar fifth house of lovers and playmates, Taurus, you have probably been having the time of your life. Well, the good times will be even better on January 13 and 14, as the Sun and Mercury add their two cents to the mix from their spot in your solar ninth house of long-distance relationships. Someone may be moving...

Money and Success

Venus rules money matters, Taurus, and she is in your solar eighth house at the moment, all done up in benevolent Sagittarius. Now, this house refers to joint finances, loans, and inheritances, so if you're waiting for news about something in that category, you'll probably hear about it on January 17, and the news should be good.

Tricky Transits

Expect the unexpected on January 31, as Mercury gets into a testy, action-oriented square with shocking Uranus. Sudden announcements and surprise missives from afar could be on your agenda, or someone you love may be recoiling from some rather startling news. Either way, a very private conversation may be in order.

Rewarding Days

7, 9, 13, 19, 29

Challenging Days

4, 5, 18, 20, 25, 31

Taurus | February

Relaxation and Recreation

Loving Venus will hook up with benevolent, fun-loving Jupiter on February 9, Taurus, and since they both will be in earth signs like your own at the time, you can count on having some amazingly good luck. You should probably also not expect to be a veritable font of willpower, since when these two planets get together, their motto is "Nothing exceeds like excess." Ah, well. Enjoy yourself!

Lovers and Friends

Happy Valentine's Day, Taurus! You can count on February 14 being absolutely delightful for you, thanks to the emotional Moon in your solid, sensual sign, who will make contact with generous Jupiter—who, you'll remember, is on duty in your solar fifth house of lovers. Oh, yes. Possible scenarios include flowers, candy, or an overnight stay at a five-star hotel—with a hot tub, of course.

Money and Success

You may think a financial matter has gone terribly, terribly wrong on February 5, Taurus, or at the very least that you are in over your head. Not to worry. Get yourself an appointment with a trusted professional the next day, and find out, once and for all, exactly what you need to do to get this situation solved. It won't be long before you see positive results for your efforts.

Tricky Transits

Red-hot Mars has been making his way through your solar seventh house of one-to-one relationships, Taurus, and this passionate fellow is wearing sexy Scorpio. Well! Needless to say, you have probably not had much sleep recently, and you won't get much rest this month, either. Your natural sensuality coupled with Scorpio's appetite for pleasure is a recipe for...well, you know.

Rewarding Days

4, 6, 8, 9, 14, 25

Challenging Days

7, 10

Taurus | March

Relaxation and Recreation

An unexpected invitation to a party or outdoor gathering will probably arrive around March 15, Taurus, and you really should go. Fun-loving, larger-than-life Jupiter and quick-witted Mercury are the astrological culprits that will be on duty, and when these two get together, there's no such thing as boring. Exhausting, maybe, but for all the right reasons.

Lovers and Friends

The really big astrological headline this month is the easy trine that will be formed by Jupiter and Pluto on March 16, Taurus—and in your case, this is really good news. Both planets will be in earth signs like your own, which are famous for sensuality—oh, and remember, Jupiter is still in your solar fifth house of lovers, and Pluto is pretty darn sexy. Nice!

Money and Success

If you've been thinking of applying for an authoritative position within your current company, Venus will be happy to help. She's on duty in your solar tenth house of professional dealings and relationships with higher-ups, and her legendary ability to charm anyone into anything will certainly come in handy. Schedule a chat with your boss right now.

Tricky Transits

Chatty Mercury and loving Venus will get together this month in woozy, dreamy, romantic Pisces, and since both planets are in your solar eleventh house of groups and friendships, an introduction around March 14 could put you face to face with someone sexy who is quite a bit older or younger than yourself. If that's the case, forget the math.

Rewarding Days

2, 6, 12, 14, 15, 16

Challenging Days

4, 5, 8, 23, 25

Taurus | April

Relaxation and Recreation
Around April 14, you'll be in the mood to party, Taurus—big time. You might be celebrating, or you might simply want to reward yourself for all your recent efforts on the job. Either way, with Mercury in your sign set to trine Jupiter—the King of Excess, you'll remember, who's in your solar fifth house of recreation—it's obviously time for one of those totally hedonistic three-day weekends.

Lovers and Friends
Mercury will set off for your sensual sign on April 5, Taurus, just as loving Venus storms off into impulsive Aries. Yes, it certainly does sound like pillow talk is on your agenda, quite out of the blue. Not to worry, though. This won't be a fleeting thing. Solid, grounded Saturn will form an easy trine with the Sun, bringing out the practical side in just about all of us.

Money and Success
Right around April 17, Taurus, your workload could become quite heavy, possibly because someone at work has dropped the ball. These added responsibilities could be handed over to you quite suddenly, but if you put your backbone into it, you'll rise to the occasion and impress the higher-ups. That raise, bonus, or promotion you want is well within reach.

Tricky Transits
April Fools' Day will be nothing if not surprising, Taurus, thanks to Mercury—who is the Trickster, after all—and startling Uranus, who just loves to bring along the last thing on earth you'd ever expect. And since both planets are all done up in impulsive Aries, the sign that lives for adrenaline rushes, someone could take you quite off guard. Have a good laugh!

Rewarding Days
1, 5, 12, 14, 17, 18

Challenging Days
4, 6, 10, 15, 16, 28

Taurus | May

Relaxation and Recreation

From May 10 through May 13, Taurus, the party at your place will be on. A pack of planets in your sign—famous for its love of physical delights and creature comforts, by the way—will make contact with excessive Jupiter and sexy Pluto. If you're attached, you two should probably throw your guests out early, but if you're not—well, don't you just love a parade?

Lovers and Friends

Loving, charming Venus, your ruling planet, is all done up in your sign, Taurus, which just so happens to be her favorite. Venus loves love, and your sign is ultra-sensual, so she'll be happy to bring along quite a few delectable new admirers for your perusal. Look to May 10 through May 13 for the chance to hook up with someone absolutely delicious.

Money and Success

With the Sun, Mercury, and Venus on duty in your sign—which is known for being a money magnet, Taurus—you'll have plenty of attractive offers, possibly from different employers who are more or less trying to woo you away from your current position. Meet with them and discuss the situation, but don't make any moves until well after May 22, when Mercury will go direct.

Tricky Transits

Mercury turned retrograde on the 28th of last month, Taurus, so he'll be moving in reverse right up until May 22. He's in your sign and your solar first house of personality, so communicating your needs could be a bit tougher than usual. This is a time for reevaluation, but not for starting new projects, especially any of a financial or romantic nature.

Rewarding Days

1, 2, 10, 11, 12, 13, 30

Challenging Days

4, 5, 22, 24, 26, 27

Taurus | June

Relaxation and Recreation

Venus will set off for home- and family-oriented Cancer on June 17, Taurus, and for the first time in a long time, you'll probably be able to actually stay home and put your feet up. If you have personal days or vacation time coming, this is the perfect time to cash it in and have a "staycation" at your place with family and dear friends.

Lovers and Friends

An argument with your sweetheart could be on the agenda around June 9, Taurus, and since Mars in Scorpio will be involved, you should take it very seriously. Your words will carry great weight, whether you intend it or not, and Scorpio planets are famous for carrying a grudge. Be very, very careful not to let your temper get away from you, and think before you speak.

Money and Success

Up until June 17, Venus, your ruling planet, will be spending her time in Gemini, a sign that can often be a bit scattered. Now, this will put Venus in your solar second house of finances and money matters, and while you are ordinarily quite well organized in this department, it might be tough to pull off at the moment. Relax, though.

Tricky Transits

Right around June 18, Taurus, you might start feeling a bit cranky, especially around your primary partner. The thing is, you might not know why you're feeling this way. It will take some doing for you to figure it out, but it will be time well spent. In the meantime, try not to pick on your partner over tiny details that really have nothing to do with the real issue.

Rewarding Days

19, 26, 27, 28

Challenging Days

4, 8, 9, 10, 17, 18

Taurus | July

Relaxation and Recreation

Once again, Taurus, a host of Cancer energies will inspire you to stay home, stay put, and enjoy the company of your dear ones. Now, this doesn't mean you necessarily have to be at your place. In fact, family gathering or cookouts with friends will keep you contented and comfortable—which, in your book, is what life is all about. Enjoy every minute.

Lovers and Friends

If you're ready for some passion, Taurus—and when aren't you?—you can have your fill of it this month. With sexy Mars in Scorpio on duty in your solar seventh house of one-to-one relationships, excessive Jupiter in your solar fifth house of lovers, and all those Cancer planets set to make contact with romantic Neptune, it's not hard to imagine you grinning. A lot.

Money and Success

The Full Moon on July 18 will occur in Capricorn, an earth-sign cousin of yours that has a way with authority figures—and that same day, talkative Mercury will form an easy trine with Saturn, the planet of business and career matters. Needless to say, if you're up for a review or on your way to an interview, you really don't have much to worry about!

Tricky Transits

You've never been especially fond of surprises, especially when they wreak havoc on your normally well-organized agenda—so you might have a bit of trouble adjusting to some surprise announcements around July 7, 10, and 16. If a family member is involved, you might also need to come to their rescue on the double.

Rewarding Days

3, 4, 5, 9, 18, 20

Challenging Days

7, 10, 11, 16, 28, 29

Taurus | August

Relaxation and Recreation

The heavens will be filled with earth energy this month, Taurus, your very own element, so just this once, you'll probably feel as if the rest of the world is actually on the same practical page you're on. Venus, Mercury, and the Sun will join fun-loving Jupiter in Virgo in your solar fifth house of fun. Yep. A month to remember, for all the right reasons.

Lovers and Friends

If you need to make some changes within your current relationship, Taurus, you won't be happy about it, but you will see the need for it. On August 6, two angry squares could bring along the final straw—and since permanence-loving Saturn is involved, it could be time to say goodbye. If you've invested a lot of yourself, you might hesitate, but remember, you're never alone for long.

Money and Success

With Venus—your ruling planet—set to spend from August 5 through August 29 in practical, well-organized Virgo, you can pretty much count on having an especially prosperous month. A loan to finance a new project could be tough to get on August 6 and 13, when Saturn could toss some roadblocks in your way just to see what you're made of and how much you want this thing.

Tricky Transits

Again, Taurus, the astrological agenda for August 6 could be a bit problematic for you. The thing is, talkative Mercury and lovely Venus will square off with stubborn Saturn and angry Mars—which certainly does sound like arguments over money and love. Don't stick around if a situation turns volatile, and remember, just because you're invited to an argument doesn't mean you have to accept.

Rewarding Days

1, 5, 10, 17, 22, 23

Challenging Days

3, 6, 12, 13, 14, 25, 26

Taurus | September

Relaxation and Recreation

That pack of planets in your solar fifth house of recreation, lovers, and playmates will keep you busy, Taurus, but squares passed out by Saturn could put unexpected difficulties in your way—if you let them, that is. Don't be cranky. If you're stuck or delayed, take a look around you and see what you would have missed if you weren't where you are right now.

Lovers and Friends

If you're still miraculously single as of September 23, Taurus, not to worry. The lovely lady Venus—your very own ruling planet—will set off for your solar seventh house of one-to-one encounters, and the parade will begin. The thing is, Venus will be all done up in sexy, magnetic Scorpio, so all you really have to do to enjoy this buffet is show up. Fair enough?

Money and Success

It's impossible to mention success—astrologically speaking, that is—without mentioning Jupiter, the benevolent, generous Roman god. That said, since he will begin his year-long trek through partner-oriented Libra on September 9, you might want to think seriously about taking on a professional partner. Don't be manipulated into shaking hands on September 12 or 13. Take your time.

Tricky Transits

On September 12 and 13, expect confusion, followed by fireworks, in rapid succession. Even if you do your level best to steady everyone and everything around you, the day could be tough. Before you make any official decisions or give up your signature, remember that Mercury will be retrograde until September 21, and be sure you understand the fine print.

Rewarding Days
2, 6, 19, 20, 23, 27

Challenging Days
1, 10, 11, 13, 14, 15

Taurus | October

Relaxation and Recreation

A metaphysical group may catch your attention on October 1 or 2, as Venus and Mercury team up to visit ultra-spiritual Neptune in your solar eleventh house of groups and friendships. If you're searching for answers to The Big Questions, these folks may be able to point you in the right direction, or at least give you some idea of where to start.

Lovers and Friends

Venus will stay on duty in your solar seventh house of personal encounters until October 17, still all done up in Scorpio, a very sexual sign. Considering your expertise in this tender department, if you're attached, your partner will be one very happy camper. If you're not, you definitely won't have to worry about being lonely.

Money and Success

Good news! A lucky turn of fate regarding either a work situation or a loan or inheritance will arrive around October 14, when thoughtful Mercury will get together with practical Saturn, who never passes out presents you haven't earned. Keep an eye open for any and all subtle kudos or slaps on the back from higher-ups—and enjoy it.

Tricky Transits

Fiery Mars will square off with unpredictable Uranus on October 28, creating a volatile, passionate energy that could cause you to lose your legendary cool. If you've been stewing about something that happened weeks ago, you will stew no longer—and it won't take much to get you riled. Clear the area of any innocent bystanders as soon as you feel your face getting warm.

Rewarding Days
3, 4, 5, 11, 26

Challenging Days
1, 2, 7, 8, 13, 19, 23, 28

Taurus | November

Relaxation and Recreation

Ah, yes. Your ruling planet, lovely Venus, will take off for earthy Capricorn on November 11, just in time to make the holidays warm and fuzzy. She'll be making her way through your solar ninth house of far-off friends and long-distance relationships, so don't be surprised if a long-missing loved one calls, texts, or even knocks on your door around November 24 or 25.

Lovers and Friends

Venus will get together with dreamy Neptune on November 19 to put sweet romance on your agenda, Taurus. If you're attached, you two should make time to get away from it all together, even if it's only for an overnight stay at your favorite five-star hotel. Be sure to get the room with the hot tub—and a "privacy, please" notice for the doorknob.

Money and Success

Mars will storm into your solar tenth house on November 8, Taurus, and for the next two months, you'll be a force to be reckoned with. If you're already in a position of authority, you'll want to make some major changes in your work environment. If not, you might find that the higher-ups are making moves that will benefit you in the long run.

Tricky Transits

If you're having trouble talking things over with your sweetheart around November 6, it might be best to table the discussion before one of you says something you might come to regret. Wait until November 15 or 26, when Mercury will be happy to arrange for clear communications. Serious financial decisions will be easy to make on November 23, so sit tight until then.

Rewarding Days

1, 2, 7, 11, 14

Challenging Days

16, 17, 18, 29, 30

Taurus | December

Relaxation and Recreation

Happy holidays, Taurus! The Universe has arranged for a truly delightful month. In particular, December 24 through December 28 will be warm, loving days, and family gatherings will be peaceful. It will be a surprising month—for only the best of reasons—thanks to Venus and Mars in unpredictable Aquarius, who'll create a flow of interesting, unusual visitors.

Lovers and Friends

No less than three astrological heavy-hitters—generous Jupiter, surprising Uranus, and stabilizing Saturn—will make contact with your ruling planet, affectionate Venus, on December 25. You're especially susceptible to her moods, and when she's happy, you're happy—so you can expect to be just about delirious with joy around that time, and pretty much for the entire month.

Money and Success

If unexpected expenses come up around December 7, you'll be well equipped to handle them, Taurus. You've always had a good head on your shoulders, and that goes double for your finances. You might be asked to help a friend in need, and as per usual, you won't refuse. Expect your kindness to come back to you a dozen times over.

Tricky Transits

Be careful if you're out and about on New Year's Eve, Taurus. If you're planning on indulging in a few adult beverages, leave your keys at home and call a cab or choose a trustworthy designated driver. Fast-acting Mars will collide with woozy Neptune that night, and accidents could happen. Be sure that you and yours are safe and sound.

Rewarding Days

10, 11, 12, 24, 25, 26, 27, 30

Challenging Days

18, 19

Taurus Action Table

These dates reflect the best—but not the only—times for success and ease in these activities, according to your Sun sign.

	JAN	FEB	MAR	APR	MAY	JUN	JUL	AUG	SEP	OCT	NOV	DEC
Move	2, 3				22, 23							8, 9, 11
Start a class			4, 5			2, 3			1, 2, 3	22, 24		
Join a club		13, 14									9, 10, 11, 12, 17	
Ask for a raise			9, 10		4, 5			14, 15				
Look for work	23, 24			7, 22			8, 9, 10					8, 9, 10
Get pro advice		13, 14, 17, 18					4, 5			1, 5, 17		
Get a loan			21, 22		17, 19, 23	10, 11, 12					25, 26	
See a doctor			23, 24						1, 2			
Start a diet	23, 24, 25									30		
End relationship	5, 6			22, 23				18, 19, 30				19, 20, 21
Buy clothes		22, 23							16, 17, 18			
Get a makeover					19, 20		17					
New romance		26, 27		4, 5		11, 12						
Vacation							15, 16	9, 10, 11, 12, 13				

Gemini

The Twins
May 20 to June 20

Ⅱ

Element: Air

Quality: Mutable

Polarity: Yang/masculine

Planetary Ruler: Mercury

Meditation: I explore my inner worlds

Gemstone: Tourmaline

Power Stones: Ametrine, citrine, emerald, spectrolite, agate

Key Phrase: I think

Glyph: Pillars of duality, the Twins

Anatomy: Shoulders, arms, hands, lungs, nervous system

Colors: Bright colors, orange, yellow, magenta

Animals: Monkeys, talking birds, flying insects

Myths/Legends: Peter Pan, Castor and Pollux

House: Third

Opposite Sign: Sagittarius

Flower: Lily of the valley

Keyword: Versatility

The Gemini Personality

Your Strengths and Challenges

Your ruling planet is Mercury, the ancient Messenger of the Gods, who whizzes around the Sun in a record 88 days. He had to learn to move quickly because it was his job to shuttle information between the heavenly deities and we mere mortals—which tends to be time-consuming. He's endowed you with his fleet-footed abilities and his talent for rapid-fire communication and quick navigation, so if anyone knows shortcuts, it's you. Needless to say, patience probably isn't your strong suit.

You're happiest when your mind is engaged and your body is moving, and since you folks wrote the book on multitasking, it's not unusual to find you doing two things at once—at least two. That said, if you absolutely must sit still, you absolutely must keep your mind busy. When you're not attached to your vehicle, your phone, or your computer, you'll be chatting in person with someone interesting, one of your favorite sports. In fact, although waiting in line is torturous for you, it's actually bearable if you can strike up a decent conversation—and by decent, I mean fast-paced at the very least and informative and funny at the very best. You're constantly on the lookout for new information and you have a terrific sense of humor, so you can easily chat with just about anyone on just about any topic at just about any time. You're a perpetual student and also a wordsmith, qualities that allow you to tell terrific stories and keep your friends endlessly amused and amazed at your verbal gymnastics. Oh, and yes, you do tend to change your mind a lot, which only makes sense, since your symbol is the Twins.

Your personal motto is "Variety is the spice of life," and you live by it. You're famous for your versatility and adaptability, as well as your perpetual curiosity, and while you do tend to be easily distracted (Look! Kittens!), you somehow manage to get all your chores done and all your projects accomplished—in record time, too. You might seem to be scattered at times, but those who know you understand that it's just your way. You love surprises and tangents, and just can't stand stop signs, red lights, and periods at the end of sentences. You are a quick study and a terrific teacher, and are capable of getting along with just about anyone. You tolerate a whole lot from others and accept them as they are—as long as they don't bore you. Boredom is the one thing you can't and won't tolerate.

Your Relationships

You fast-moving, easily bored critters are way too much fun to be around, Gemini, which is why you're rarely alone. You tend to be surrounded by fun-loving, outgoing friends who share your curiosity and restlessness and keep your brain actively engaged. Your friends come from all walks of life and are usually a variety of ages, races, and beliefs—because, after all, you do love variety. The only thing you just can't tolerate is being bored, so you're happy to accept others exactly as they are, with no strings attached and no expectations, as long as they're interesting. The good news is that you're so open-minded that others are happy to return the favor.

When it comes to love—well, it's not exactly that you're fickle, but if you're not amused, you might find yourself glancing over their shoulder to see who that was who just came into the room. The "interview process" for anyone who wants to capture your heart involves a whole lot of Q & A sessions—with you asking the Qs and mentally recording the As—but it won't take long. You know what you like and what you don't like. Matter of fact, speed dating might be a terrific way for you to get through those first dates even faster.

You're a youthful sign, so no one ever guesses your age correctly, and you do tend to enjoy the company of younger folks—including younger partners. In general, you tend to gravitate toward the other air signs, Libra and Aquarius, who also specialize in communication and conversation. Libras are fun and share your love of socializing, but they're often a bit too focused for your tastes. Your Aquarius friends and lovers are word wizards like you, and are just as fond of their computers and electronic gadgets. Oddly enough, it's your opposite sign, Sagittarius, who often makes the best match, since you two never get tired of talking, moving, and looking at things. All kinds of things. Seashells. Birds. Plants...

Your Career and Money

When it comes to money, Gemini, you tend to consider it something that you can trade for fun gadgets and interesting experiences—and while you do give in occasionally to impulse purchases, more often than not, you're far more likely to purchase something that has a purpose and to shop around before you buy. Shopping in general—including window-shopping—is great fun, anyway. So much to look at!

Of course, you're naturally drawn toward electronic gadgets, so getting your hands on the latest computer or phone absolutely delights you.

There are myriad ways you might choose to earn your daily bread, but ideally, your work should give you personal freedom and the ability to make your own schedule. On the other hand, if you're working with information on a computer or you spend your days chatting with others in a customer service position, your mind will be happy and you'll keep on learning. Since you love chatting and making short trips, you might drive a cab or a bus, too—where your ability to find shortcuts also comes in handy. Any occupation that guarantees you that no two days will ever be the same will do just fine.

Since you folks are the word wizards of the zodiac, writing, speaking, and teaching are also ideal. You make a terrific teacher because you're far from boring. Children in particular adore you.

Your Lighter Side

What's fun for you, Gemini? Well, all kinds of things. Life is pretty much a carnival in your mind, full of colors and sounds and smells and all kinds of interesting people—so naturally, carnivals and fairs are one of your favorite ways to spend the day. When you're indoors, there's nothing like a good game of Trivial Pursuit, Scrabble, or Pictionary to make you smile. That's if you can get anyone to play with you more than once, because winning against you is no easy task! Dancing and walking are right at the top of your list, not to mention gymnastics and amusement parks. Overall, however, nothing beats chatting with someone who knows something you don't. You walk away from them feeling as if you've just had a great meal.

Affirmation
New experiences keep my mind, body, and spirit happy and healthy.

The Year Ahead for Gemini

If you were born at the tail end of May or the first few days of June, you're due for a truly exciting and passionate spring season—to say the very least. Mid-March, fiery, assertive, and often angry Mars will begin slowing down to turn retrograde on April 17, when he'll station opposite your Sun from his spot in your solar seventh house of one-to-one relationships. Now, planets that station are trying to make a point, so if you find that one of your primary relationships has suddenly become a bit too volatile for your tastes, don't think twice about ending it. You have a very keen mind and a way with details, so it might just be little things that tweak your antennae, but regardless of what it is that sets off those warning bells, pay attention. On the other hand, however, intense passion can also be quite delightful, so if you're happily involved, you two won't be able to keep your hands off each other and your friends will probably beg you to get a room. At any rate, this will go on until the first week of May. Now that you know what's coming up, make plans to use all this red-hot energy as positively—and enjoyably—as possible. The rest of you aren't off the hook, either. You, too, can expect sparks, if not all-out fireworks, to be a part of your world—and you, too, need to decide how to use this energy productively.

And speaking of being productive, with expansive Jupiter in hard-working Virgo and your solar fourth house of home and family matters, you might use the first four months of the year to redo your home, add on a room or two, or welcome a new arrival. No matter what else is going on, a serious spring cleaning is definitely in order. A long-distance move is also a possibility, so if you've got the urge to go, and a way to earn your daily bread when you're there, what's the holdup? No one says you have to stay forever, so you might want to think of it as an extended vacation until you decide if it feels like home.

Oh, and lest we forget, it's not just Mars who'll be making his way through your solar seventh house of committed relationships. Serious Saturn, who just loves permanence and stability, is also on duty there, so if you haven't settled down yet with someone delightfully interesting, don't worry. The thing is, Saturn often brings along relationships with others who are either much older or much younger. In that case, don't fixate on the numbers. Concentrate on what you've got between you, realistically. If it's made to last, who graduated first won't matter at all. Mars and Saturn will both be wearing travel-loving Sagittarius, by the way, so expect your ears to perk up—and maybe your pulse rate too—at the sound of an enchanting accent.

What This Year's Eclipses Mean for You

Eclipses arrive in pairs, Gemini, two weeks apart and once every six months. The Solar Eclipse is a supercharged New Moon, and the Lunar Eclipse is an equally powerful Full Moon. The first set of eclipses will start on March 8 with a Solar Eclipse in tenderhearted, spiritual Pisces and your solar tenth house of career, publicity, and reputation. You might decide to champion your favorite cause or use your beliefs to recreate your profession. This sign does tend to be in the neighborhood when we're looking for an escape hatch from reality, however, so do be careful not to get caught up in addictions or unhealthy habits. Distract yourself in positive ways. If you've been thinking about making a major move, use the next six months to think things over and see what your work prospects might look like in your new location.

The Lunar Eclipse in Libra on March 23 will open your eyes—big time—to what's really going on within a relationship that's been part of your life for quite some time now. Don't panic. Yes, you might suddenly realize that you've been going through the motions and are not really invested in the future of a current partnership, and yes, in that case, you'll want out, ASAP. On the other hand, someone you've only seen as a friend or an associate could also say or do something that gives you a whole new perspective about them—and a whole new tingle, too. If you're single, consider the fact that this lunation will occur in your solar fifth house of lovers, playmates, and recreation, so even if you two are deliriously happy together, don't fly off to Las Vegas right away. See what happens after you spend a whole lot of time alone together.

On September 1, the second Solar Eclipse of the year will shake things up in your solar fourth house of home, family matters, and domestic situations. This lunation will occur in earthy, practical Virgo, an extremely well-organized sign that likes things to be just so. That said, this would be a terrific time to renovate, redecorate, add a room, or even move, if you're so inclined. At the very least, you'll do some serious fall cleaning! Be careful what you do with paperwork. Be sure that anything you're tossing isn't something you'll need in the future for financial or business matters.

The Lunar Eclipse will arrive on September 16, and since it will illuminate your solar tenth house of career and professional matters, you might just find that vocational changes you set into motion back in early March have actually taken—and taken well. In fact, at this time, you should expect to be made aware of just how much you've changed in the eyes of the world—for the better! Your mission is to keep up the good work, and if someone decides to make a public display of their admiration and gratitude for your efforts, smile pretty and say thank you. You've earned this!

Saturn

Your solar seventh house of one-to-one relationships will continue to host Saturn, who tends to be a rather conservative, discriminating energy, but not so much when he's wearing his favorite business-casual outfit in Sagittarius, as he is now. Yes, you might need to tighten things up in this department, and as per Saturn's love of rules, regulations, and guidelines, you might need to lay down the law in a certain relationship (or two), but in this sign, you'll be able to do it in an easygoing way. If you've got to make a total break, be honest, open, and completely positive. Imagine a parting of the ways with no guilt, no regrets, no looking back, and no hard feelings. That sure would make it easier to keep someone in your life on a different level, rather than banishing them from your life forever. Now, Saturn also has a penchant for bringing others into our lives who are much older or much younger than ourselves, so if you find yourself desperately attracted to someone but nervous about the age difference, stop that. Really. Concentrate on what you two have in common. If anyone realizes that variety is truly the spice of life, it's you, so enjoy your differences. In fact, you should celebrate them! This goes double for dear friends who are in the process of making huge life changes. Be supportive and optimistic. After all, if they're happy, you're happy.

Uranus

This unpredictable guy will spend yet another year in your solar eleventh house of group affiliations, peer circles, and gatherings, so if you think you've seen it all, you might not want to say that out loud. Uranus loves nothing more than to bring along the very last thing we'd ever, ever expect, and he's pretty darn good at it, too. In your case, it might be that you've been investigating different groups of friends for a few years now, and that you're eager to keep dropping in on new groups, too. The possibilities are endless, and you're interested in just about everything, from metaphysics to knitting to earth sciences, so you owe it to yourself to let this quirky, unconventional energy introduce you to all kinds of new people who can answer all the myriad questions you'll ask. Of course, Uranus is in red-hot Aries, so even if they have amazing answers for you, not too many of these new associations might actually become a part of your life for the long haul, but who cares? Your mission in life is to take just a taste of everything, like a butterfly flitting from flower to flower. You've only got another couple of years to enjoy this eye-opening planet's energy, so don't waste it. Oh, and regardless of how taken you are with a certain pack of idealists at the moment, keep in mind that Uranus's energy is a bit like a light switch. When it's on, it's on. When it's not, it's not. All this goes double if you were born between June 6 and 17.

Neptune

If you were born between May 27 and June 4, Gemini, you're currently laboring under a testy square from Neptune, who's in Pisces and especially powerful now—even though she's even more invisible than ever. This subtle but potent ultra-intuitive planet is working her magic in your solar tenth house of career, profession, and reputation, and since she tends to carry around a pink smoke machine and a bucket of pink fairy dust, you'll have no problem whatsoever operating under the radar, but if you're doing something that might not be entirely on the up and up, it's time to put an end to it. Whether or not you're willing to admit it, something isn't sitting right with your conscience, and your dreams will give you a bird's-eye view of exactly what that might be. Make it a point to record your dreams, and be as diligent about the details as possible. If anyone can look back and recognize the symbolism a week or so later—or longer—it's you. But you'll need the facts. Now, Neptune is also a big fan of altered states, from infatuation to depression to alcohol or drug addiction—basically, anything that will smooth out the rough edges of reality and make your life a whole lot easier to deal with—for now. The thing is, Neptune lulls us into believing that life is already just as we want it, when in fact we're just literally living a dream. Be sure to touch base with someone eminently practical and realistic who knows you well and loves you even more.

Pluto

This intense, determined energy is only halfway done with his trek through with hard-working Capricorn, Gemini, which he began back in 2008. Yes, it's been seven years that he's been making his presence known in your solar eighth house of shared resources, loans, and inheritances, and since he's so very fond of urgent circumstances, you've probably been dealing with more than a few financial power struggles and lots of unexpected cries for financial help. This is also the house where issues of intimacy are handled, so betrayal may have also been an issue—and quite possibly a very painful one. The good news is that no matter what Pluto removes, he replaces it with something shiny and brand-new—something that suits you much more than whatever you were holding on to. Willpower is also handled in this house, so if you need some, not to worry. You are in the middle of a major Plutonian process specially designed to make you stronger from the inside out. Your mission is to cooperate with the process. The thing is, it's happening so slowly that you might not even notice it if you don't pay attention. But let's get back to the issue of intimacy again. Pluto wrote the book on passion, sexuality, and focus. If you're seeing someone, it's got to be hot and heavy or you'll get bored—which, as we all know, is the one and only deal breaker in your book.

Gemini | January

Relaxation and Recreation

The star of your show this month is charming Venus, who'll be in fiery, funny Sagittarius and your solar seventh house of one-to-one relationships up until January 23. Venus is quite sociable and especially outgoing in Sagittarius, so you probably shouldn't expect to get much rest. Fortunately, you don't need much and you don't mind yawning the next day if the evening was worth it. Enjoy!

Lovers and Friends

Venus, the Goddess of Love herself, will spend most of the month in your solar seventh house of one-to-one relationships, Gemini, all done up in funny Sagittarius, a sign that shares your curiosity and restlessness. This bodes well for all your encounters, but if you're single, that status could change quite quickly around January 12. Keep an ear out for a storyteller with a delightful accent.

Money and Success

Venus also rules money matters, Gemini, and since her Sagittarius outfit is making her feel extremely generous, one of two things is possible. You might offer someone a loan, or a gift disguised as a loan for someone too proud to accept what they see as charity. On the other hand, if you need some financial help yourself, you won't have to look far to find it.

Tricky Transits

Your ruling planet, Mercury, will turn retrograde on January 25 from his position in your solar eighth house of intimate partners, so if you get the feeling someone is sending you mixed signals, you might be reading them wrong. Try to be patient, and wait at least three weeks before you make any permanent decisions about the relationship.

Rewarding Days
6, 12, 13, 14, 23, 30

Challenging Days
5, 7, 24, 25, 26

Gemini | February

Relaxation and Recreation

The New Moon in Aquarius on February 8 will plant a seed in your solar ninth house of education, Gemini, so you might have a sudden urge to sign up for a class to improve your resumé or even learn an entirely new profession. With Aquarius energy in the mix, chances are good that computers will be involved, so you're sure to enjoy yourself, no matter what the subject.

Lovers and Friends

The Sun, Mercury, and Venus in unpredictable Aquarius will keep your solar ninth house an active place this month, Gemini. Now, this is where long-distance friends and far-off dear ones are handled, so if you're missing someone who's far from you, the temptation to drop everything and go to them will be darn near impossible to resist. If there's any way you can, be spontaneous.

Money and Success

Venus rules money matters, Gemini, and she'll be in your solar eighth house of shared resources and financial arrangements as the month begins. If you need a loan, apply before February 16. If a family member comes to you in need around February 6 or 7, you'll need to make up your mind in a hurry. Is this the first time—or the first of many times?

Tricky Transits

The Full Moon on February 22 will set up shop in your solar fourth house of home, family, and domestic issues, Gemini, all done up in practical, respectable Virgo. The problem is that woozy, dreamy Neptune will be exactly opposite this lovely lunation, and Neptune does tend to be in the neighborhood when misunderstandings occur. Make communication a priority.

Rewarding Days
2, 3, 8, 13, 16, 25

Challenging Days
5, 7, 22, 23

Gemini | March

Relaxation and Recreation

Venus in Aquarius and your solar ninth house of travel and education will absolutely insist—charmingly, of course—that you broaden your horizons this month. Maybe a spontaneous long-distance trip? Maybe classes to master a new computer program? It doesn't matter what you choose, as long as it feeds your curious mind and restless spirit.

Lovers and Friends

The Sun and Mercury will set off for your solar eleventh house of friendships on March 19 and 21, Gemini, and they'll be wearing fiery, assertive Aries. Now, this could mean that fireworks will fly amid a group you're keeping company with, but then again, Aries is quite a passionate sign, so someone you have only thought of platonically in the past may suddenly be quite appealing.

Money and Success

Money matters may be a bit confusing this month, Gemini, especially if you've been working toward a raise, bonus, or promotion and it just isn't happening. The astrological culprits responsible are Mercury and Venus in woozy Pisces and your solar tenth house of career matters. Get the facts straight before you burn any bridges. Something could be in the works for you behind the scenes.

Tricky Transits

On March 20, Venus will collide with Neptune. Now, this is a very romantic team, so you might just run into the love of your life, and it might be a higher-up or superior. On the other hand, you might cross paths with someone who seems just perfect, but if your antennae keep twitching, don't fly off to Vegas just yet.

Rewarding Days

1, 2, 7, 16, 24, 31

Challenging Days

4, 5, 10, 14, 20, 30

Gemini | April

Relaxation and Recreation

Talk about a good time! Venus will join unpredictable Uranus in Aries on April 5, Gemini, in your solar eleventh house of friendships and groups. This romantic lady will form an easy trine with passionate Mars on April 12, who just so happens to be in your solar seventh house of relationships, so be prepared for some spontaneous fun!

Lovers and Friends

A New Moon will occur in Aries and your solar eleventh house of friends on April 7, and someone new and extremely exciting may join your group—and strike your fancy. Now, this person may have arrived last month, in which case, you two are probably an item by now. All your casual relationships will take on a more serious tone around April 18—for all the right reasons.

Money and Success

Venus will get into an uncomfortable aspect with expansive Jupiter around April 16, and you may find it tough to figure out exactly where your money is going. Don't try to settle money matters around that time. Wait a day or so and straighten things out with a trusted professional who understands the fine print and won't miss any details.

Tricky Transits

On April 10, thoughtful Mercury will spar with impulsive Mars, and if you're not careful, misunderstandings could spiral into major arguments. Mercury is in solid, stubborn Taurus, and Taurus planets play for keeps, so it won't be easy to work this thing out. Be sure of your facts before you accuse or challenge anyone. That goes double for your significant other.

Rewarding Days

1, 3, 5, 12, 18, 30

Challenging Days

2, 4, 15, 16, 19, 27

Gemini | May

Relaxation and Recreation

The Sun, Venus, and Mercury will takes turns trining fun-loving Jupiter in your solar fourth house of home and family, so if you haven't planned a family gathering yet, get busy! May 10 and 12 look wonderful, but if you need to wait till the weekend, so be it. Have everyone over to your place, and break out the barbeque.

Lovers and Friends

Once Venus sets off for your sign on May 24, she'll bring all her magnetism and charm to your already sociable, appealing personality, and invitations and offers are sure to be plentiful. On May 24 itself, however, she'll face off with Mars, so sparks might fly, but remember— Mars rules passion, so there are plenty of ways for this opposition to work out nicely.

Money and Success

All Taurus planets will form easy trines this month with generous Jupiter and determined Pluto, and since Taurus is a natural money magnet, opportunities to make some solid cash will abound. This is also a terrific month to handle loans, inheritance issues, and joint finances, especially around May 10, 11, 12, and 30. If you're into research, a position in that field could open up after May 27.

Tricky Transits

Outgoing Jupiter and cautious Saturn will get into a testy square on May 26, and since the signs they've chosen as their battleground are detailed Virgo and not-so-detailed Sagittarius, you could miss something if you're not listening carefully to a teacher or an authority figure. Pay attention! This is the type of energy that turns molehills into mountains.

Rewarding Days

1, 2, 9, 10, 11, 20, 30

Challenging Days

4, 5, 24, 25, 26, 27

Gemini | June

Relaxation and Recreation

If you're in the mood for a road trip, the weekend of June 10 would be a fine time to go. Venus in your sign will get together with spontaneous Uranus, urging you to forget about a schedule and just wing it. Pile the whole gang into the car and head off for destinations unknown. Just be sure to check the oil before you leave!

Lovers and Friends

Relationships could be tricky this month, Gemini, since the Sun and Venus will take turns squaring off with serious Saturn in your solar seventh house of one-to-one relationships. If you're dealing with geographic obstacles, you might need to decide whether a long-distance relationship can really work out. If someone is trying to control you—well, needless to say, you won't tolerate it.

Money and Success

Venus rules money matters, Gemini, and around June 2 and 3, it seems that she'll be battling with both confusion and roadblocks, thanks to Neptune and Saturn. Don't panic, and don't try to settle anything on June 6. Wait until June 12 and 13, when you'll have the information you need to make a sound choice—and expect that information to arrive from a very surprising source!

Tricky Transits

The New Moon of June 4 and the Full Moon of June 20 will activate your relationship axis, Gemini, and you might find that someone has not been forthcoming with you. You'll need to do some digging to find out exactly what's been going on, but thanks to lucky Jupiter and determined Pluto, you should have the answers you need on June 26.

Rewarding Days
8, 12, 13, 25, 26, 27

Challenging Days
1, 2, 4, 6, 14, 30

Gemini | July

Relaxation and Recreation

Several planets in home-loving Cancer will make this the perfect month for family outings and trips with the kids, Gemini. As soon as July 1, you might also receive happy news about a new arrival. Of course, once the Sun, Mercury, and Venus set off for playful Leo mid-month, recreation will be at the very top of your priority list—and maybe a bit of romance, too.

Lovers and Friends

Speaking of romance, let's talk about charming Venus in Leo, who'll arrive on July 11, setting up shop in your solar third house of conversations and communications. With this magnetic energy on duty, it's not hard to imagine how every syllable you utter could turn into an irresistible invitation to get to know you better. Enjoy!

Money and Success

If you've been having money problems lately, not to worry. Stability will be restored to your work situation around July 20, thanks to a conversation with a higher-up that goes quite well. You might even hear something definite about a new position you've applied for within your current workplace that offers better pay and benefits—or a whole new career.

Tricky Transits

Pluto is on duty in authoritative Capricorn and your solar eighth house of joint financial matters and intimate encounters, and your ruling planet, Mercury, is in lavish, impulsive Leo. These two signs have trouble communicating, so expressing your needs could be tough around July 21 and 24, and you'll have to find a way to get your point across without offending those closest to you.

Rewarding Days

1, 3, 8, 16, 20, 26, 31

Challenging Days

2, 7, 10, 11, 16

Gemini | August

Relaxation and Recreation

If you've been meaning to visit with an older friend or elderly relative, make it your business to see them on August 1. Saturn will get together with the Sun in playful, bighearted Leo, and you two are sure to have a fine time together. Likewise, if a friend you haven't seen for a while is in town around August 16, cancel your plans and get together with them.

Lovers and Friends

Mars will storm the borders of Sagittarius and your solar seventh house of one-to-one relationships on August 2, Gemini, and Mars brings passion and excitement with him wherever he goes, so you definitely won't be bored. There may be a few arguments on the agenda, but it's good to clear the air. Besides, Mars in any fire sign gets over things fast!

Money and Success

Around August 13, you could get into a bit of a dispute about money with your business partner or significant other, but don't worry, because it won't last long. The best thing you can do to work it all out is to make sure that they understand their responsibilities—but establishing a set date for their monthly contribution wouldn't hurt, either.

Tricky Transits

On August 24, impulsive Mars will collide with cautious Saturn in your solar seventh house of one-to-one relationships, Gemini. Now, both of these planets rule uniforms and occupations that require them, so be on your toes! No speeding and no texting while driving. And if someone strikes you as trouble, trust your instincts and avoid them.

Rewarding Days

1, 2, 10, 18, 27, 28

Challenging Days

5, 6, 7, 19, 20, 30

Gemini | September

Relaxation and Recreation

Oh, my! On September 9, outgoing, fun-loving Jupiter will set off for Libra, your air-sign cousin, Gemini, and one of the signs that is just as sociable, friendly, and outgoing as yours. This will put generous Jupiter in your solar fifth house of lovers and playmates, so for the next year, it might be hard to focus on work—but your weekends will be incredible. Enjoy!

Lovers and Friends

The really big news is Jupiter's entry into partner-oriented Libra. This generous planet doesn't pay much attention to limits and tends to frown on rules, so if you're single, you can expect a veritable parade of "applicants" for the positions of lovers and friends. If you meet someone delicious who's not like anyone you've ever dated, you'll be enthralled.

Money and Success

A power struggle over money matters could erupt around September 11, Gemini, and you absolutely won't stand for it. As per usual, at first you'll try to be fair and unbiased, but if you're dealing with someone cranky or selfish, that might not be possible. Don't beat yourself up about it. Some people just refuse to be satisfied.

Tricky Transits

The eclipses on September 1 and 16 will rattle your solar axis of home and family matters versus work and career, Gemini, and for a while, you might feel as if you're being pulled in two directions—at least two. If you've been working more than usual lately and accepting any overtime you can get, your family might be upset. Juggle!

Rewarding Days

7, 8, 9, 19, 25, 30

Challenging Days

1, 2, 12, 13, 14

Gemini | October

Relaxation and Recreation

With risk-loving Jupiter on duty in Libra and your solar fifth house of lovers and playmates since last month, Gemini, you're probably already having the time of your life—but you'd better fasten your seat belt, because Mercury is about to join forces with him. Yeehaw! Talk about a good time! Expect short trips, long trips, interesting conversations, and lots of new friends.

Lovers and Friends

If you're not currently attached, Gemini, you'll have plenty of opportunities to meet the Right One this month. The thing is, the Universe will present you with quite an assortment of interesting, unusual people who will keep your curious mind fascinated, so you'll need to remind yourself that you can afford to be picky! Have some fun and enjoy "shopping"!

Money and Success

Impulsive Mars will spend the month is your solar eighth house of shared resources and financial dealings, Gemini, which might ordinarily mean that you'd be willing to take chances with your money. Mars is in cautious Capricorn, however, so conversely, you'll probably be a lot more careful about your spending and quite concerned about where every cent you earn ends up.

Tricky Transits

Venus will enter your solar seventh house of one-to-one relationships this month, Gemini, which can be absolutely wonderful or a bit on the troublesome side. If you're attached and happy, you two simply need to plan some adventures together to keep the passion alive. If you're on the market for a new partner, you might run into a few who people aren't exactly reliable. Take your time.

Rewarding Days
1, 4, 6, 14, 17, 26

Challenging Days
2, 12, 13, 19, 22, 23

Gemini | November

Relaxation and Recreation

Here's another month full of fun, Gemini, brought to you courtesy of a sky full of Sagittarius planets and Jupiter in Libra. You definitely won't get a lot of rest, but you won't want to miss a single moment of what the Universe has on tap for you. In fact, startling Uranus will bring some lovely last-minute U-turns to your plans that will turn out to be delightful. Enjoy!

Lovers and Friends

Well! Loving, magnetic Venus will stay on duty in your solar seventh house of one-to-one relationships until November 11, Gemini, and since she's all done up in lucky, funny Sagittarius, you'll probably enjoy the company of generous, outgoing people—both lovers and friends. And let's not forget that Jupiter is on duty in your solar fifth house of lovers. Better double up on those vitamins.

Money and Success

This could be a tricky month for you, Gemini, financially speaking, especially as November winds down. Venus rules money, and she'll be setting off for cautious, frugal Capricorn on November 11, which puts her right smack dab in the middle of your solar eighth house of joint resources and financial affairs. From November 24 through November 26, you may need to decide where to cut a few luxuries.

Tricky Transits

The New Moon of November 29 will set up shop in your solar seventh house of one-to-one relationships, Gemini, indicating that a change is on the horizon. That same day, Venus will get into a testy square with Uranus, who never fails to bring along the last thing on earth you'd ever imagine possible. It might be a new lover, or it might be the end of something, too.

Rewarding Days

4, 5, 15, 16, 29

Challenging Days

3, 6, 24, 25, 30

Gemini | December

Relaxation and Recreation

The skies are fairly bursting with air energies like your own, Gemini, as well as planets in fire, an element you find fun and exciting—so you can count on being extremely active socially, which always makes you happy. The news is even better toward the holidays, when lots of peaceful trines and exciting sextiles will bring you joyous reunions and exciting new friends.

Lovers and Friends

A pack of planets in unpredictable Aquarius will dash through your solar ninth house of long-distance relationships and far-off loved ones, Gemini, so just in time for a terrific holiday season, you can expect to see some faces you've been dearly missing. Whether you travel to them or they to you, there will be no shortage of warm hugs and I love you's.

Money and Success

Generosity and abundance are on your astrological agenda for the month, Gemini, thanks to expansive, extravagant Jupiter in Libra. The thing is, you'll definitely be tempted to overspend, which could be a burden in the very near future. Resist the urge to get too crazy. The best gift you can give others is your time, attention, and love.

Tricky Transits

Your ruling planet, Mercury, will turn retrograde on December 19, Gemini, and since you're a bit more susceptible to his moods than most of us, you might need to deal with a few travel problems or miscommunications for the rest of the month. Troubleshooting is the key. Gas up the car, check the oil, and make sure your spare is set to go. Oh, and don't forget the directions.

Rewarding Days

1, 3, 6, 9, 11, 24, 25

Challenging Days

10, 19, 31

Gemini Action Table

These dates reflect the best—but not the only—times for success and ease in these activities, according to your Sun sign.

	JAN	FEB	MAR	APR	MAY	JUN	JUL	AUG	SEP	OCT	NOV	DEC
Move				15, 16		10, 11		24, 25, 26				
Start a class		5, 6, 7, 9, 10			27, 28		16, 17, 18		1, 2, 3		2, 3	
Join a club	15, 16		1, 2, 3	2, 3				17, 18, 19				4, 5, 6
Ask for a raise						18, 19, 20			11, 12			
Look for work		5, 6, 7			25, 26		18, 19, 20	15, 16		8, 9, 10, 19, 20		
Get pro advice	10, 11			12, 13				15, 16			5, 6, 7	
Get a loan		12, 13, 14				16, 17, 18		10, 11, 12				
See a doctor							8, 9			26, 27		24, 25
Start a diet			9, 10						1, 2, 3			
End relationship	24, 25		23, 24			20, 21			16, 17			29, 30, 31
Buy clothes							1, 27, 28			1, 17, 18		
Get a makeover				9, 10				3, 4, 23, 24			13, 14, 15	
New romance		13, 14					10, 11, 12					7, 8
Vacation				19, 20					9, 10			

Cancer

The Crab
June 20 to July 22

Element: Water

Quality: Cardinal

Polarity: Yin/feminine

Planetary Ruler: The Moon

Meditation: I have faith in the promptings of my heart

Gemstone: Pearl

Power Stones: Moonstone, Chrysocolla

Key Phrase: I feel

Glyph: Crab's claws

Anatomy: Stomach, breasts

Colors: Silver, pearl white

Animals: Crustaceans, cows, chickens

Myths/Legends: Hercules and the Crab, Asherah, Hecate

House: Fourth

Opposite Sign: Capricorn

Flower: Larkspur

Keyword: Receptivity

The Cancer Personality

Your Strengths and Challenges

Home. Family. Security. Privacy. Any questions? The description of your sign might end here, Cancer. You know you're mega into your family, and they're probably just as into you. You're also quite familiar with how much your home means to you, and how hard you work to protect it and keep it safe for all your loved ones under its roof. As far as privacy goes, well, anyone who knows you knows it's just plain foolish to bother you when you ask for alone time—which doesn't happen often. You tend to devote a whole lot of your time, energy, and attention to the ones you love, but once you say "I'm outta here" and that bedroom door shuts, all becomes quite still in your kingdom. No matter who you live with or what your official titles are, don't kid yourself: you're in charge here—and that goes double for the kitchen, and the kitchen table, in particular. Anyone with half a lick of sense will ask before they pull up a chair—and if you're cooking, everybody out! No, you don't want help. They can help by cleaning up. You have your very own system in the kitchen and in your home, and actually for scheduling your life in general, and you really, really don't like for it to be tampered with.

Now, as far as this whole "moody" thing goes, you can stop shaking your head, because you most definitely are moody. Cranky, even, at times. The thing is, it's your astrological job to be cranky, moody, and utterly emotional, no matter where you are or what's going on. Your ruling planet is the emotional Moon, after all. As she waxes, wanes, changes signs, and forms eclipses, her moods change—and so do yours. We may be just a wee bit jealous of your ability to let your feelings out, by the way. Most of us have been trained from birth to do the opposite— so thanks for the inspiration!

There's no better comforter, nurturer, or caretaker than you on the planet, by the way, so if someone dear to you insists on only you doing something for them—well, what can I say? You spoiled them, you knew you were doing so, and you have to admit, it feels good to be needed. Just watch out for a tendency to get into relationships held together by codependency. It might be flattering to have someone so attached to you at first, but after a while it gets very, very old.

Your Relationships

Whether you're choosing a friend or a lover, Cancer, you always follow your gut—which is the right thing to do. In fact, if you think about it, the only time your gut has gotten you into trouble is when you haven't listened to it. That said, it's easy to see how first impressions mean a lot to you. You're really not all that interested in what someone looks or sounds like; you're far more interested in the vibes you get from them. First off, are they safe? Can you be alone with them without being on guard and crawling back into that shell? Most importantly, can you trust them around your home and the people you love?

That's what a potential friend or lover is up against, and whether or not you mean to, you don't go on first dates—you go on first interviews. It's the emotional screening process, and it doesn't take long. You're a cardinal sign, so patience isn't up there on your list of most famous qualities. No, you're a big fan of cutting to the chase. Do try to cut us some slack if we're taken off guard by your rapid-fire, intense questioning. Who knew someone with such a great big heart would be so interested? It's flattering—and scary.

That said, when you're out looking for love, Cancer, you're looking for someone who's in touch with their feelings, and not afraid of yours—no easy task. The other water signs are usually who you'll go to first, both for friendship and love, not just because you share an element, but because you share the ability to go beyond the five senses for information. Water signs have extremely keen antennae, and it's tough to explain those antennae to anyone who's not a proud owner.

Now, Scorpio and Pisces are your water-sign cousins, both gifted with instinct and intuition that you admire and respect. Other Cancers will make you feel smothered, so keep them on board as friends but resist the urge to cohabitate. Only one of you can own the kitchen, after all. As for Scorpio, they're a bit intense at times, but if they love you, they'll fire-walk for you, and when it comes right down to it, that's what you're after. Pisces are wonderful friends. You two will pick up on the same silent signals at the same time and finish each other's sentences, too.

Your Career and Money

Obviously, if there's any way you can work it out, being self-employed and working at home would always be ideal for you. You love being around your loved ones and your things, so a home-based business is right up your alley. Failing that, bet you're interested in real estate—dressing up homes for new families, that is. Yes, it's perfect. Renting or leasing your own property would be the best of all worlds. Then, too, you love kids and you love to be around them, so working at a daycare center is great fun. Oh, and let's not forget about water. Talk about being "in your element"! What could possibly be less like work than being by a lake, beach, or pool all day?

Your Lighter Side

Well, it's easy to figure out what qualifies as a good time for you, Cancer: family, close friends, and lots of time to spend hugging them. Oh, and cooking for them, too. Nothing gives you greater satisfaction than hearing the happy, pleased sounds of loved ones who are enjoying your efforts. Of course, you might also enjoy having them cook for you every now and then, so please do mention that fact at your next cookout.

Affirmation
Being surrounded by my loved ones is truly nirvana.

The Year Ahead for Cancer

Two things, Cancer: First off, your solar fifth house of love affairs and sexy playmates will be hosting fiery, passionate Mars as of January 3, and for a whole lot longer than his usual stay of two months. Now, speaking of passionate, did I neglect to mention that Mars will be all dolled up in sexy Scorpio? Well! Obviously, you're going to be pretty darn busy with your love life, and it's wonderful that you'll be occupied with such tender pursuits. The thing is, Scorpio planets tend to get a little over-possessive every now and then, and maybe just a little bit obsessed, too, so if you're seeing someone and nothing is definite between the two of you yet, call a friend and distract yourself. Yes, even though obsessing on this sort of thing strikes you as a delicious type of torture, step back and get your head right.

Okay, second up: Mars will set off for fiery, funny Sagittarius and your solar sixth house on March 5, and he'll stay put there until he retrogrades back into Scorpio on May 27. In a nutshell, since this house is where work and relationships with coworkers are handled, what this might mean is that your work situation is due to change—à la Sagittarius, in a very big way. If you're not happy in your current situation, you probably already can sense what's coming. Fortunately, you also know where you want to be, work-wise, so get going on that path. And please do have plan B in place before you stalk out and slam the door behind you. The good news is that you'll have those fabulous antennae of yours to point you in the right direction—and if a heavy dose of Mars can't inspire you, nobody can!

Oh, and by the way, from May 27 through June 29, Mars will retrograde back into Scorpio and your solar fifth house of lovers—ahem!—so you might find yourself trying to tie things up between you and someone you've recently dismissed from your life. If you're unhappy with the relationship but you really miss the physical connection you two shared, you'll need to be brave. It won't be easy, but you'll need to refuse to do it all over again. If it didn't work once, it won't work twice—unless, of course, you have new solutions to the old problems that split you up in the first place.

Now, let's talk about Jupiter, who'll spend the year—up until September 9, anyway—in your solar third house of neighbors, conversations, and communication with siblings, all done up in detail-oriented Virgo. Now, he's been here since last August, so you're probably used to all the activity and lovely chats this guy has inspired, and I'm sure you've come to love the energy, too—especially if you've just reconciled with a sibling. You might even miss it. Fortunately, you'll get over it, because Jupiter's next stop won't exactly be a hardship. He'll take off for cooperative, balance-loving Libra on September 9, which just so happens to put him in your solar fourth house of home, family, and domestic situations. Needless to say, if there's been trouble on the home front, it's time to deal with it.

What This Year's Eclipses Mean for You

Eclipses arrive in pairs, Cancer, over a two-week period, and then again six months later. Now, we're all affected by eclipses on an emotional level, but that's even truer for you. Your ruling planet is the emotional Moon herself, and since you're so susceptible to her moods, the influence of these super-duper lunations is usually pretty darn substantial.

This time around, the first Solar Eclipse will occur on March 8, bringing the Moon together with the Sun in spiritual, sensitive Pisces and your solar ninth house of travel, education, and new adventures. This eclipse will inspire you to learn something new about metaphysics, spirituality, or religions—something that will give you the answers you need. Pisces planets are of the water element, like your own, so if you do travel, it might be across the ocean, to distant horizons, possibly even on a cruise ship. Your mission is to allow yourself the luxury of relaxing. You've certainly earned it.

On March 23, the first Lunar Eclipse of the year will occur, and this time out, this super-charged New Moon will illuminate Libra, the sign of partnerships, cooperation, and compromise. It will land in your solar fourth house of home, family, and domestic situations, so if you've been considering a move, this may be when you hear about a place that's just perfect for you and yours. Then, too, if you've been at odds with a dear one, it will definitely be time to either extend or accept an olive branch—and you'll be gracious and fair, either way.

The second set of eclipses will begin on September 1, when the second Solar Eclipse of the year will plant a seed in your solar third house of conversations, thoughts, and decisions. Since this will bring the Sun and Moon together in hardworking Virgo, your job will probably be very much on your mind. If you're done with your current work, it's time to get out there and investigate your options. If you've perfected a craft or other personal hobby, you might think about making it into a part-time business. Bet it doesn't stay part-time for long.

Finally, on September 16, the last Lunar Eclipse of the year will arrive, once again in the sign of Pisces. Now, this seems to be the natural culmination of what you began back in early March. If you feel you've learned enough to teach others, take your show on the road. Promote yourself and let the world know what you have to share. You'll find that you're drawing others to you who are eager to learn from you and quite respectful of your time and talents. If you were only able to plan a trip back in March and haven't yet taken it, this would be the perfect time to do so.

Saturn

Saturn will spend yet another year in your solar sixth house, Cancer, where issues of health and work are handled. Now, this guy just loves schedules, so you've probably been keeping to yours pretty darn carefully, but if you haven't—well, it's time to change all that and bring some structure into your daily life. Might be that you're after a job with more regular hours, or that you're working toward a promotion. The good news is that Saturn rules authority figures, so keep them happy by being reliable and thorough, and rewards will certainly follow. Saturn may not be easy, but he's fair. You can count on receiving exactly what you've earned, so invest some effort and watch what happens. Now, let's talk about health. With Saturn's self-disciplined energy in this house, an exercise routine is easy to stick to. If you're already on one, kudos. Keep up the good work. If you're not, get thee to a gym or start walking with a friend. You might also be toying with the idea of changing your eating habits, which will also be easy to do now. Saturn is a no-frills kind of planet, so he'll continue to inspire you to cut out the fat—literally. It takes only three weeks to change a habit. Get some healthy ones going and ditch whatever isn't helping you feel your best.

Uranus

This rebellious planet has been making his way through your solar tenth house of career matters for years, Cancer—ever since March of 2012, matter of fact. For the duration, your patience has probably been tested, to say the very least, by some pretty darn erratic behavior on the part of the authority figures at work. If that has caused you to consider changing careers—well, then, Uranus has done his job. His mission is to shake you out of situations that are repressive or confining and push you toward personal freedom. If you were born between July 7 and 19, you've also been experiencing this unpredictable energy via a high-energy and often irritating square to your Sun. Now, squares insist on action. They make us edgy and restless, until we become so exasperated we finally decide to change—or better yet, we rebel mightily and dramatically against whoever or whatever it is that's causing our discomfort. In short, if you need to get away from an uncomfortable or stifling situation—and this includes relationships of all kinds, personal and professional—it's time to do it, and make a quick, clean, and guiltless getaway. The good news is that you'll end this adventure feeling like an entirely new person—the one you've known was in there all along.

Neptune

Your solar ninth house of travel, education, and new adventures has been playing host to woozy, dreamy Neptune for roughly five years now, Cancer, and since she's so fond of water, if you haven't yet indulged in a cruise or a seaside or lakeside vacation, this is the year to do so. As a water sign, you'll not only enjoy yourself, you'll also be recharging your emotional batteries by being around—or, better still, in—your own element. If you've been thinking about taking some classes, this is also the right time for it. That goes double if the subject you're fascinated with happens to be spiritual or metaphysical, or related to world religions, all of which will come easily to you now.

If you were born between June 28 and July 6, your intuition will be pretty darn flawless this year, and you'll be able to find the perfect niche to explore developing your psychic abilities. If you're interested in music or art, get yourself some training. You'll probably run into someone from another state, coast, or even country who'll be happy to point you in the right direction. Mentors and gurus are all around you now. Be sure to take full advantage of what they have to offer—and don't be afraid to offer the benefit of your experience to others. Remember, we're all students here on Planet Number Three, but we're also teachers.

Pluto

Pluto will spend yet another year in your solar seventh house of one-to-one relationships, Cancer, turning up the intensity on all your encounters. Pluto just loves to clean house and take out the trash, so you'll probably find that harmful or negative relationships are actually leaving your life. Even if you're not initiating these changes consciously—and you should be, by the way—you're still putting out the vibes. If you've lost someone dear to you, take comfort in the knowledge that Pluto also rules regeneration, so your heart will heal—albeit slowly—and new relationships will be along shortly. That said, if you're single and looking, Pluto's presence here will bring along some really intense types. On the plus side, you could meet a soul mate, and if you do, it will be feel far more like recognition than an introduction. On the negative side, you'll need to be careful not to become attracted to anyone who seems a bit dangerous. They might be truly dangerous. Trust your antennae—and, of course, your gut. If you were born between July 5 and 10, Pluto will form an opposition with your Sun, so any or all of these scenarios may be happening right now or just finishing up. Remember, you're in the midst of the huge process of deciding what you want from others and learning how to ask for it and attract it.

Cancer | January

Relaxation and Recreation
Fiery, impatient Mars will spend the month in your solar fifth house of lovers, playmates, and casual relationships, Cancer—so you might not get much rest, but you definitely won't be bored. His very presence here is enough to motivate you to make that call, but let's not forget that he's all done up in sexy Scorpio. Yep. Definitely not boring.

Lovers and Friends
You've already been alerted to the fact that Mars is in intense, sexy Scorpio, so if you're not seeing anyone, you'll certainly be in the mood to get out there and look around. Luck will be with you on January 17, 18, or 19, and you just might meet someone who'll fascinate you—big time. Make sure you have a friend with you to offer up their opinion.

Money and Success
Dealing with joint finances will keep you on your toes this month thanks to the Sun and Mercury, who'll make their way through your solar eighth house of loans, inheritances, and shared resources, Cancer. The thing is, they'll be all done up in startling Aquarius, so you'll have to be ready for anything. That goes double because Mercury will do the retrograde dance from January 5 through January 25.

Tricky Transits
On January 7, the Sun in Capricorn and your solar seventh house of one-to-one relationships will square off with unpredictable Uranus in impulsive Aries—who just so happens to be in your solar tenth house of authority figures and career matters. Someone dear to you may not be happy about all that time you're spending on the job, especially if you're on call more often than not.

Rewarding Days
13, 14, 18, 19, 30

Challenging Days
5, 6, 7, 20, 22, 29, 31

Cancer | February

Relaxation and Recreation

Passionate Mars in sexy Scorpio will spend yet another month in your solar fifth house of lovers, playmates, and casual relationships, Cancer, so if you're not currently seeing someone, you should expect a delightful buffet of admirers, all of whom will be quite intent on getting to know you better. A lot better.

Lovers and Friends

Valentine's Day looks just delightful, Cancer, thanks to an easy trine between the Moon (your ruling planet) and Jupiter, who never fails to bring presents, hugs, and good feelings when he visits. If you don't have a steady Valentine and a sibling or neighbor offers to introduce you to someone they're sure is just perfect for you, give it a shot—no matter what happened last time.

Money and Success

Venus is in charge of money matters, Cancer, and she'll spend half of the month in your solar seventh house of one-to-one relationships, all done up in practical Capricorn. If you're thinking about cohabitating, she'll be on duty to help you come up with a fair financial arrangement you both can stick to. Be sure you iron things out before the moving van arrives.

Tricky Transits

A high-intensity meeting between loving Venus and sexy, relentless Pluto will take place on February 5, Cancer, so fasten your seat belt. These two create "interesting" relationship scenarios, ranging from obsession to instant, irresistible infatuation. If you meet someone new who seems a bit dangerous, take your time getting to know them—and as per usual, trust your gut.

Rewarding Days

3, 4, 9, 14, 28, 29

Challenging Days

5, 7, 22, 23, 27

Cancer | March

Relaxation and Recreation

There may be a bit of travel on your agenda this month, Cancer, thanks to Venus, Mercury, Neptune, and the Sun, who'll spend an awful lot of time in your solar ninth house, all done up in nostalgic Pisces. If there's someone out there who's been much too far from you for much too long, make it your business to see them. You'll be glad you did.

Lovers and Friends

If a relationship hasn't been going too well lately, you might decide to terminate it around March 4 or 5, Cancer, but before you do, make sure it's what you really want to do. Now, if there's any kind of abuse going on, whether physical or mental, disregard that bit of advice and go—immediately, if not sooner.

Money and Success

If things have been a bit shaky in your financial life recently, you can probably expect that to end now, Cancer—or at least to get a whole lot easier. By the end of the month, all those planets in quirky, unpredictable Aquarius will leave your solar eighth house of joint money matters behind—and not a moment too soon for your tastes!

Tricky Transits

Your ruling planet, the emotional Moon, has scheduled two eclipses for this month, Cancer, both of which will most definitely be tricky for all of us to handle. The thing is, the Moon has an awful lot to do with your moods, so if you're a bit out of sorts around March 8 and 23, force yourself to relax and take some time alone to think things over.

Rewarding Days
6, 10, 11, 12, 16, 17

Challenging Days
4, 5, 8, 14, 23

Cancer | April

Relaxation and Recreation

A pack of fiery Aries planets will liven up your month in a very big way, Cancer, and, along with the New Moon in that same sign on April 7, could put you in the mood to pack up for a few days and hit the road, quite on impulse. If you can, you really should. After all, when was the last time you gave yourself some time off?

Lovers and Friends

Some nice, solid Taurus energies will spend a good part of the month in your solar eleventh house of friendships and groups, Cancer, so if you're in the mood to play, you can count on having all the right companions only too happy to join you. Venus will jump into that sign and house on April 29, and romance with a friend of a friend may be on your agenda.

Money and Success

From April 5 through April 29, Venus, the Goddess of Love and Money, will spend her time in fiery, impulsive Aries. Needless to say, if you're out shopping, especially around the New Moon of April 7, you really should have a sensible friend along with you to keep you out of financial trouble. Matter of fact, let them hold on to your plastic.

Tricky Transits

Oddly enough, April Fools' Day will play host to some astrological transits that are just perfect for this offbeat holiday, Cancer, so be on your toes and if your antennae tell you that someone is trying to prank you, believe it. Your best bet? Be prepared with a couple of surprises yourself! Nothing hurtful, of course. Go easy.

Rewarding Days
1, 4, 5, 14

Challenging Days
6, 7, 19, 27, 28

Cancer | May

Relaxation and Recreation

A sky full of mellow earth energies will make the first half of the month pretty darn pleasant for you, Cancer, bringing along lots of opportunities for making new friendships. And since three planets in solid, practical Taurus will be on duty in your solar eleventh house, you can count on them being the kind that last.

Lovers and Friends

Loving Venus will set off for lighthearted, playful Gemini on May 24, Cancer, which will put her in your solar twelfth house of Privacy, Please. Now, the first thing she'll do that day will be to form a rather testy opposition with fiery Mars, so you might need to fight the urge to pout or hide out. If someone hurts you, let them know about it!

Money and Success

Arguments over money matters may be on your agenda during the last week of the month, Cancer, so if you've been simmering over someone's lack of responsibility in this department, you won't stew much longer. If you can, hammer things out early in the month—say, around May 10 or 11. You'll save yourself a whole lot of stress and tension.

Tricky Transits

Jupiter just loves to expand things, Cancer. It's what he does best. Saturn, on the other hand, frowns upon indulging in anything that isn't necessary. What a team. They'll square off on May 26, so you should probably expect a bit of tension around that time, mostly with regard to work or work-related relationships. If you feel that someone is deliberately pushing you around, put your foot down.

Rewarding Days

1, 2, 7, 10, 11, 12, 13

Challenging Days

4, 5, 21, 22, 24, 26

Cancer | June

Relaxation and Recreation

This has got to be your favorite time of year, Cancer, when the parade of planets in your sign and your solar first house of personality and appearance begins. That said, you'll probably be spending a whole lot of time with your family, and the kids will be especially entertaining, not to mention affectionate. Next month will bring more of the same. Get out the grill.

Lovers and Friends

Loving Venus will set off for your very own soothing sign on June 17, Cancer—and just in time, too. That same day, realistic Saturn will get into an irritating square with dreamy Neptune, and that means that all kind of fantasies might just be shattered. If a friend comes to you with a serious relationship-oriented problem, hugs will most definitely be in order.

Money and Success

The Full Moon of June 20 will occur at the very last degree of Sagittarius and in your solar sixth house of work situations. If you've just about had it with conditions on the job, it won't take much to convince you to storm off into the sunset, slamming the door behind you. Please do be sure you have other options before you go.

Tricky Transits

If you feel you're not getting your point across around June 5, 6, and 7, Cancer, you're probably right. The Sun and Venus in chatty Gemini will get into inconjunct aspects with intense, demanding Pluto—which does not bode well for conversations and communications. Don't make any important decisions, and hold off on announcements.

Rewarding Days
26, 27, 28, 29

Challenging Days
5, 6, 7, 14, 15, 17, 22

Cancer | July

Relaxation and Recreation

You might actually be able to kick back and enjoy life this month, Cancer—provided you warn the kids that the hours you'll spend as their personal chauffeur will be drastically reduced. Of course, someone may be just getting their license or all excited about a new vehicle, too, which would make your announcement a whole lot easier.

Lovers and Friends

With loving Venus, the Sun, and chatty Mercury on duty in your home- and family-loving sign for most of the month, Cancer, you should probably get ready for some wonderful weekends at your place. It's time to gather together with loved ones and enjoy the sun and the outdoors. Why, you might even get a bit of a tan!

Money and Success

Venus rules money matters, Cancer, and she'll spend the first eleven days of July in your sign and your solar first house of personality and appearance. The first thing that comes to mind is that dressing for success will earn you all kinds of rewards, so if you're looking to climb a few steps up the ladder, give it a shot. At the very least, you'll feel confident. At best, you'll find the job you've been looking for.

Tricky Transits

Uneasy aspects between fiery Mars, the Sun, and surprising Uranus on July 13 and 14 could cause your world to be a bit less than calm, Cancer. If someone is obviously mad about something but not willing to share what the problem might be, don't play into this passive-aggressive nonsense. Your mission is to refuse to be shaken up, controlled, or manipulated.

Rewarding Days

1, 3, 5, 6, 8, 9, 17

Challenging Days

2, 10, 11, 16, 29

Cancer | August

Relaxation and Recreation

It's time to enjoy life, Cancer, and forget about any recent unpleasantness that may have occurred between you and a loved one. Matter of fact, putting old resentments to bed wouldn't be a bad idea, either. If you run into someone you left on less-than-happy terms, do the right thing. Either extend or accept the olive branch.

Lovers and Friends

The heavens will be passing out warm hugs and lots of laughter on August 27, Cancer, as loving Venus and generous Jupiter come together in your solar third house of conversations and communications. Now, these are inarguably the most benevolent planets, so having them side by side will be delightful for us all. You, however, will receive some very happy news.

Money and Success

The Sun will be in Leo until August 22, Cancer, which puts this lavish fellow in your solar second house of money matters. That said, you should probably not be out shopping for gifts without a chaperone, since Leo planets are famous for pulling out all the stops to put a smile on someone's face. Your mission is to be sensible.

Tricky Transits

Mercury will turn retrograde on August 30, Cancer, from his spot in detail-oriented Virgo and your solar third house of short trips. Now, this transit could bring problems with traveling to the places you visit frequently, perhaps in the form of traffic or roadwork, but it might also be that your vehicle needs some help. Troubleshoot for mechanical problems before you leave the house.

Rewarding Days

1, 2, 10, 14, 17, 22, 27, 28

Challenging Days

6, 7, 13, 25, 30

Cancer | September

Relaxation and Recreation

Mercury will spend the first three weeks of the month moving retrograde, Cancer, so if you have plans to travel with the kids and other family members, you really should prepare for unexpected delays. If you're traveling by vehicle, have it looked over by a mechanic you trust before you hit the open highway. Most of all, if you do get stalled, don't be cranky.

Lovers and Friends

On September 23, Venus will tiptoe discreetly into sexy Scorpio and your solar fifth house of lovers, Cancer—and yes, the news could certainly be worse. The thing is, someone recently introduced to you by a family member may, oddly enough, be just as perfect for you as they said. If so, stage two of your relationship will proceed in a most delightful way.

Money and Success

Try not to buy anything electronic or invest in new vehicles until Mercury turns direct on September 21, Cancer. Matter of fact, it might be best to wait until next month for either adventure. The thing is, Mercury isn't just retrograde, he's retrograde in your solar third house of short trips, conversations, and communications. If you must make a purchase, save the receipt—and get the warranty.

Tricky Transits

If you've recently had vehicle trouble, Cancer, I hate to tell you this but it might not be over just yet. First of all, Mercury is still retrograde and will remain so until September 21, but then, too, there's a Solar Eclipse scheduled for your third house of short trips on September 1, and Saturn will step in to provide even more in the way of delays and roadblocks. Try to remain calm. This, too, shall pass.

Rewarding Days

6, 7, 23, 25

Challenging Days

1, 2, 10, 12, 20, 21

Cancer | October

Relaxation and Recreation

On October 22, the Sun will set off for your solar fifth house of lovers, playmates, and fun times, Cancer, followed shortly by chatty, thoughtful Mercury. Now, they'll both be in sexy Scorpio at the time, so your idea of playtime will probably change—from hanging out at your place to dressing up and heading out to hunt for someone delicious. Good luck!

Lovers and Friends

Mars set off for your solar seventh house of one-to-one relationships at the end of last month, Cancer, and he'll stay on duty there until November 8. Now, this is a very passionate fellow, so wherever he goes, he likes to stir things up. He's also pretty good at inspiring arguments. Now that you know he's in the neighborhood, you can use his energy for better things.

Money and Success

Careful there, Cancer. Right around October 19, you could get into it with a family member or partner who hasn't been carrying their share of the financial burden for some time now. The good news is that you'll be quite calm as you present the situation, and even more matter-of-fact when you lay down the law, complete with "due by" dates.

Tricky Transits

An argument could be in the offing on October 28, Cancer. Yes, another one. Hot-headed Mars will square off with unpredictable Uranus—an explosive team, to say the least. Mars will still be in your solar seventh house of relationships, so if you feel things heating up—unpleasantly, that is—between you and your sweetheart, do yourself a favor and put some distance between you for a few hours.

Rewarding Days

1, 2, 3, 4, 30

Challenging Days

5, 7, 13, 15, 16, 28, 29

Cancer | November

Relaxation and Recreation

Loving Venus will get together with your ruling planet, the emotional Moon, on November 3, Cancer, so it's not hard to imagine you in the mood to spend every possible minute with the ones you love. And since both planets will be in Sagittarius, the sign that's so fond of long-distance travel, you might even be joined by someone you haven't seen in a very long time. Enjoy!

Lovers and Friends

A fling could turn into something far more meaningful this month, Cancer—as soon as November 1, in fact. The Sun in intense Scorpio is in your solar fifth house of lovers, and even though this house is usually reserved for playmates and casual affairs, keep in mind that Scorpio energy plays for keeps. If you're ready to get involved, this could be it.

Money and Success

Be careful with your money around November 4, Cancer, when Venus will get into a square with dreamy Neptune. It will be easy for you to get distracted and lose actual cash, and even easier for you to be taken in by someone with a plan for your finances. If your antennae tell you this situation is too good to be true and the person offering it isn't trustworthy, refuse.

Tricky Transits

A conversation could turn rather fiery in a hurry around November 6, Cancer, so if you feel your face beginning to burn, you should probably just walk away, as quickly as possible. Startling Uranus will be one of the astrological culprits involved, and this guy most definitely has a hair-trigger temper, especially now that he's in impulsive Aries. Table that discussion—permanently, if need be.

Rewarding Days
1, 2, 3, 7, 11

Challenging Days
5, 6, 17, 18, 24

Cancer | December

Relaxation and Recreation

Happy holidays, Cancer! As family-oriented as you are, this is undoubtedly your favorite time of year—and this year in particular will be especially delightful. Loving Venus will form an easy trine with generous Jupiter and an exciting sextile with surprising Uranus on December 25, setting the stage for parties, gifts, and even a surprise appearance. Enjoy!

Lovers and Friends

Wow! Talk about a great month, Cancer. With the possible exception of December 26 and 31, just about all the planets will be in cooperative, fun-loving relationships with one another, inspiring you to do the same. It's hard to imagine you not seeing your loved ones frequently. Of course, everyone will need to come to your place to party—but that's what they live for.

Money and Success

As far as money goes, Cancer, you can expect the usual circumstances. You'll head out to do some sensible shopping, determined to stick to your list and, more importantly, your budget. And as per usual, if you spot something a loved one would just adore, you'll forget all about both. Ah, well. It's only once a year.

Tricky Transits

There's really only one day this month that sticks out as possibly tricky, Cancer, and oddly enough, it's New Year's Eve. That night, impulsive Mars will collide with woozy, dreamy Neptune, both of them in Pisces—Neptune's own dreamy sign. That said, if you're impaired from the party, don't drive, and don't let anyone drive you if you're not sure of their condition. Don't forget your seat belt.

Rewarding Days

Pretty much all month.

Challenging Days

26, 31

Cancer Action Table

These dates reflect the best—but not the only—times for success and ease in these activities, according to your Sun sign.

	JAN	FEB	MAR	APR	MAY	JUN	JUL	AUG	SEP	OCT	NOV	DEC
Move	7, 8						3, 4, 5				5, 6	
Start a class		15, 19		23, 25, 26				12, 13, 14		1, 2, 3		
Join a club	11, 12		6, 7, 8			7, 8			1, 2			5, 6, 7
Ask for a raise	10, 11			1, 27, 28			6, 7, 8				26, 27	
Look for work	9, 10, 11		4, 5, 6		6, 7, 25, 26			5, 6, 17, 18, 19			4, 5	
Get pro advice		6, 7, 8				21, 22			11, 12			
Get a loan				23, 24			13, 14, 15					27, 28, 29
See a doctor	1, 27, 28				15, 16, 17				1, 2, 3		22, 23	
Start a diet		8, 9				6, 7, 8				16, 17, 18		14, 15
End relationship	24, 25		22, 23				19, 20		16, 17			
Buy clothes	18, 19							3, 4, 23, 24			14, 15, 16	
Get a makeover			8, 9		6, 7				28, 29, 30			
New romance	18, 19					26, 27						
Vacation		3, 4, 5			22, 23					7, 8, 9		27, 28, 29

Leo

The Lion
July 22 to August 22

♌

Element: Fire

Quality: Fixed

Polarity: Yang/masculine

Planetary Ruler: The Sun

Meditation: I trust in the strength of my soul

Gemstone: Ruby

Power Stones: Topaz, sardonyx

Key Phrase: I will

Glyph: Lion's tail

Anatomy: Heart, upper back

Colors: Gold, scarlet

Animals: Lions, large cats

Myths/Legends: Apollo, Isis, Helios

House: Fifth

Opposite Sign: Aquarius

Flowers: Marigold, sunflower

Keyword: Magnetic

The Leo Personality

Your Strengths and Challenges

Let's get one thing straight right away, Leo. You are indeed royalty, and you do indeed deserve to be treated as such. Your symbol is the lion, the legendary King of the Jungle, and it's a terrific fit. The lion was a symbol that carried a whole lot of weight back in medieval times, when having one on your family crest would automatically get you the best seat in the house. Yes, being treated well by others is absolutely mandatory, but you're quite willing to do the same for them. You're a terrific playmate and an unforgettable lover, always game to try something new. You have an adventurous nature, in all departments. Makes sense. After all, lions have adventures all the time—comes with that King of the Jungle territory. Lions are very brave, like you, too—which certainly comes in handy when you hop up on that stage, full of confidence, ready to entertain us once again. You're so good at your job that you're very rarely alone unless you want to be, and new fans are easy to come by. Like the lion, you're also quite protective of your "pride"—which consists of anyone you love. And speaking of love, your sign rules the heart in the physical body. When your pride gets bruised, your heart gets broken, and it's not a pretty sight. However, those who love you and are lucky enough to be loved by you know exactly how to state their point without hurting your feelings.

Now, let's talk about the challenging part of your nature. To start with, you probably just cringed at the very thought of hearing what's not positive about yourself. You are a very proud sign, so you don't often take criticism well—but you can tuck that lip back in, because you don't often have to, and your "faults" are really quite endearing. Sure, you like to be the star of the show, but you're really good at entertaining us. Besides, the warmth of your attention is more than worth the price of admission. You do tend to be a bit on the vain side, especially concerning that mane of yours, but hey—you've got to look your best for the fans, right?

Your Relationships

You're a spoiler, Leo. Anyone who's ever enjoyed the pleasure of your full attention can most definitely attest to that. It's not just that you go out of your way to make them smile, be they friend or lover, but more so that way you have of making someone feel like they're the most important person in the world. Your ruling planet is the Sun, and when you've taken a shine to someone, the warmth you offer is irresistible. You don't ask for much in return, either. Just appreciation and affection. Okay, and a few compliments every now and then. That's all. Okay, and maybe some applause. And a standing ovation every now and then wouldn't hurt, either. Basically, you want to be the star of the show to the ones you love, and you're willing to return the favor. Big time. You're quite lavish with gifts, in addition to attention. If you spot something a loved one would adore, they'll soon have it. If there's somewhere they want to go, you'll get them there and see to it that it's a five-star experience.

Romance is your business, and you're really good at it. What you're looking for is a lover, a playmate, and a friend, all rolled up into one person. The other fire signs make excellent friends and even better partners. You adore the energy and impulsiveness of Aries. Plus, they're always up for an adventure, and adventures are right at the top of the list for you. Sagittarius makes a terrific playmate, especially as a traveling companion. It's tough to partner up with another Leo, though, but then, that's understandable. The spotlight is only so big, after all. Quite often, you'll find yourself in the loving arms of a Libra, for obvious reasons. Their specialty is one-to-one relationships, so when they're involved with you, you're the center of their world and you always come first. Yep. Certainly sounds like a match made in the heavens.

Your Career and Money

Regardless of what type of work you choose, Leo, you'll need a stage. Might be a great big one, complete with a spotlight and thousands of screaming fans in the audience. Might be a schoolroom, too. Teaching little ones is a nice fit. Keeping their attention by performing is fun, and you're quite fond of the warmth and affection that children extend so easily. Then, too, you might have done a stint as a bartender, which would also be great fun for you. After all, what's not to love about hosting a party for a few hundred of your closest friends? No matter what you choose to do to earn your daily bread, you'll need frequent reassurance that you're doing a good job. Nothing will chase you out the door faster than feeling unappreciated or ignored. Now, let's talk about money—which you see as something to be traded for adventures, new experiences, and spoiling the ones you love. You're quite lavish with gifts, especially if you're newly in love. The thing is, you're not afraid to work hard so that you can have the best—which, of course, is what royalty deserves. You're also not afraid to keep your own books, and with meticulous Virgo on the cusp of your solar second house of finances, you're usually pretty darn good at it.

Your Lighter Side

You're into creating things, Leo, and you're often really good at creating art and music—so that even when you're not performing, your talents are on display. And speaking of which, crafting the perfect performance is really, really fun and really, really important to you, too. You're also into sweet romance, and you're good at it. You love coming up with ideas for the perfect evening out or the perfect vacation. You'll pull out all the stops and go for the five-star treatment if you know it will please someone you adore—and cost will not be a consideration. You're very playful, and you're determined to make as much of your time here on our lovely planet pleasurable and fun.

Affirmation
My natural abilities fill me with confidence.

The Year Ahead for Leo

Fiery Mars will extend his stay in Scorpio and Sagittarius this year, Leo, so your solar fourth and fifth houses will host him straight through the end of September. Mars will be in intense, perceptive Scorpio when he storms into your solar fourth house of home, family matters, and your domestic situation, so if you have the feeling that something is brewing, you're probably right. In fact, you should probably prepare yourself for a bit of drama on the home front, especially from January 3 straight through early March and again from late May through early August. Mars will retrograde from May 27 through June 29 in this sign and house, so you might find that old power struggles are coming up again and demanding to be dealt with, or you might discover that someone hasn't been totally honest with you. Either way, try not to fixate on the issue. You'll have bigger fish to fry come March, April, May, August, and September, anyway, when Mars will be in fiery, fun-loving Sagittarius and your solar fifth house of love affairs. If you're not yet attached, keep an ear out for someone with a delightful accent who's not exactly from your neck of the woods. At the very least, you'll have a wonderful new playmate.

Now, let's talk about Jupiter, the King of the Gods—royalty, like yourself—who'll pass from Virgo into Libra on September 9. For most of the year, Jupiter will take up residence in your solar second house of finances, wearing Virgo, quite the detail-oriented energy. If you need to straighten out any troubling money matters, you'll have plenty of opportunities, and you really should invest your energy in organizing your affairs in this department. In particular, if you're not sure where your money is going, it's time to start collecting receipts and keeping records. Fortunately, Jupiter often brings benevolent, helpful higher-ups into our lives, so if you need help with this project, you won't have to look far to find it. On the other hand, you may need to advise someone on their finances, or at least give them your opinion on how to make things better.

Now, when Jupiter enters Libra in September, he'll be making his way through your solar third house of conversations and communications, so you should expect to be doing a whole lot of chatting—for the entire coming year, by the way. During that time, you'll probably also have some decision-making to do. The thing is, Libra planets can make us quite indecisive, so take your time, consider all your options, and don't allow yourself to be rushed into anything. You might also expect at least one of your conversations to be about settling down. Libra is, after all, the sign that rules one-to-one relationships, so taking a formerly casual relationship to the next level seems to be on your agenda.

What This Year's Eclipses Mean for You

Every six months, a pair of eclipses arrives, two weeks apart. Solar Eclipses bring the Sun and Moon together in a supercharged New Moon. They inspire beginnings—of a rapid-fire variety. Lunar Eclipses are equally energetic Full Moons that inspire quick endings. In your case, it seems that the eclipse cycle will involve partnership and financial negotiations, so you can definitely expect some action in those departments.

The first set of eclipses will begin with a Solar Eclipse on March 8, bringing the Sun and Moon together in Pisces and your solar eighth house of joint finances and matters dealing with inheritances, loans, or shared possessions. If you're unclear about the details of an important transaction, have a professional look over all your documents and records. Don't sign anything until you know exactly what you're agreeing to and don't let anyone rush or intimidate you. That goes double for an ex-spouse or business partner.

On March 23, a Lunar Eclipse in partner-oriented Libra will arrive, illuminating your solar third house of thoughts, conversations, and communications. You'll definitely be thinking about what you want from relationships, and if you're happily attached, you two might suddenly decide to make it official and head down to the courthouse. If you're single, be very careful with online dating sites. You certainly could meet someone special, but just in case, make sure any introductions take place in public. Now, paperwork is also handled in this house, so you may be at the tail end of negotiations begun recently. The thing is, eclipses are erratic critters, so you might think matters are settled, only to find that someone has stalled or delayed them. Libra energy inspires fairness and compromise, so if things haven't gone very well up until now, expect a quick U-turn.

On September 1, the second Solar Eclipse of the year will occur in detail-oriented Virgo and your solar second house of finances. Yes, that certainly could mean you're wading through more paperwork, but New Moons indicate beginnings, so this time around the reason might be that you've decided to start something—say, perhaps, your own business. If that's the case, your mission is to be precise and specific when you're negotiating leases, loan agreements, and contracts. If you're doubtful about anything, consult a pro—maybe the person you used back in March.

The last eclipse of the year will be a Lunar Eclipse, set for September 16. This one will occur in Pisces and your solar eighth house of joint finances and matters dealing with inheritances, loans, or shared possessions. If that sounds familiar, it's because the Solar Eclipse of March 3 was also in this sign and house in your solar chart. The Moon will be full this time out, however, and since culmination and closure are her specialties during this phase, you might actually be looking at the end of a very long, drawn-out, and possibly unpleasant situation.

Saturn

Saturn will spend the year in Sagittarius, which puts him right smack dab in your solar fifth house of recreation, playmates, and dealings with children. This serious, practical planet could toss some added responsibilities your way, which will prevent you from socializing as much as you usually do. Now, don't panic. No one's saying you can't go out and play, only that you'll need to do your homework first. Besides, there's something about actually earning a break or vacation that makes it even sweeter. Now, let's talk about romance. If you're happily attached, you two can count on the bond you have growing even deeper. If the situation isn't good, however, you may consider ending it. If you're single, you're probably looking, but working so hard and taking care of others will make it a bit tougher for you to meet a new flame. When you have time to socialize, then, don't waste it. Be sure you're spending your precious leisure hours with your kind of people. Saturn also often brings along relationships with others who are either much older or much younger, so don't automatically discount someone for that reason. Forget about doing the math. Focus on what you have in common, and remember, you have every right to be picky. Of course, it's also quite possible that you're not even interested in dating at the moment. If that's the case, don't worry about it. You're not losing your edge, just waiting for quality versus quantity.

Uranus

You've been enjoying the company of this eye-opening energy in your solar ninth house since March of 2012, Leo—and what a ride it's been. The ninth house is where issues to do with education and traveling come up, and with Uranus on board, I'm willing to bet you've learned a lot about some pretty darn odd and unusual subjects. You've probably also traveled to places most people don't ever think of visiting—which undoubtedly made it more fun. Uranus's mission here is to activate your curiosity and push you toward situations that will allow you to broaden your horizons. He's all done up in impulsive Aries—your fire-sign cousin—so whatever adventures Uranus has tossed your way have allowed you to experience the adrenaline rush of brand-new experiences that Aries energy craves. Of course, this house also has a lot to do with our opinions on The Big Subjects, so you've probably changed your mind pretty darn drastically about politics, religion, and how the world should be run in general. If you were born between August 8 and 19, you are also currently experiencing Uranus's energy via an easy, fiery trine to your Sun. The Sun represents your sense of self, and when Uranus drops by, a whole lot changes. Just about everything, matter of fact—so the one thing you can be sure of is that you'll end this transit as an entirely different person. Stay open to the unusual—and have fun rediscovering yourself!

Neptune

For the past five or so years, dreamy, woozy, and oh-so-romantic Neptune has been making her way, silently and invisibly, through your solar eighth house of intimate partners, Leo, and she'll stay on duty there for all of 2016, too. Now, she travels with a pink bucket of stardust and a pink smoke machine wherever she goes—it's her Reality Diffusion Kit. In this house, her efforts can go two ways. First off, there's nothing like love to turn reality into a truly wonderful place to be, so if you're attached, it's pretty much a given that you two can't stop looking at each other, much less bear to be physically separated for more than a few hours. Your love life has probably been intense, passionate, and tender, and you'll find that the connection you two share regenerates your soul and makes you more of who you really are, way down inside at your very core. On the other hand, all that pink stuff can make it tough to see clearly, so you also stand a chance of experiencing fraud, confusion, or downright betrayal at the hands of someone you thought you knew. When in doubt, ask for the opinion of a friend who loves you enough to be truthful.

Now, if you were born between July 28 and August 5, your Sun is also currently under the spell of an inconjunct aspect with Neptune, which can be a bit problematic, not necessarily with regard to relationships (although that's definitely possible) but more so when it comes to joint finances. You'll need to be very sure that no one is taking advantage of your kind heart simply because they can.

Pluto

Your solar sixth house is where issues of work, health, and your daily routine are handled, Leo, and right now, it's currently playing host to powerful, transformational Pluto. This means that a whole lot of changes either have been or will be happening in these departments. While you might not realize what's going on at first, when you look back at your current situation in a few years, you'll see that you were in the middle of a major process. Pluto is subtle but relentless. Wherever he is, it's best to let go of what's not working and replace it with something better. In your case, it's health habits that may need to be changed, and changed drastically. The good news is that if you've abused your body in any way and you stop that nonsense now, you'll have the full benefit of Pluto's regenerative powers at your disposal—so get right on that. Likewise, if you're not feeling appreciated at your current place of employment, you've probably been backing away from it gradually. If it's time for a change, you'll know it. All you have to do is put the wheels in motion. If you were born between August 6 and 12, Pluto will also form a tricky inconjunct aspect to your Sun this year, and since planets in this aspect have absolutely nothing in common, this can be a time of confusion. On the plus side, however, you'll need to learn a new skill set to get your point across and make your way, so in the long run, this, too, will prove beneficial.

Leo | January

Relaxation and Recreation

You may not be ready to stop partying just yet, Leo—but then, you may not have to. Work will definitely take up a good amount of your time, but Venus in Sagittarius will see to it that you have plenty of energy—not to mention a host of playmates—once you close the office door behind you.

Lovers and Friends

A voice from the past? You betcha, Leo—maybe even more than one. Mercury will turn retrograde on January 5 in your solar seventh house of one-to-one relationships, and suddenly, someone you haven't heard from in a very long while may decide to give you a jingle. Don't get too excited just yet, though. Circumstances may keep you apart until next month. Hang in there.

Money and Success

Mercury's retrograde through your solar sixth house of work could mean you'll be starting the new year by retracing your steps a bit, but try not to get too frustrated. Think of this as an opportunity to perfect a project that has your name on it. You know how much your professional reputation means to you. Don't be cranky. Be grateful for the second chance.

Tricky Transits

Mercury will set off for your solar seventh house of one-to-one relationships on January 1, Leo, all done up in unpredictable Aquarius. On January 5, however, he'll stop in his tracks to begin a three-week retrograde period. Now, this is the stuff that second chances are made of, so if you recently finished up a project and find that something has been left undone, get back to it on January 8.

Rewarding Days

11, 12, 13, 14, 15

Challenging Days

3, 5, 17, 25, 31

Leo | February

Relaxation and Recreation

Mercury's retrograde last month probably brought someone back into your life, Leo, but if you didn't have a chance to get together, you can change that as of February 13, when this chatty, personable energy will reenter your solar seventh house of relationships. Loving Venus will also be on duty there as of February 16, so if you two were once an item, you might give them a second shot at the title.

Lovers and Friends

As you're working away together around February 9, it may suddenly strike you that a coworker or higher-up is pretty darn attractive. Well, now. What to do? If the feeling is mutual—and you'll be able to tell immediately—don't let an age difference dissuade you from getting to know them better. Forget the math. Focus on that lovely spark.

Money and Success

Jupiter's position in your solar second house of finances has probably treated you quite well, Leo. Jupiter's motto is "Much, Many, More," and he's quite the generous guy. This month, a few more financial goodies will come your way around February 9, most likely through partnering up with someone from the past whom you've worked well with before.

Tricky Transits

Talking things over may not be an easy task around February 27, Leo, thanks to an uneasy aspect between chatty Mercury and Jupiter. If you just can't understand where the other person is coming from and it's obvious that they're befuddled by you as well, take a breather—and maybe a walk. You might be asking the wrong questions, and a bit of perspective will make that clear.

Rewarding Days

3, 9, 14, 16, 25, 26, 29

Challenging Days

6, 7, 22, 27

Leo | March

Relaxation and Recreation

Careful now, Leo. Loving Venus will tiptoe off into your solar eighth house of shared finances, loans, and inheritances on March 12, all done up in dreamy Pisces—a sign that's not always good with details. If you need to sign papers, have someone who knows what they're doing look them over for you first, and don't allow yourself to be rushed.

Lovers and Friends

The eighth house also rules intimate relationships, Leo, so Venus's journey through here could have quite the upside to it. Pisces planets dissolve boundaries, so you and your sweetheart will share some especially tender and almost mystical moments. And talk about romance—which just so happens to be one of your specialties. March 26 in particular will bring you a great big heaping dose of it.

Money and Success

Jupiter will get together with intense, determined Pluto on March 16, Leo, urging you to think about pursuing a management or supervisory position. If you're trained and prepared for it, wonderful. If you're not, don't jump into anything that won't end well. Pick the brain of someone who's been there, and take the time to learn all you need to know.

Tricky Transits

Two eclipses this month could mean you're due for some great, big changes you weren't expecting, Leo—but don't panic. Change is good for the soul, and it certainly makes things interesting. Besides, an easy trine between Jupiter and Pluto will help you stabilize things fast. Keep that in mind if a certain higher-up throws a huge project your way and wants it done yesterday.

Rewarding Days

2, 6, 7, 26, 28, 29

Challenging Days

4, 5, 8, 14, 23, 30

Leo | April

Relaxation and Recreation

A sky full of bold, fiery Aries energies will see to it that you're far from bored. April 1, 2, and 3 look to be especially fun, and an Aquarius Moon will bring just the right amount of spontaneity into the mix. She'll be back on duty in your solar seventh house of relationships around April 30, too. Don't even bother to make plans. Just enjoy what the Universe tosses your way.

Lovers and Friends

Is it time to make things more permanent between you and your current lover, Leo? Bet it is. Bet that urge will be especially strong around April 18, when loving Venus will form an easy trine with Saturn, who just adores commitments. Both planets will be in fire signs like your own at the time, too, an added bonus. Sounds like passion, excitement, and contentment all mixed together.

Money and Success

If you have a financial deal to finalize, April 18 looks terrific for that, too. It's hard to beat a Venus-Saturn trine for money matters, so this would also be the perfect time to apply for a new position or sit down with the higher-ups and talk about a raise. Of course, if you've already done all that, you'll probably receive some very happy news.

Tricky Transits

An older relative could become quite demanding this month, Leo, especially around April 6, when the Sun squares off with Pluto. This could mean that your responsibilities toward them have increased to the point that you are no longer able to do it all alone. We all know how proud you are, but there's nothing wrong with asking for help if you need it.

Rewarding Days
2, 3, 5, 12, 18

Challenging Days
4, 6, 10, 15, 16, 28

Leo | May

Relaxation and Recreation

The heavens above will host a pack of practical Taurus planets this month, Leo—which certainly does bode well for your financial situation. They'll be making their way through your solar tenth house of career matters, to start with—but Taurus planets attract resources without even trying. If you're thinking of making a career change, check out your options now.

Lovers and Friends

Mercury will turn direct on May 22, Leo, just a day after the Full Moon in Sagittarius shines her bright light into your solar fifth house of lovers. A friend you haven't seen for some time could make an appearance, or you might hear an interesting accent and be quite fascinated by the owner.

Money and Success

If you put the wheels in motion last month for a promotion, Leo, and you haven't yet received it, look to May 7 through May 13 for the news you've been waiting for. Venus in your solar tenth house of career—who's all done up in earthy Taurus, by the way—will hook up with Jupiter in your solar second house of money matters. Yep. Time to celebrate.

Tricky Transits

A testy square between Jupiter and Saturn will occur on May 26, Leo, pitting your solar second house of money matters against your solar fifth house of lovers and playmates. You're generous to a fault, but every now and then, it's nice if someone else pitches in to help pay the tab. If you're living with someone, it might also be time to have The Talk about money.

Rewarding Days

1, 2, 7, 9, 10, 11, 12

Challenging Days

4, 5, 24, 26, 27

Leo | June

Relaxation and Recreation

There may not be much time for recreation this month, Leo. The Sun, Venus, and Mercury in fast-moving, restless Gemini will take turns squaring off with expansive Jupiter in your solar second house, so making money will probably be your priority. If you're self-employed, this will be a very busy time for you. Go for it. Strike while the iron is hot.

Lovers and Friends

The Full Moon of June 20 could be tricky, Leo. It will occur in your solar fifth house of lovers in the very last degree of Sagittarius, and planets in this condition tend to carry an urgent tone. If you're not satisfied with your current relationship and you know you've done everything you can to make it work, it might be time to split the sheets.

Money and Success

Red-hot, aggressive Mars is in intense, determined Scorpio at the moment, Leo, which means he's storming through your solar fourth house of family matters. This could indicate that it's time to vent about someone's behavior—and you'll want them there when it happens. Remember, however, that Mars in Scorpio plays for keeps. Don't say anything in anger that you'll come to regret.

Tricky Transits

You may feel as if you're in the middle of a tug of war this month, Leo, especially around June 8, 9, and 10. If family members aren't happy with the amount of time you're spending at work, sit them down and explain that you can't play if you can't pay, so they'll just have to be patient.

Rewarding Days
8, 12, 13, 19, 26

Challenging Days
1, 2, 3, 4, 17, 30

Leo | July

Relaxation and Recreation

Okay, Leo. You can return to your normally active social life now. You worked really hard last month and you've certainly earned the right to have some guilt-free fun—no easy task with serious Saturn hanging out in your solar fifth house of playtime. Fortunately, the yearly parade of planets through your fun-loving, playful sign will override Saturn as of July 11.

Lovers and Friends

That same argument about the amount of time you spend away from family members could come up again this month, Leo, right around July 7 in particular. If they have a point, you might want to give them some quality time—and all your attention. Not to worry. Your friends won't forget you.

Money and Success

Ready for a pat on the back from a higher-up, Leo? Well, get ready for one around the Full Moon of July 18. The Moon will be in your solar sixth house of work and all done up in Capricorn, a sign that specializes in a strong work ethic. Your efforts to get something right will pay off now, and might even show up in your paycheck.

Tricky Transits

A problematic domestic situation could cause you a bit of stress around July 13, Leo. If this has been brewing for some time, you'll need to put your foot down and make it clear that you're in charge. It may not be easy getting others to cooperate, but Mars in determined Scorpio will inspire you to refuse to budge an inch.

Rewarding Days

1, 3, 19, 20, 26, 31

Challenging Days

7, 10, 11, 16, 21, 24, 29

Leo | August

Relaxation and Recreation

Forget about relaxing, Leo. Fiery Mars will set off for your solar fifth house of playmates and playtime on August 2, all done up in fun-loving, adventurous Sagittarius. Now, Mars inspires a craving for adrenaline, and you just love adventures, so this is a match made in heaven. Get ready to try something new—and love it.

Lovers and Friends

A Full Moon in unpredictable Aquarius will charge up your relationship axis on August 18, Leo, and you might suddenly decide you don't want to share that sexy new lover. If that's the case, you don't necessarily have to put a ring on it, but you should let them know that you'd like to be exclusive. Who could possibly resist you?

Money and Success

A debt could come due around August 13, Leo, as authoritative Saturn stations to make a point and squares off with Venus at the same time. This is energy you won't be able to avoid feeling, so expect a bit of tension, but don't let it go too far. Just do what you can do. As long as it's truly your best, you can relax.

Tricky Transits

Saturn's station on August 13 may also be problematic when it comes to freeing yourself up for some playtime, Leo. This guy brings responsibilities with him—added ones, that is—and in this house, that's not such a good thing. There is good news, though. If you get your homework done and done well, a spontaneous adventure might be on the agenda for August 16.

Rewarding Days

1, 2, 15, 16, 29

Challenging Days

6, 7, 13, 14, 22, 30

Leo | September

Relaxation and Recreation

On September 9, Jupiter will take off for partner-oriented Libra and your solar third house of conversations and communications, Leo—which means that for the entire coming year, you'll be positively lethal in the department of charm. Prepare to easily convince just about everyone of just about anything. Think of it as being temporarily endowed with a superpower, and use it only for good.

Lovers and Friends

As if Jupiter in Libra weren't enough of an excuse to find you flirting up a storm, affectionate, magnetic Venus will also be in that sign this month. Well! You most certainly won't be lonely, but you will need to keep in mind that once you turn on the charm, you may not be able to turn it off. Don't aim it at anyone you're not really interested in.

Money and Success

An urgent situation that comes up at work around September 11 or 12 might not be as bad as you think, Leo. So before you hop in the car and rush off in a frenzy, take a deep breath. You can mull over what to do when you get there, but if you're on the road, concentrate on the road.

Tricky Transits

It's time for Mercury retrograde again, Leo, and this time out, he'll spend his time in Virgo and your solar second house of money matters. You may need to revisit a financial situation, or it might be time to collect on a debt. This is no time to apply for credit, so if you're out shopping and see something you just have to have, force yourself to wait.

Rewarding Days

6, 7, 8, 9, 19, 25

Challenging Days

2, 10, 11, 12, 13, 15, 16

Leo | October

Relaxation and Recreation

Ready to do some traveling, Leo? Well, if you're not at the moment, you will be after October 17, when Venus will slip into something more comfortable—Sagittarius, that is—and lure you away from your usual routine. Try not to travel from October 28 on, though, when getting where you're going won't be easy. Drive safely.

Lovers and Friends

If you're currently and happily attached, Leo, you should probably warn your friends that they won't be seeing much of you for the first half of the month. The lovely lady Venus will spend that time in ultra-sexy Scorpio and your solar fourth house of home, and you two will be doing a whole lot of ordering in.

Money and Success

All that work wasn't for nothing, Leo, as you'll soon discover. It seems that a higher-up has taken notice of your efforts and wants to reward you for them—and the good news could arrive as soon as October 14. You might get a promotion, but be careful not to bite off more than you can chew. Be honest about what you're capable of. They'll love you anyway.

Tricky Transits

Mars and Pluto will collide on October 19, Leo, a very volatile team that's often in the neighborhood when anger turns to rage. If you feel yourself getting hot under the collar, put some distance between you and whoever is irritating you. If you explode before you can even think about leaving, however, don't beat yourself up. It happens to all of us. Now mend those fences.

Rewarding Days

5, 6, 11, 14, 26

Challenging Days

7, 8, 13, 15, 19

Leo | November

Relaxation and Recreation

Venus, Mercury, and the Sun will all spend time in your solar fifth house of recreation, Leo. They'll all be wearing fun-loving, playful, and extremely adventurous Sagittarius, your fire-sign cousin. This would be a terrific time to travel, if you can, but if not, you can at least satisfy that urge by making some plans. Focus on new experiences.

Lovers and Friends

Red-hot Mars will take off for your solar seventh house of relationships on November 8, Leo—and wherever this fiery fellow goes, passion is sure to follow. The thing is, he'll be in unpredictable Aquarius, a sign that tends to bring along interesting and unusual types who aren't like anyone we've ever known. Might be fun, right? Don't rule out any new admirer just because their appearance is startling.

Money and Success

It's tough to go wrong financially when Venus is in your solar sixth house of work, Leo. That goes double since she'll be in hardworking Capricorn, a sign that's never been afraid of getting its hands dirty. That said, if you've been searching for a way to make a tad more cash—for playtime, of course—you might be offered a part-time position or hired to do a one-time project.

Tricky Transits

Mercury will square off with dreamy Neptune on November 18, Leo, which can go several ways. Might be that Neptune puts stars in Mercury's eyes—and in yours, of course—so sweet romance could be on the agenda. On the other hand, you might miss some important paperwork details if you're not careful. Your mission is to find another set of eyes. A reliable pair, please.

Rewarding Days

4, 5, 15, 22, 23

Challenging Days

6, 18, 24, 25, 29, 30

Leo | December

Relaxation and Recreation

What a fabulous month, Leo! Just about every planet in the heavens will be in a terrific mood, just in time to make the season merry. Now, you just love this time of year. There's the kids' excitement and the shopping for something perfect for your sweetheart—not to mention all those warm and wonderful gatherings with friends. Enjoy!

Lovers and Friends

A surprise visit around December 10 or 11 is on your agenda, Leo, but since unpredictable Uranus will be involved in the situation, it's hard to say whether you'll be showing up at someone's door with presents or they'll be showing up at yours. Either way, you'll be delighted. You might even get to see someone you've missed mightily.

Money and Success

Mercury will turn retrograde on December 20, Leo, all done up in Capricorn and preparing to retrace his steps through your solar sixth house of work. This might ordinarily be troublesome, but if you're smart, you can make it work for you. Check on anything you've recently finished to be sure you won't need to redo it while you're trying to enjoy the holidays.

Tricky Transits

Mercury's station on December 19 could make traveling a bit tricky, Leo, so before you leave the house, make sure you have the GPS—or good, solid directions. That goes double for December 31, when Mars will get together with Neptune in dreamy-eyed Pisces. If you're up for a party, having it at your place would be best. Tell your friends to bring sleeping bags.

Rewarding Days

Just about all of them.

Challenging Days

19, 26, 31

Leo Action Table

These dates reflect the best—but not the only—times for success and ease in these activities, according to your Sun sign.

	JAN	FEB	MAR	APR	MAY	JUN	JUL	AUG	SEP	OCT	NOV	DEC
Move			16, 17, 18			6, 7, 8			24, 25		18, 19	
Start a class		3, 4, 5					15, 16, 17			6, 7		4, 5
Join a club	11, 12							16, 17, 18			7, 8	
Ask for a raise		5, 6, 7		2, 3, 4		3, 4, 21, 22				8, 9, 10		
Look for work	9, 10, 11		10, 11, 12		24, 25, 26		18, 19, 20		28, 29, 30		4, 5, 6	
Get pro advice				17, 18, 19		11, 12, 13		4, 5, 6			22, 23	
Get a loan		1, 28, 29			20, 21					3, 4, 5, 31		24, 25
See a doctor	26, 27, 28		21, 22				7, 8		1, 2			
Start a diet		22, 23		22, 23				18				
End relationship	24, 25		23, 24		21, 22				16, 17		29	29, 30
Buy clothes		13, 14				3, 4, 5				17, 18		
Get a makeover	18, 19			9, 10			11, 12		3, 4, 5		24, 25, 26	
New romance		10, 11	8, 9			14, 15		7, 8, 9		1, 28, 29		17, 18
Vacation				14, 15, 16				2, 3, 4			2, 3, 29, 30	

Virgo

The Virgin
August 22 to September 22

♍

Element: Earth

Quality: Mutable

Polarity: Yin/feminine

Planetary Ruler: Mercury

Meditation: I can allow time for myself

Gemstone: Sapphire

Power Stones: Peridot, amazonite, rhodochrosite

Key Phrase: I analyze

Glyph: Greek symbol for containment

Anatomy: Abdomen, gallbladder, intestines

Colors: Taupe, gray, navy blue

Animals: Domesticated animals

Myths/Legends: Demeter, Astraea, Hygeia

House: Sixth

Opposite Sign: Pisces

Flower: Pansy

Keyword: Discriminating

The Virgo Personality

Your Strengths and Challenges

Well, Virgo, as you well know, your sign has a bit of a reputation for being "picky"—which I'm sure you're all too aware of and probably quite sick of hearing about. I totally defend your right to be mad about all that, but it's actually quite a compliment. In my humble opinion, "picky" means "detail-oriented and meticulous," which are much-needed and much-appreciated qualities (especially by us fire signs). You're also pretty darn good at cutting to the chase and getting to the meat of the matter. The true bent of your sign is discrimination, and you're smart enough to know that not everything deserves your keen attention. And speaking of paying attention, your short-term memory and ability to retain details are absolutely amazing. Heaven help anyone who questions your memory, your spelling, or your math—especially if you offer to make a bet with them. Yep. Like shootin' fish in a barrel.

Now, about the "clean" thing. Are you really all clean-freaks who stay up until midnight re-alphabetizing your CDs? Well, yes and no. Yes, you do love to be in clean, fresh environments, but when yours isn't, you might often find yourself wondering why someone doesn't take care of that—as you walk on by. It's only natural. You're a mutable sign, so you're easily distracted and endlessly restless. You do tend to pay special care to keeping what's important to you well organized and in good working order. That goes double for tools, equipment, and supplies you need for work, not to mention the clothes you wear on the job.

Like your Gemini cousins, who are also ruled by Mercury, you're also interested in everything. That's only natural, too. Mercury was the Messenger of the Gods, whose job it was to shuttle information back and forth between the immortals and us mere mortals. The difference between you is that Gemini adores all details, while you know which are important and which are not. Geminis do make terrific playmates, though, and they're good at word games and puzzles, so you're often in their company.

Your Relationships

Here's a fun fact, Virgo: you're a "fixer." That goes for puttering around with things that aren't working, but it also pertains to your relationships. When you meet someone new and you're interested in them, even if they have a couple of rather glaring character flaws, you won't be deterred. You see their potential and immediately start thinking of how brightly you could make that rough diamond sparkle. That's a lovely quality, but it might not be the right tack to take. If what you notice first about someone is their imperfections, that might well mean that they're not perfect for you. You'd be much better off spending your time with others you can accept exactly as they are—and who'll return the favor.

Obviously, you connect with others who are either good detectives—as per the discovery of clues, I mean—or quite interesting and informative, thanks to the influence of your ruling planet, cerebral Mercury. When it comes to choosing a mate, Scorpio may choose you—and if so, you know exactly what I'm saying here—and honestly, this can be a very nice match. You two can regale each other with tales of intrigue and research. The conversation will be terrific, and the mental stimulation will go on and on. Much as you might like to sign up with a funny, witty Sagittarius, resist the urge. In the long run, you will make each other crazy. Think *The Odd Couple*. Think about your love of details and their fondness for the big picture. Could be tough. Getting together with another earth sign—Taurus or Capricorn—usually works out quite well for you, since you're both interested in the comfort and quality of life on the physical plane. Other than Scorpio, the other two water signs can also be very good matches. Cancer will keep the home fires burning and the kitchen clean, and Pisces will sit and have ethereal discussions with you for hours.

Your Career and Money

Serious Saturn will spend the year in fiery, impulsive, and not notoriously self-disciplined Sagittarius, which can't help but put him in the mood to loosen up, just a bit, Virgo. The thing is, he's the planet in charge of career situations, and he's in the mood to do something different. That said, so are you, thanks to the presence of Jupiter in your sign and your solar first house of personality and appearance. If you have been doing your best to impress a higher-up and get yourself a raise, bonus, or promotion, it could very well happen over the next month or so. The thing is, the more you resist the urge to grow and expand, the more Jupiter will push you toward it. Resistance is futile, and you know how easily bored you are. Why not give reaching out a chance? At the very least, you might find that you're interested in travelling for work,

especially if your family members are game to come along and entertain
you. If you have any control whatsoever over where you go and when,
put it into play now.

Now, things in the department of joint finances will be going along
as usual, Virgo, at least until Jupiter leaves your sign behind in August—
at which point, he'll enter your second solar house of personal finances
and money matters. The King of Excess in this house? What could possibly go wrong?

Your Lighter Side

Your sign is nothing if not cerebral, which is an odd fit for an earth sign.
The thing is, earth signs are practical and focused on life in the material
world—which includes the creature comforts that we all are occasionally
allowed to enjoy. That said, you should know that with intense Pluto in
your solar fifth house of lovers and casual playmates—well, there will be
no such thing as a casual anything! Better plan on becoming infatuated,
in a very big way.

Affirmation
I accept myself and others without conditions.

The Year Ahead for Virgo

Mighty Jupiter will be on duty in your sign and your solar first house
of personality and appearance as the year begins, Virgo, and he'll stay
put there until September 9. This trek started last August (in 2015),
and since Jupiter expands everything, for better or worse, life has either
been very good or very challenging. That goes double if you were born
between September 14 and 18. That trend will continue, but if life has
been a bit rough, you'll have an opportunity for a do-over as of January
7. Jupiter will stop in his tracks to back up and turn retrograde on that
day, and you'll have until May 9 to set things straight. Of course, Jupiter
is best known for being the heavens' answer to Santa Claus, so chances
are good that you have been and will continue to enjoy this transit.
What's not to love about being showered with goodies? Of course,
Jupiter does tend to be a tad excessive, and you may have put on a few
pounds recently, so use that retrograde period to take off what you put
on. The good news is that you've probably ditched at least one bad habit
by now, but if there are others you'd like to tackle, you'll have until September to get rid of them all.

Now, let's talk about Mars, who'll spend an awful lot of time in Scorpio and Sagittarius this year. This fiery fellow will enter Scorpio on January 3, which puts him in your solar third house of conversations and communications straight through March 6 and then again from May 27 to August 2. Now, Mars has never been known to be especially patient, and he does have quite the temper, so heaven help anyone who starts an argument with you during this time—because you will most certainly finish it! The ancient God of War doesn't tolerate fools, either, so you might be a bit more terse than usual with someone who just doesn't seem to be getting your point. Of course, Mars's energy is useful for far more than fighting—and it's not so much the fight this planet relishes as much as it is the adrenaline rush. Obviously, you'll be craving that rush during his visit here, so if you have a tough project to tackle, this is the time to do it. Now, when Mars storms back into Scorpio, from May 27 through August 2, you'll probably need to tie up a few financial loose ends. Don't ignore the issue. The point of visits from the God of War is to inspire you to charge right up to the problem and deal with it. Now, Scorpio planets are extremely perceptive and determined, so if you have a decision to make, trust your gut above all else. They're also a bit obsessive at times, so if you end up lying in bed one night, wondering what someone meant by a simple comment, it's time for some pleasant distraction. Get right on that.

What This Year's Eclipses Mean for You

Two sets of eclipses come along every year, Virgo. In a nutshell, Lunar Eclipses are mega-mighty Full Moons, often specializing in closures of the sudden variety. Solar Eclipses are equally energetic New Moons that arrive two weeks apart, every six months. Taken as a whole, these super-lunations often point out themes for each Sun sign. Now, you're pretty darn clever and you notice little things that most of us miss, so I'll bet you've already seen the signs of what's coming your way and can guess what your theme for the year might be. But just in case, here it is: relationships, relationships, and relationships. The thing is, two of the four eclipses scheduled this year will land right smack dab in your solar seventh house of relationships. As if that weren't enough to initiate some serious changes in the department of partnerships—personal, platonic, and professional—consider the fact that a third eclipse will be all done up in Libra, the sign that's famous for being most focused on and attentive to The Beloved—even if they happen to be an ex-Beloved. Oh, and then there's one eclipse in your own sign.

Let's start with the Solar Eclipse—the first mega-powered New Moon of the year, due to touch down on March 8. This lunation will occur in intuitive Pisces and your solar seventh house of one-to-one relationships. Since the Moon will be new and oh so eager to meet kindred spirits and soul mates, you can expect new friendships. Lots of them. If you're single and looking, the parade will be on and new admirers will be plentiful. You might fall in love at first, too. The thing is, eclipses move fast, so some of these new people may not be around forever. Your mission is to learn everything you can about relating to others. What are you really looking for in a partner? What are you simply not willing to tolerate?

On March 23, a Lunar Eclipse will occur in partner-oriented Libra and your solar second house of values. If you're seeing someone at the time, it will be very important to you that you share everything, as true partners do. That includes financial responsibilities. Don't be afraid to bring up the subject.

The second Solar Eclipse will occur on September 1, in your very own sign. If that just so happens to be your birthday, this will most certainly be a year to remember. This lunation will set up shop in your solar first house of personality and appearance, urging you to get yourself healthy, fit, and happy. That said, this is yet another indication that you might be at the very beginning of a new relationship. After all, what's more inspirational than a new love to get us thinking about our appearance? You might also be starting a new job or even a business of your own.

The final eclipse of the year will be a Lunar Eclipse and will arrive on September 16. Just like the first eclipse last March, this one will take place in Pisces and your solar seventh house of one-to-one relationships, and a secret that's revealed might entirely change your mind about someone dear to you.

Saturn

Saturn will spend the year in your solar fourth house of home, family matters, and domestic situations, Virgo, which might be considered a tough transit by some. In your case, however, since you're ordinarily quite fond of order and not at all tolerant of chaos, you'll probably enjoy it. Saturn loves to straighten, organize, and fix—which just so happens to be at the very top of your list, too. Saturn also inspires us to lay down a solid foundation and build something stable from it. In that case, you might actually be building a home or looking for a place that's more practical or better tailored to your needs. One way or another, you'll want more stability, safety, and security in this tender department—and you won't be afraid to work hard to have it. Speaking of security, you might also have a system installed in your home or make a move to a gated community. Now, about the family. Saturn brings responsibilities wherever he goes, so you might need to spend a bit more time with the kids or take care of an elder relative. As per usual, you'll be willing to help, and if someone dear to you needs a grounding influence in their life, you'll be happy to provide it.

Uranus

Uranus has the astrological market cornered when it comes to spontaneity and surprises—hands down. He's been making his unpredictable way through your solar eighth house since March of 2012, which is when you probably first noticed that your tastes were changing in the department of intimate relationships. Might be that someone new and entirely different from anyone else you've ever known made their way into your heart—and probably your boudoir as well. Might be that you suddenly discovered something shocking about someone you thought you knew—so shocking, in fact, that it caused a major shift in the connection between you. Of course, there are many kinds of intimacy, so it might just be that you suddenly decided to share your deepest, darkest thoughts with a trusted confidant. Now, this house also rules joint finances, loans, and inheritances, so a sudden loss or gain in one of those categories may have rocked your world recently and caused you to reexamine what's really important. You may also have had to deal with the sudden loss of a loved one, either to death or the end of a committed relationship. All this goes double if you were born between September 8 and 18, since you've also been dealing with the erratic and uncomfortable energy of an inconjunct from Uranus to your Sun. In that case, you're probably trying to incorporate highly unusual or confusing circumstances and people into your life. It's time to stop holding on to what's not working just because it's familiar to you. You'll be relieved when it's over.

Neptune

Neptune is currently on duty in your solar seventh house of one-to-one relationships, Virgo, where she's been holding court for the past five years. Now, her specialty is dissolving boundaries, which can be terrific—or not. It depends on whether or not you're with the right people. If you're in a committed relationship with someone you adore, with kindred spirits, or with others who truly care for you, you're probably having the time of your life. In this case, you'll feel totally connected with others, and you'll know that they're in tune with your energy, too. If not, you might be involved with those who use Neptune's energy another way—perhaps by abusing alcohol or drugs. In that case, run. Now. No arguing. Don't let someone else's addiction weigh you down and rob you of your spirit. No fair feeling guilty, either. They managed before you and they'll manage once again. You might also be doing them a tremendous favor by withdrawing your support and forcing them to face reality. What you need is someone who loves you enough to get you to wake up and smell the roses. If you were born between August 29 and September 6, all this goes double. No, triple. Neptune will also be forming an opposition with your Sun, which tends to manifest in relationships. The best of all worlds is the effect this transit can have on your spirituality, which will be easy for others to see. Consider yourself an honorary guru and mentor.

Pluto

Pluto may do his work invisibly, but the effects are extremely noticeable. In your case, Virgo, he's been working his way quite patiently through your solar fifth house of lovers, playmates, and dealings with children, so a lot has changed or will change in this ordinarily lighthearted house. To start with, you've probably found that your idea of fun has changed, and pretty darn drastically, too. You may have developed an intense fascination for detective stories, mysteries, or medical dramas. You might also be a bit too fascinated with someone who's sexy because they're dangerous—in which case, you should definitely get personal references before you sign up for anything long-term or serious. Really. Ask around and listen up. Pluto gives us the ability to take charge of our lives when he visits, and it's your turn to take charge of what you do for excitement and who you choose to spend your leisure time with. Choose carefully. If you were born between September 6 and 11, you're also under the influence of a trine aspect to your Sun from this potent guy—and people pay big bucks for Pluto trines, believe you me. Yes, it's time to transform, but no, it won't be at all difficult. All you have to do is get the show on the road—which actually might be difficult, if you give in to the easy, lazy energy of the trine and spend this transit reading Stephen King novels. Don't do that—or at least keep it to a minimum. You have bigger fish to fry.

Virgo | January

Relaxation and Recreation

As of January 8, your solar fifth house of playmates, lovers, and recreation will play host to Mercury, your ruling planet. Mercury will turn retrograde from that spot, making it more difficult than usual for you to get to your favorite playground, even if you troubleshoot. If anything stalls or delays you, don't think for one second that it's your fault. Relax and enjoy the view.

Lovers and Friends

The Sun, Venus, and Mercury will pass through your solar fifth house, Virgo, so your social life stands to be lively. The thing is, with Mercury set to retrace his steps here from January 8 through January 25, an old lover could well return, asking for a second shot at the title. Think long and hard before you agree. Do you have new answers to those old problems?

Money and Success

On January 23, Venus will set off for practical Capricorn and your solar fifth house, Virgo. Now, this house has everything to do with speculations of the monetary sort, so if you're inclined to buy a lottery ticket—just one, mind you—use those numbers you've been playing for years. On January 27, you might have some very, very good news.

Tricky Transits

There are some who say that the asteroid/planetoid Chiron is your ruler, Virgo, and it just might be true. You folks are "fixers," and Chiron was the ancient inspiration behind chirurgery, which led to surgery, so it's a good fit. Pay attention to what comes your way on January 19, especially with relation to your significant other. You might find that you can heal and help them like no one else can.

Rewarding Days
13, 14, 18, 28, 29, 30

Challenging Days
5, 7, 17, 20, 25, 31

Virgo | February

Relaxation and Recreation

You may not get much relaxing done around February 3, Virgo, but you will certainly be quite amused and entertained. It seems that Mars in passionate Scorpio will team up with intense, unrelenting Pluto on that day to inspire you to make a statement. A serious statement. Complete with fireworks, if need be. When Mars passes through the solar third house, enthusiasm is a given. In Scorpio, all bets are off!

Lovers and Friends

You're due for an especially delightful Valentine's Day, Virgo, thanks to generous, benevolent Jupiter and the emotional Moon, both of which will be in earth signs—so you will quite literally be in your element. What delightful timing, especially since Jupiter is in your sign and your solar first house of personality and appearance.

Money and Success

A sudden windfall around February 6 may cause a bit of a stir in your neck of the woods, Virgo—especially since there may be a debate about who actually brokered, negotiated, or initiated the deal. If you wish you had an extra day to think about things, take heart. On February 29—a most unusual day—you'll be able to restore stability to you and yours. What a great feeling!

Tricky Transits

If you were born on or around August 26, Virgo, the Full Moon of February 22 will be quite illuminating. It will occur in your sign, right on top of your Sun, shining a light on your feelings and wishes for your physical body. The thing is, woozy Neptune will be opposite to it. Bet you'll intuitively discover something wonderful about yourself—like a hidden talent you didn't know you had.

Rewarding Days

3, 8, 9, 14, 16, 29

Challenging Days

5, 6, 7, 22, 23, 27

Virgo | March

Relaxation and Recreation

Mars will take off for blunt, truthful Sagittarius and your solar fourth house of home and family matters on March 5, Virgo, so the pace of life at your place will pick up—big time. In this sign, Mars never, ever travels without attracting attention, which will be quite different from his recent passage through Scorpio and your solar third house, when "shh..." was pretty much all you could say.

Lovers and Friends

By March 13, the Sun, Venus, and your ruling planet, Mercury, will all join Neptune in Pisces in your solar seventh house. Now, you have a propensity for seeing the best in others and wanting to fix them. But on March 14, a situation with authority figures could come up, and you won't be able to do anything for a loved one. Don't beat yourself up.

Money and Success

Venus will be on duty in your solar sixth house of work and work-oriented relationships until March 12, Virgo. Now, she's brought along her special talent for soothing troubled waters and making nice, so if you left things on less-than-pleasant terms with a coworker/friend, you'll have a chance to make things right. And with Venus on duty, all you really have to do is show up and smile.

Tricky Transits

March 14 may be problematic for you, Virgo, thanks to some really irritating squares between chatty Mercury and loving Venus (both on duty in your solar seventh house of relationships) and serious Saturn and angry Mars. Now that last team is in Sagittarius and your solar fourth house of home and family, so don't be surprised if a child or other family member has a whole lot of complainin' to do.

Rewarding Days

2, 6, 15, 16, 17, 24

Challenging Days

4, 5, 8, 11, 21, 22, 23, 31

Virgo | April

Relaxation and Recreation

With mighty Jupiter on duty in your sign and your solar first house of personality and appearance, Virgo, you've been really hard to miss lately—even though you're usually the very soul of discretion and modesty. Jupiter insists that we strut our stuff, and whether or not you're aware of it, you've attracted the attention of someone delicious. Guess who?

Lovers and Friends

Your ruling planet, Mercury, will station to turn retrograde on April 28, Virgo, in your solar ninth house of long-distance loved ones. Now, this certainly could mean that you're due to run into someone you haven't seen in a very long time. Since Mercury will be in sensual Taurus, however, you'll probably remember quite well how it felt to snuggle up with them. Want to do it again? Bet you do.

Money and Success

Between April 5 and 9, several planets in Aries and your solar eighth house of shared finances will get together with the New Moon to plant a seed in this house, Virgo. If you've been thinking about investing in your own business, this is definitely a good time to do it, but be sure not to get tied up in anything permanent—on paper—until well after April 28.

Tricky Transits

The Sun in impulsive Aries will square off with intense, brooding Pluto on April 6, Virgo, activating a bit of tension between your solar eighth house of intimate relationships and your solar fifth house of lovers, playmates, and leisure time. That said, you should keep in mind that tension between you and a certain someone is a surefire way to know that you're attracted. An investigation is definitely in order.

Rewarding Days
2, 3, 12, 13, 14, 29

Challenging Days
4, 10, 15, 16, 27

Virgo | May

Relaxation and Recreation

You're going to be in the mood this month to travel, Virgo, so if you haven't yet made your plans, get right on that. Do yourself a favor, however, and avoid trying to get from point A to point B at the end of the month. A host of planets will be doing battle, and the tension can't help but spill over into our lives.

Lovers and Friends

Speaking of tension, Virgo, we really should talk about May 26—because you might be experiencing some right around that time. It might be that family members are testy because they want more time with you than you can spend right now, due to overtime or an added project. Remind them that this is temporary and you'll be back shortly.

Money and Success

Venus rules money as well as love, Virgo, and she'll be off for Gemini on May 24. Now, this sign is ruled by Mercury, just like your own, so you have a lot in common, and with all that chatty, witty energy on duty, there's really no way you won't be able to talk someone into finally giving you the raise, bonus, or promotion you've been after.

Tricky Transits

An uneasy inconjunct aspect between the lovely lady Venus and serious Saturn will occur on May 5, Virgo, and since this will cause a bit of confusion between your solar fourth house of family and your solar ninth house of travel, you might feel a bit uneasy yourself. If you need to leave for a few days to take care of a work situation, don't you dare feel guilty.

Rewarding Days

1, 2, 7, 9, 10, 12, 30

Challenging Days

4, 5, 24, 25, 26, 27

Virgo | June

Relaxation and Recreation

Jupiter will form an easy trine with Pluto on June 26, Virgo, linking your solar first house of personality with your solar fifth house of lovers. Now, when these two superpowers link up, anything becomes possible—so if you've been trying to figure out how to afford that trip you and yours have been dying to make, the answer will be along shortly.

Lovers and Friends

Several awkward aspects will occur between loving Venus and serious Saturn this month, Virgo, and since Saturn is such a big fan of being polite, well mannered, and respectable, showing your affection to the one you love might be tough to do, especially in public. The good news is that by the time June 27 rolls around, you'll be able to let your hair down, no matter where you are.

Money and Success

That raise you've been trying so hard to get will be well within your grasp this month, Virgo, especially around June 12. Venus will set up shop in your solar tenth house of career matters—which bodes well, right from the start—and she'll also make contact with sudden-acting Uranus in your solar eighth house of financial resources. Sounds like congratulations will be in order when you least expect it.

Tricky Transits

The Full Moon on June 20 will occur in your solar fourth house of home and family matters, Virgo. If you're at all inclined to move, the urge to get going will be tough to resist. The thing is, Mercury will form some irritating aspects with both Saturn and Neptune, so before you pack up and leave, be sure you're clear on exactly how much you'll be paying every month.

Rewarding Days

7, 8, 25, 26, 27

Challenging Days

1, 2, 3, 4, 18, 30

Virgo | July

Relaxation and Recreation

Venus will be on duty in your solar eleventh house of friendships and group affiliations, Virgo, right up until July 11. Until then, she'll be all done up in nurturing Cancer, and you might just decide that you're ready to take on the leadership duties of a group that's currently rudderless because you're ever so fond of the members. Becoming a den mother or den father might be fun.

Lovers and Friends

July 7 stands to be a rather tense day with regard to balancing your time between your friends and your current sweetheart, Virgo, so prepare for some fireworks. It seems that Venus, Mercury, and the Sun will all get into it with startling Uranus and intense Pluto—and this, friends, is the stuff that power struggles are made of. Your mission is to count to ten before you speak.

Money and Success

Uranus will get into action-oriented squares with the Sun, Mercury, and Venus in Cancer this month, Virgo. Since Uranus happens to be on duty in your solar eighth house of shared resources and joint finances, getting a push from all these home-loving energies might mean you're in the market for a place of your own. Bet you find it around July 20.

Tricky Transits

The Full Moon will arrive on July 18, Virgo, all done up in practical, responsible Capricorn, a sign that's quite fond of commitments and permanence. That said, if you've been thinking about taking a friendship to another level, talk it over and be sure you two can return to a platonic relationship if it doesn't work out.

Rewarding Days

1, 3, 5, 6, 8, 9

Challenging Days

2, 7, 16, 21, 24

Virgo | August

Relaxation and Recreation

You won't get much rest this month, Virgo, but the cast of heavenly planets that will be keeping you up will suit you just fine. Mercury and Venus will join Jupiter in your sign and your solar first house of appearance and personality, followed by the Sun on August 22. Talk about being in your element! If you're into a craft or hobby, you might just be able to turn it into a part-time business.

Lovers and Friends

If you have the feeling that someone is trying to take advantage of you this month, Virgo, pay attention to it. On August 7 and 14, Neptune will receive oppositions from Mercury and Venus, respectively, making you a bit more vulnerable than usual. That said, don't be paranoid, but do be careful.

Money and Success

If you've been thinking about asking for a raise or applying for a promotion, you might want to avoid August 6 and 13, Virgo. You'd be better off scheduling your meeting for August 10 or 17. If you can't manage to connect with the powers that be until after August 22, not to worry. A host of energies in your sign will see to it that you make a terrific impression.

Tricky Transits

Mars will square off with dreamy Neptune on August 25, Virgo, and all of a sudden, you might start to feel pretty darn cranky with your partner—with no idea why. Huh. Well, Mars is a passionate fellow, and he does crave adrenaline, so if you're bored, that could be the problem. Smart as you are, though, I'm quite sure you can think of a way to spice things up.

Rewarding Days

5, 10, 22, 23, 27, 28

Challenging Days

3, 6, 13, 14, 19, 25

Virgo | September

Relaxation and Recreation

Mighty Jupiter will head off into Libra and your solar second house on September 9, Virgo—and since this house rules your financial affairs and Jupiter never does know when to quit, you might be a bit excessive over the coming year. If you can afford it and you've worked hard to get the things you want, go for it.

Lovers and Friends

The Lunar Eclipse of September 16 will set off your solar seventh house of one-to-one relationships, Virgo, so fasten your seat belt and prepare for some changes. Now, you might initiate change yourself, by deciding that you're not willing to stay in this relationship any longer. The good news is that you might just fall in love at first sight.

Money and Success

With generous, lucky Jupiter in your solar second house of money matters as of September 9, Virgo, it's not hard to imagine you winning something. Something big, of course—after all, Jupiter is quite the excessive guy. If you're so inclined, get yourself a lottery ticket around September 18. Just one, please. Hey, that's all it takes.

Tricky Transits

The Solar Eclipse on September 1 will activate your sign and your solar first house of personality and appearance, Virgo, in a very big way. If you've been thinking about dieting or starting a new exercise program, this is the time to do it. Grab your earbuds and head off to the gym, or take regular walks with friends.

Rewarding Days
6, 7, 9, 19, 20, 23

Challenging Days
2, 10, 11, 12, 13, 21

Virgo | October

Relaxation and Recreation

Mysteries will fascinate you this month, Virgo, and you might even turn into a bit of a detective, thanks to Venus and Mercury in Scorpio and your solar third house of thoughts, communications, and conversations. If you have any research to do, this is the time for it. You will enjoy digging around for clues, and will know exactly where to look to find them.

Lovers and Friends

Someone may approach you with a very, very smooth line around October 5, Virgo, and if you're interested, you should know that this was inspired by intense Pluto and sexy Venus in Scorpio. The thing is, this combination doesn't mess around when it comes to love. You're either in or you're out. Ready to make that choice so soon?

Money and Success

On October 14, Mercury in Libra and your solar second house of personal finances will get into an easy sextile with practical, reliable Saturn. Now, this is the stuff that sound financial decisions are made of, so go ahead and make investments confidently. You're also due for a raise or bonus that will nicely stabilize your budget.

Tricky Transits

On October 2, the Sun and Mercury will get into some rather uncomfortable aspects with Neptune and Uranus, making it tough to see someone else's point of view. If you really don't understand their motivations, talk to someone who knows them well. You might just be happily surprised at what you find out.

Rewarding Days
1, 4, 14, 26

Challenging Days
2, 7, 12, 13, 23

Virgo | November

Relaxation and Recreation

This will be an interesting month for you, Virgo, so buckle up. As soon as November 4, you might find that a family member is rather insistent about you spending less time at work and more time at home. Now, that would be just fine if it weren't the holiday season and you didn't want to make a few extra dollars. Explain the situation patiently.

Lovers and Friends

If you're thinking about making a commitment to the person you've been seeing lately, Virgo, you can relax and feel confident that you've made the right choice. Loving Venus in practical Capricorn and your solar fifth house of lovers bodes quite well for settling down. If you're after true stability, this may be the month you find it.

Money and Success

With generous Jupiter in your solar second house of money matters, Virgo, it's easy to see how you might be just a tad excessive every now and then. Around November 24 and 25, however, you'll need to rein in that urge as Pluto in Capricorn brings along a rather urgent financial situation involving a child or a partner.

Tricky Transits

Mercury will get into an uncomfortable aspect with startling Uranus on November 6, Virgo, and without even knowing why, you might have the feeling that someone is holding something back from you. If that's the case, your best bet would be to ask them directly about it, but if that's not possible, the least you can do is talk to someone with an objective opinion.

Rewarding Days

1, 2, 7, 22, 25

Challenging Days

6, 18, 24, 29

Virgo | December

Relaxation and Recreation

What a terrific month, Virgo! It seems that the Universe has arranged an absolutely wonderful holiday season for you and yours. The fun starts on December 1, when you'll probably be invited to a gathering of coworkers—say, an office party. By the time December 24 and 25 roll around, you'll have seen your fair share of mistletoe and blinking lights, but enjoying them with friends and family is what it's all about.

Lovers and Friends

Mercury and the Sun will pass through your solar fifth house of lovers this month, Virgo, all done up in respectable, reliable Capricorn. If you've been seeing someone for a while now, you might glance over at them and decide that you don't want to share their attention. You might even put a ring on it. Ah, yes. Another reason to celebrate.

Money and Success

Happy news regarding your work situation will arrive on December 24 or 25, Virgo, and you might end up starting the New Year with a bit more in your paychecks. Not only that, but if you've been trying for a promotion, that may come through in time for the new year as well. Congrats! A celebration is definitely in order. Yes, another one.

Tricky Transits

Outside of the fact that travel around December 19 could be tricky, thanks to Mercury's retrograde station, the only day that really looks troublesome this month is December 31. The thing is, impulsive Mars will collide with woozy Neptune that day in your solar seventh house of relationships, so if you're out celebrating, don't get into a car with anyone who's not in any condition to drive.

Rewarding Days

Pretty much the entire month.

Challenging Days

19, 26, 31

Virgo Action Table

These dates reflect the best—but not the only—times for success and ease in these activities, according to your Sun sign.

	JAN	FEB	MAR	APR	MAY	JUN	JUL	AUG	SEP	OCT	NOV	DEC
Move		18, 19, 20		13, 14, 15		7, 8, 9		1, 2, 28, 29		21, 22, 23		15, 16
Start a class	22, 23		6, 7		27, 28		21, 22, 23			11, 12		
Join a club		8, 9, 10		3, 4, 5		23, 24, 25			13, 14, 15		7, 8	
Ask for a raise	18, 19		4, 5, 31	17, 18, 19	25, 26		18, 19, 20			17, 18, 19		11, 12, 13
Look for work		6, 7, 8				11, 12		5, 6	11, 12		5, 6, 7	
Get pro advice	27, 28	22, 23, 24	26, 27, 28		15, 16		8, 9, 10			26, 27, 28		19, 20, 21
Get a loan	4, 5					16, 17, 18		10, 11, 12			27, 28, 29	
See a doctor	27, 28				23, 24				1, 2, 3			
Start a diet				22, 23		20, 21		18, 19		30, 31		
End relationship	24, 25		23, 24		20, 21		18, 19		15, 16, 17		28, 29, 30	
Buy clothes		14, 15				14, 15, 16			20, 21			10, 11, 12
Get a makeover	2, 3, 29, 30			20, 21, 22			6, 7, 27, 28				13, 14, 15	
New romance			8, 9		12, 13, 14, 29, 30, 31			19, 20		1, 2, 3		
Vacation	7, 8, 9			25, 26, 27		18, 19			8, 9, 10			26, 27, 28

Libra

The Balance
September 22 to October 22

Element: Air

Quality: Cardinal

Polarity: Yang/masculine

Planetary Ruler: Venus

Meditation: I balance conflicting desires

Gemstone: Opal

Power Stones: Tourmaline, kunzite, blue lace agate

Key Phrase: I balance

Glyph: Scales of justice, setting sun

Anatomy: Kidneys, lower back, appendix

Colors: Blue, pink

Animals: Brightly plumed birds

Myths/Legends: Venus, Cinderella, Hera

House: Seventh

Opposite Sign: Aries

Flower: Rose

Keyword: Harmony

The Libra Personality

Strengths and Challenges

Okay, Libra, let's talk about the real you instead of the usual stuff you read about how "balanced" your life is. Not. In fact, your life is in constant need of rebalancing—but it's not your fault. We're not automatically in possession of the qualities of our Sun sign. The Sun is our mission and our goal, so our lives are all about learning our skill. Your specialty is, indeed, balance: keeping things balanced, restoring balance to whatever happens to be out of whack at the moment, and anticipating what might need balancing in the future. The thing is, you can't learn your skill if everything is just hunky-dory all the time and everything is going along smoothly, so you gravitate toward situations and relationships that are lopsided in some way. You also tend to attract that kind of energy. No, it's not an easy job you've chosen, but please do keep at it, because the rest of us love being around you while you learn. You're as charming as the day is long, friendly, poised, and sociable. You can talk to just about anyone about just about anything, and very few of us have a bad word to say about you.

You're probably also tired of reading about how "indecisive" you are. Okay, pretend you're looking me in the eyes. Don't blink or look away, and tell me you're not. See? To be fair—and if anyone is, it's you—you have to admit that the decision-making process is not one you enjoy. But that's perfectly understandable, so stop beating yourself up about it. Your symbol is the scales, and again, they always need to be balanced. The problem is that once you make a choice, you're tipping the scales. And it's your job to keep them balanced. And you can't if you keep making decisions. Yep. It's a dilemma, all right. Maybe that's why yours is also the sign of partnerships—because, after all, it's a whole lot easier to choose when someone else's preferences are involved. The thing is, you need to remember that you're perfectly entitled to your own opinions, likes, dislikes, and tastes. Do yourself a favor and spend just a bit of time alone. Stop shuddering and let me explain why. When we're alone, we don't need to please anyone but ourselves. So take yourself shopping or out to lunch once in a while—and don't you dare ask anyone for their thoughts on what you should get!

Your Relationships

Well, now, Libra, this just so happens to be your favorite part of life on the planet. Spending time with a partner—pretty much all the time, if you can manage it—is your goal. You don't like to do anything alone, and you tend to put the needs and likes of your partner well before your own. Now, that kind of devotion is totally appealing to others, mostly because it's so rare but also because it's flattering—and who doesn't like to be flattered? If you have the right people around you, it will serve you well, and you'll earn lifelong friends and forever partners—in which case, you're at the top of your class. If you're in the midst of those who come and go, however, listen up. There's absolutely no need for you to please someone just because they're in your proximity. Do yourself a favor and save all that good stuff for those of us who adore you, appreciate you, and try our best to be just as good to you as you are to us. Believe it or not, you're not the honorary cruise director wherever you go (although that may well be your job). Take time to enjoy yourself every now and then. Oh, and please don't forget about your friends once you've fallen in love. You can live without your sweetheart for one night a week.

When it comes to choosing friends, or more importantly, a partner, I'm willing to bet that you usually end up with either Leo, Sagittarius, or Gemini, for the following reasons. As for Leo, well, Leo loves to be worshipped, doted on, and made to know—on a seriously regular basis—that they're loved and appreciated. Obviously, you're perfect for the job, and if you have your very own Leo, enjoy! They'll never, ever bore you, which is worse than death for you air signs. Same goes for Gemini, your air-sign cousin who's every bit as sociable as you are, and every bit as keen to mingle and chat. Same thing goes double for Sagittarius, who always makes you laugh.

Your Career and Money

As skilled as you are at one-to-one interaction, Libra, you do tend to choose occupations that allow you to practice your specialties. Individual counseling is particularly appealing to many of you, especially if it's a long-term commitment of sorts. Your true forte, however, is exercising that newfound knowledge about restoring balance and order. Obviously, when it comes to negotiating, mediating, or restoring peace to warring factions, you're the one for the job. If you can earn your daily bread in one of these ways, so much the better. You'll never dread going to work, and you'll always be proud of yourself. Oh, and let's not forget how much you like to be with others. That said, if you don't already have a partner at home and a partner at work, you'll find one of each this year, so relax. In the meantime, let's get back to indecision. If you have shopping to do, please take along a friend who knows you well enough to know what you actually like, and more importantly, who knows that expressing their opinion will only muddy up the process.

Your Lighter Side

On the subject of having fun, let's just say, right up front, Libra, that if you're not sharing an experience with someone else, it tends to become rather tedious for you. After all, who are you going to bounce your thoughts off of if you're all alone? Your love of beauty and balance is brought to you by your ruling planet, lovely Venus herself, so art, music, and aesthetically beautiful surroundings are important to you. Be kind to yourself, and spend as much time as possible in peaceful, pleasant places with happy, stable people who won't put you in the position of mediating petty battles. Even cruise directors get a day off every now and then.

Affirmation
I accept myself exactly as I am.

The Year Ahead for Libra

The good news is that Jupiter will be leaving your solar twelfth house of secrets and alone time this September, Libra, when he'll set off for your very own sign and your solar first house of personality and appearance. The tough part may be deciding what to do with yourself in the meantime. The thing is, Jupiter is larger than life. He expands the house and sign he visits, so being cooped up in a closet obviously isn't his cup of tea. Your mission, while he's in this private, dimly lit place, is to resist the urge to gossip—which won't be at all easy, since you'll be privy to some seriously amazing secrets right around now, most of which most definitely won't be fit for public consumption.

Once September arrives, however, you'll suddenly feel like a brand-new guy or gal—no kidding. There's something about hosting Jupiter in your sign that just turns on the energy/fun/enthusiasm meter inside us, and there's always much rejoicing in the kingdom. That said, you should know that Jupiter is an excessive kind of guy who believes that more, most, and much are the only way to go. In your solar first house, he'll expand everything about you—all those qualities your sign is famous for wielding so well. That includes your charm, sociability, and willingness to cooperate. Obviously, once September 9 arrives, you won't be lonely—so if you've been feeling a little blue or underappreciated lately, not to worry. The Universe has your back. Send your thank-you notes to Jupiter.

Now, let's talk about Mars, who'll spend all but the last three months of 2016 in Scorpio and Sagittarius. First of all, that's not usually the case. Mars tends to stay put in a sign for two months at the very most, at which point he's bored and ready to move on. This year, however, he apparently has work do—which means that you do too. Mars will begin this trek on January 3, when he storms off into sexy, intense Scorpio and your solar second house of money matters, possessions, and values. Now, Scorpio is far from shallow, so if you suddenly have the urge to purge, go right ahead. You know what you need and what you don't—and yes, that goes for both things and people. Stop stopping yourself.

Mars will dash off into Sagittarius and your solar third house of conversations and communications on March 6 and stay there until May 27. The thing is, he'll spend a heck of a lot of time moving in retrograde motion from this spot, so you may need to repeat yourself—and as per Mars, you won't appreciate having to do that. Now, prepare yourself, because what I'm about to reveal may be a bit of a shock, but when Mars is in the area, we're assertive, to say the very least—and when Sagg planets are around, we're blunt. I rest my case.

What This Year's Eclipses Mean for You

There will be two sets of eclipses this year, in March and September. These high-energy New and Full Moons occur two weeks apart. Solar Eclipses occur at New Moons and usually indicate a sudden new beginning that makes a great big change in your life. Lunar Eclipses are extra-powerful Full Moons and tend to point to culmination and closure. Regardless of which type they are, eclipses act fast, so buckle up.

The first Solar Eclipse will occur on March 8, in magical, mystical Pisces and your solar sixth house of work and relationships with coworkers. If you've been thinking about a career in counseling—which is a terrific job for you, by the way—this is the perfect time to get the show on the road. If you are interested in but not proficient at tarot, astrology, or feng shui, take classes. In the not-too-distant future, incorporating those skills into how you earn your daily bread could become quite important to you.

On March 23, a Lunar Eclipse will occur in your partner-oriented sign and your solar first house of personality and appearance. If your birthday is in the early degrees of Libra, this will be a very significant year, but all of you balance-loving folks will receive a bit of a wake-up call from the Universe. In this house, the issue may be your physical body, in which case it might be time to start that diet or stop a bad habit that's not doing your health any favors. You'll probably also become a bit pre-occupied with the first impression you make on others—and all of this certainly could mean that you're at the end of one relationship and the beginning of another.

On September 1, a Solar Eclipse will plant a seed in your solar twelfth house of secrets, Libra—and this one could be tricky. If you're attached and not at all happy in the relationship, you'll definitely be looking for greener pastures, and you really don't like being without a partner, so it might be tempting to begin an affair before you've actually closed the door on your current relationship. Keep in mind that secrets don't stay hidden forever, and weigh the consequences before you do anything that could become public knowledge and work against you in the future.

The final Lunar Eclipse of 2016 will occur on September 16, once again in Pisces and your solar sixth house of work. If you've been taking classes on spiritual or metaphysical topics, it will suddenly occur to you that you've learned an awful lot. If you feel confident enough to teach, take on a protégé who shows promise in this field and share your knowledge. This energetic eclipse will bring out the guru and spiritual mentor in you. Take the responsibility seriously.

Saturn

Bet you've been a bit sarcastic lately, Libra, or that you've come to love dry humor. The astrological culprit responsible for this is Saturn, who just so happens to be marching through your solar third house of conversations and communications, all done up in Sagittarius, the sign that most loves humor. With this serious guy in this not-so-serious sign, there will be laughter in your life, but it won't happen if the humor is sophomoric or slapstick—both of which will earn the performer a very strict "tsk, tsk." You're thinking practically now, making serious plans for the future and taking on more responsibility. That can get heavy after a while, however, so please don't get depressed—and if you do, don't hibernate. Talk to a trusted confidant about it, and get thee to a doctor. Saturn rules professional people, and with this planet in open-minded Sagittarius, you can count on finding help if you look. Now, the third house also refers to your neighborhood and your neighbors, so authority figures, older folks, or someone in a uniform may be moving in next door. Then, too, your block may be going through a restructuring process and roadwork or construction may tie up traffic and make it tough to get around. Don't get frustrated. Take a look around and see what you would have missed if you weren't right where you were. There are lessons everywhere for you now. Don't miss a single one.

Uranus

Well, Libra, you've certainly had some rather "interesting" encounters lately, haven't you? Of course you have. Uranus just loves to hook us up with highly unusual people, so ever since he set off for red-hot Aries and your solar seventh house of one-to-one relationships back in March of 2012, you've probably had some eye-opening new friends or lovers come into your life. Now, this might mean you're spending your time with someone whose hair is purple—on the side of their head that's not shaved—or, if that's your style, that you've taken a liking to someone who dresses in tailored beige suits and sensible shoes. One way or the other, your eyes have been and will continue to be opened by an inside view into the world of someone completely different from you. This is a fun, exciting time, and you'll learn an awful lot about the myriad ways others express themselves. If you were born between October 8 and 19, your Sun is currently being opposed by Uranus, and since oppositions tend to show up in our relationships—which just happens to be your specialty—you've been experiencing a double dose of the erratic, unpredictable, and unusual, in most if not all of your encounters. This energy can be easy and fun, but it can also be quite unsettling. You may have just ended a relationship rather abruptly, or you may be considering that right now. One thing is for sure—with this unpredictable planet in a sign as impulsive as Aries, whatever happens will happen in an instant.

Neptune

Your solar sixth house has to do with issues of work and work-oriented relationships, Libra, and Neptune has been on duty here for right around five years. The thing is, she's a magical energy, and magic can be used for all kids of reasons and to achieve all kinds of aims. In this spot, she may inspire you to literally become interested in performing magic as an occupation—and what fun that would be! Of course, Neptune also casts some serious spells herself, and since relationships with coworkers are also handled here, it's not hard to imagine you, at some point, having one serious, heavy-duty crush on one of them. The good news is that Neptune's influence is plenty potent enough for both of you, so if you're infatuated, they probably are too. On the other hand, you might find that a certain person you work with isn't quite what they seemed to be. Remember, Neptune rules glamour, and back in the day, casting a glamour on someone meant changing their appearance. Be on guard, but don't get paranoid. If you see them do something you don't like, ask about it. Now, if you were born between September 29 and October 7, all that goes double, since Neptune is also currently visiting with your Sun. The thing is, she's forming an uneasy aspect with it—an inconjunct. The problem with these transits is that it's easy to get confused and end up searching for answers to the wrong questions. It's also possible to make yourself sick if you're around negative energies, so steer clear, and if you don't understand something, talk to someone who does.

Pluto

I'm willing to bet that you've been going through some pretty potent emotional changes over the last several years, Libra, and that all your relationships have been tricky but transformational—not to mention intense. It seems that Pluto—Mr. All or Nothing himself—has made himself comfortable in your solar fourth house of home, family, and domestic situations. Now, you'll remember that this is one relentless, focused, and often obsessive kind of guy, so if things at your place have been less than peaceful lately, it's no wonder. The good news is that you've probably done a whole lot of housekeeping, and a whole lot of charities are benefitting from your donations. The tough part might be keeping a rein on this energy with regard to family members. Pluto can bring along headlines featuring manipulation and power struggles, so if someone close to you has been working you, and you know it, it's time to put your foot down and put an end to it. That goes double for those of you who were born between October 7 and 11, since Pluto will also be locked into an irritating square with your Sun this year. Before you get upset about that "irritating" thing, however, keep in mind that change doesn't happen until we're restless enough to initiate it. This is your time to initiate domestic, emotional, and familial changes—the bigger, the better. Go for it with both guns blazing.

Libra | January

Relaxation and Recreation

Well, Libra, you may have to wait until January 12 to get any rest or have any fun. The skies above you will be hosting some rather turbulent energies until then, so you'll probably have to work hard and exercise your skills at mediation. The good news is that January 12 through January 16 looks wonderful, so you'll have a break in the action.

Lovers and Friends

If you're not seeing anyone at the moment, Libra, you'll have plenty of chances to get together with someone new this month. Oh, and that goes double for January 12, when loving Venus will form an easy, enthusiastic fire trine with unpredictable Uranus. Prepare to meet someone under highly unusual circumstances. This is the stuff of love at first sight.

Money and Success

Keep a careful eye on your wallet around January 5, Libra, when it will be all too easy to lose your money—literally, by losing your wallet, or through making an investment that isn't what it seems to be. There will be a lot of confusion in the air surrounding financial matters. Hold off on important decisions, and don't sign anything binding.

Tricky Transits

Venus will square off with generous, excessive Jupiter on January 17, putting extravagance and risk-taking on the menu for us all. Be sure not to overindulge to the point that you make yourself sick. Of course, indulging in tender touches is another story entirely. In that case, have at it. Warn your friends that you won't be around for a day or so.

Rewarding Days
12, 13, 15, 19, 30

Challenging Days
5, 7, 20, 25, 31

Libra | February

Relaxation and Recreation

The last day of the month will be February 29 this year, Libra, and that extra day looks like great fun for you. It seems that your ruling planet, loving Venus, will form a stabilizing but enthusiastic trine with serious Saturn, so if you're attached, you two will get even closer because of an event that day. If you're single, keep an eye out for someone quite a bit older or younger than yourself.

Lovers and Friends

The heavens will be relatively quiet during February, making this a pretty darn peaceful month on the home front, Libra. Oh, and as for Valentine's Day—which must be your favorite holiday—you can expect an easy trine between the emotional Moon in touch-loving Taurus and generous Jupiter to make it a very special occasion. Maybe even memorable.

Money and Success

If an argument about money matters comes up between you and yours on February 6 or 7, try not to get too worried about it. The culprits are fiery Mars and the equally fiery Sun, two astrological hotheads who act fast and then move on just as quickly. Once you've vented, it will all be over. Be sure to vent, though. No fair hanging on to something and simmering.

Tricky Transits

Communicating your needs to a loved one or child could be tough around February 10 or 27, Libra, but if there's something you really need to say, make the effort. The problem might be that you two aren't on the same page because of a past misunderstanding. It's time to lay your cards on the table and straighten it all out.

Rewarding Days
3, 9, 14, 25, 26

Challenging Days
7, 22, 27

Libra | March

Relaxation and Recreation

Loving Venus in startling Aquarius will remain on duty in your solar fifth house until March 12, Libra, which is where all kinds of fun things happen. This house describes your playmates and lovers and also your dealings with kids. With this lovely lady on duty—especially since she's your astrological ruler—you can count on lots of unexpected good times. Be spontaneous!

Lovers and Friends

If you're not seeing anyone at the moment, that could be set to change, Libra, and quickly, too. Your ruling planet, loving Venus, is making her way through your solar fifth house of lovers, all done up in Aquarius, the sign that belongs to unpredictable Uranus. Needless to say, someone quite unusual could be along shortly—under odd or unusual circumstances.

Money and Success

On March 16, mighty Jupiter will form an easy trine with powerful Pluto—and when these two combine talents, all kinds of things are possible. Pluto is in Capricorn, the sign of career matters, and Jupiter will be only too happy to provide lots of opportunities for promotions, not to mention entirely new work.

Tricky Transits

Two eclipses will occur this month, Libra, and they're very tricky creatures, so be prepared. The first, on March 8, will drop an emotional bomb in your solar sixth house of work, which could mean you'll decide that you hate your job and it isn't worth it anymore. Just be sure you have a backup plan before you storm off into the sunset.

Rewarding Days

2, 6, 16, 24, 26

Challenging Days

3, 4, 8, 9, 23, 30

Libra | April

Relaxation and Recreation

A sky full of impulsive, fiery Aries planets will make this quite the month for you, Libra—since they'll all be passing through your solar seventh house of one-to-one relationships. The thing is, in addition to sudden romance being on your astrological menu, you should also expect lots of chances to try new things with equally fiery friends.

Lovers and Friends

Mercury will lead a parade of planets through ultra-sensual Taurus and your solar eighth house of intimate matters, Libra—so obviously, the news could be a lot worse. Around April 9, the Sun and Uranus will get together in your solar seventh house of relationships, too, so don't be surprised if you're madly attracted to someone you've never met who nonetheless seems really familiar.

Money and Success

On April 29, your ruling planet, Venus, will set off for Taurus, a sign that's famous for its ability to attract money and other resources. Now, this puts her in your solar eighth house for almost a month, and since this house is where joint resources, loans, and other financial dealings are handled, things look pretty good for you and your pocketbook.

Tricky Transits

Venus will square off with intense, demanding Pluto on April 19, possibly causing a bit of a rift between your sweetheart and your family. Unfortunately, one or both of them will want you to take sides—which, of course, is out of the question, if not entirely impossible. Ah, well. It's time once again to juggle.

Rewarding Days

1, 2, 3, 18, 29, 30

Challenging Days

6, 9, 19

Libra | May

Relaxation and Recreation

All those Taurus planets will form easy trines and exciting sextiles with both generous, outgoing Jupiter and intense, determined Pluto this month, Libra—which certainly does sound like a good time will be had by all. The best part is that both career and personal matters will go along smoothly, so if you had to juggle your time last month, you'll be able to get back to normal now.

Lovers and Friends

Affectionate, partner-loving Venus will spend most of the month in Taurus, a very sensual sign, Libra, which will put her in your solar eighth house of intimate matters until May 24. If you're involved with someone, you two will most definitely rediscover the flame that brought you together. If you're single, you'll have some delightful choices to make. No hurry, either. Take your time.

Money and Success

If you've been thinking about making an investment or taking out a loan, Libra, all will go quite easily for you if you start investigating your options around May 6. Of course, Mercury will still be retrograde in Taurus, the sign most often associated with money, so feel free to do your homework and lay the groundwork, but wait until the very end of the month to finalize things.

Tricky Transits

Jupiter is a big fan of excess, Libra. In fact, his favorite words are much, more, and many. Saturn, on the other hand, is quite a frugal guy, who always goes for the no-frills option. That said, you should know that these two will form an irritating square on May 26, the stuff that push-me, pull-you situations are made of. Don't allow anyone to intimidate or rush you.

Rewarding Days

16, 19, 20, 30

Challenging Days

21, 22, 24, 26, 27

Libra | June

Relaxation and Recreation

The Sun, Venus, and Mercury will all pass through Gemini this month, your fun-loving air-sign cousin. Now, this puts them all in your solar fifth house of fun times, playmates, and dealings with kids, so you can be very sure you won't be bored. You may, however, have more invitations than time to accept them. Ah, well. Your specialty is juggling.

Lovers and Friends

If you're single, Libra, that could be set to change, and very soon. It seems that your ruling planet, Venus, has made her way into Gemini—a sign that just loves variety. That said, you can expect a veritable parade of admirers to cross your path, especially around June 6, 12, and 13. Resist the urge to choose just one right away. You can afford to be picky.

Money and Success

Mars is currently on duty in your solar second house of money matters and personal finances, Libra—and this is the kind of guy who lives for adrenaline, you'll remember. Needless to say, even if you're not ordinarily an impulse buyer, you will be now. If you can afford it, go for it. If not, consider other options more in keeping with your budget.

Tricky Transits

The Full Moon on June 20 will arrive along with a sky full of rather testy energies, Libra. Mercury in chatty, restless Gemini will oppose serious, practical Saturn and square off with dreamy, impractical Neptune as well. Full Moons are all about culmination, but if you're not sure about what to do or you're being held up by details, don't allow yourself to be rushed.

Rewarding Days
8, 12, 13, 25, 26, 27

Challenging Days
1, 2, 3, 4, 16, 17, 18

Libra | July

Relaxation and Recreation

On July 11, Venus will make her way into fun-loving, romantic Leo and your solar eleventh house of friendships and groups, Libra—and with this attractive, dramatic energy on duty, it's not hard to imagine you being the star of the show with regard to your circle of friends. If you're due to perform—regardless of where or for whom—you can count on it going very, very well.

Lovers and Friends

Chatty Mercury will join hands with loving Venus on July 16, and since they'll both be in romantic Leo at the time, pillow talk and sweet nothings will be on your agenda. The best part is that the Sun will join them there on July 22, and since he shines especially brightly in Leo, you can expect to be the focus of the attention of someone delicious.

Money and Success

Once Venus moves into lavish Leo on July 11, Libra, you'll be in the mood to pull out all the stops to make sure your loved ones know just how much you care. Fancy dinners and amazing gifts are wonderful, of course, but remember this: there's no greater, more wonderful gift than being interrupted mid-sentence by a spontaneous "I love you" from across the table.

Tricky Transits

The heavens will play host to several inconjunct aspects this month, Libra, which tend to be in the neighborhood when misunderstandings arise. That said, if you have the feeling that you and a dear one are not seeing eye to eye and you can't figure out why, table the matter until you're sure you have all the right information.

Rewarding Days

1, 3, 20, 26, 31

Challenging Days

2, 7, 11, 13, 16

Libra | August

Relaxation and Recreation

Make contact with an elder family member who's been on your mind lately, Libra, even if they're in another state, on an opposite coast, or in an entirely different country. That goes double for anyone who's going through tough times. Your voice alone will soothe their soul—and you know how good you are at reassurance. If it's possible to travel to them, so much the better.

Lovers and Friends

A relatively new friend will prove their worth to you this month, Libra, as soon as August 1, when they'll come to your aid without you ever having to ask. The good news is that you were pretty sure they would. The best part is that this act of kindness will bring you two even closer. How nice to know that someone has your back.

Money and Success

You might have a bit of a problem with money matters around August 6, Libra, especially if you or someone close to you has been trying to ignore a particularly troublesome situation. At this point, there is only one option: face this head-on and get it taken care of. You might actually find that a few missing details are all it will take to fix the problem.

Tricky Transits

The Sun will set off for Virgo on August 22, just as the Sun and Mercury get together in that very same sign. Now, this will put them all—along with Venus, by the way—in your solar twelfth house of secrets, which might well mean that you are suddenly made privy to news that isn't fit for public consumption. Your best bet? Keep quiet.

Rewarding Days
1, 2, 3, 10, 29

Challenging Days
6, 7, 12, 13, 14, 30

Libra | September

Relaxation and Recreation

Talk about a good time! Generous, outgoing Jupiter will set off for your sign on September 9, and all of a sudden, all kinds of doors will open for you—many of them involving fortunate partnerships. Your luck will also be running on high, in all departments, so if you've had a rather tough time of it lately, you can count on all that coming to an end.

Lovers and Friends

You'll be in the right place at the right time to meet up with someone just delightful this month, Libra, particularly around September 9, 18, and 19. Now, you might not see this person as someone you'd spend time with at the start, but if you take the time to work past what's on the outside, you'll just love what's on the inside.

Money and Success

Venus will set off for intense, determined Scorpio on September 23, which will put her right smack dab in the middle of your solar second house of money matters and personal finances. That could mean there will be a power struggle in this department over the next month or so. Keep a watchful eye out for signs of trouble.

Tricky Transits

There will be two eclipses this month, Libra, on September 1 and 16. Eclipses signal big changes that tend to occur quite suddenly, so if you decide you're not happy with your work, you might just decide to quit. Do yourself a favor and stay put until you make contact with others who can help you find a new path.

Rewarding Days

7, 8, 9, 25, 30

Challenging Days

1, 10, 11, 12, 17, 18, 21

Libra | October

Relaxation and Recreation

The Sun and Mercury will make their way into your sign and your solar first house, Libra, which is all about personal presentation. Now, their company will be stimulating and oh so much fun, but let's face it: with expansive Jupiter in that same spot for the upcoming year, you should pay attention to symbols and dreams now, because there will be a quiz coming along shortly.

Lovers and Friends

Venus and Mercury will collide on October 1, all done up in sexy Scorpio and set to form easy, cooperative trines with dreamy, woozy Neptune. Now, Neptune is famous for her ability to dissolve boundaries between us, so if you're with someone you've only recently gotten to know but you've already decided you're in love, it might be time to make that tender announcement.

Money and Success

Talkative Mercury and fortunate Jupiter will come together in your sign and your solar first house of personality and personal appearance on October 11—and Libra, if you have not yet allowed yourself to speak your piece, you will most certainly do it then. Matter of fact, even if you have vented before, that doesn't mean you won't do it again.

Tricky Transits

The Full Moon on October 15 will light up Aries and your solar seventh house of one-to-one relationships, Libra. Now, if you're happily attached, you two will end up spending a whole lot of time together, getting to know each other even better. If you're not happy with the situation, this may be the push you've been waiting for.

Rewarding Days
1, 4, 11, 14, 17, 26

Challenging Days
2, 5, 7, 13, 25, 28, 29

Libra | November

Relaxation and Recreation
Your very own ruling planet, lovely Venus, will spend the first eleven days of the month in fun-loving, fiery Sagittarius. She'll be bringing all her down-to-earth charm into your conversations and communications, so you'll be the life of the party. You'll also be a whole lot more blunt than usual, so prepare to raise some eyebrows.

Lovers and Friends
November 4, 5, and 6 will be terrific days for you and your sweetheart, Libra, as loving Venus forms an easy trine with impulsive Uranus in Aries. You two might even decide it's time to take a mini-vacation together, and since it's almost the weekend, why not make it a long one and hop in the car for destinations unknown? What fun!

Money and Success
November 4, 5, and 6 will also arrive with some terrific news about your personal finances, Libra. Might be that the raise you've been waiting for has finally come through—big time. Might be that you win a bit of money on the lottery. On your travels, get yourself a ticket. Just one. Don't get crazy.

Tricky Transits
Jupiter and Pluto will square off on November 24, Libra—and when these two heavy hitters are in this aspect, power struggles abound. If you're frustrated because you're not having any luck convincing someone that you're going to handle things your way, don't even bother trying again. Put some distance between the two of you and table the discussion for another day.

Rewarding Days
4, 5, 15, 19, 22, 23

Challenging Days
6, 18, 24, 25, 30

Libra | December

Relaxation and Recreation

A sky full of Sagittarius and Aquarius energies will duck in and out of exciting sextiles and easy, cooperative trines this month, Libra, making this a holiday season to remember. In particular, December 24 and 25 look like terrific days for you, with surprise guests and lots of big, warm hugs—not to mention some great gifts. Enjoy!

Lovers and Friends

Venus will set off for your solar fifth house of playmates and relationships with kids on December 7, and she'll be all done up in surprising Aquarius. This unpredictable lady will set the stage for fun—when you least expect it, of course—via spontaneous, unique friends who'll be up for just about anything. The best part is that you will be too!

Money and Success

Money matters should go along quite well for you this month, Libra. In fact, happy news will be en route, if not on December 7, then between December 24 and 26. Of course, 'tis the season for gift-giving, too, so don't be surprised if someone goes all out and presents you with something you've wanted for a very long time.

Tricky Transits

Impulsive and often reckless Mars will collide with woozy Neptune on December 31, Libra, so be very careful if you're out celebrating the new year. These two are often around when accidents occur, especially if alcohol or drugs are involved. Ringing in the new year from the safety of your home would be your best bet.

Rewarding Days

All but the three below.

Challenging Days

19, 26, 31

Libra Action Table

These dates reflect the best—but not the only—times for success and ease in these activities, according to your Sun sign.

	JAN	FEB	MAR	APR	MAY	JUN	JUL	AUG	SEP	OCT	NOV	DEC
Move	22, 23, 24		17, 18, 19			6, 7, 8	3, 4, 5, 30, 31		24, 25		18, 19, 20	
Start a class		3, 4, 5		3, 4				12, 13, 14			7, 8, 9	
Join a club	11, 12, 21		6, 7, 8		1, 27, 28		21, 22		13, 14, 15			4, 5
Ask for a raise		15, 16		27, 28, 29		2, 3		23, 24		17, 18, 19		
Look for work		6, 7, 8			15, 16		18, 19, 20				4, 5, 6	
Get pro advice	1, 27, 28		23, 24			11, 12			1, 2			19, 20, 21
Get a loan		1, 2, 28, 29		23, 24			13, 14, 15			3, 4		24, 25, 26
See a doctor			21, 22, 23		23, 24				1, 2, 28, 29, 30			
Start a diet	24, 25			22		20, 21					29, 30	
End relationship		22, 23			21, 22			18, 19		1, 30		
Buy clothes	18, 19		12, 13, 14				6, 7, 8		16, 17		22, 23, 24	
Get a makeover		13, 14		7, 8		14, 15			20, 21			11, 12
New romance	13, 14, 15, 24, 25		8, 9		29, 30, 31			2, 3, 4				
Vacation	7, 8, 9		29, 30		21, 22, 23		16, 17, 18			5, 6, 7		27, 28, 29

Scorpio

The Scorpion
October 22 to November 21

♏

Element: Water

Quality: Fixed

Polarity: Yin/feminine

Planetary Ruler: Pluto (Mars)

Meditation: I can surrender my feelings

Gemstone: Topaz

Power Stones: Obsidian, amber, citrine, garnet, pearl

Key Phrase: I create

Glyph: Scorpion's tail

Anatomy: Reproductive system

Colors: Burgundy, black

Animals: Reptiles, scorpions, birds of prey

Myths/Legends: The Phoenix, Hades and Persephone, Shiva

House: Eighth

Opposite Sign: Taurus

Flower: Chrysanthemum

Keyword: Intensity

The Scorpio Personality

Your Strengths and Challenges

You are the detectives of the zodiac, Scorpio, the one-twelfth of the population who notice what others don't. It's not that your specialty is details, like Virgo. No, you're into a far more subtle type of information collection. Yes, you watch how others work, but you also want to know why they work that way. If they interest you for some reason even you probably can't explain, you'll study them for as long as it takes. If they appeal to your libido, you might not be quite so patient. The thing is, you're perceptive, and you're very good at figuring out what a gesture, look, or movement means. You don't have to have a doctorate in psychology to know, either. This is the sort of thing that comes quite easily to you. Now, being gifted with the superpower of understanding comes with a lot of heavy responsibilities, as you well know. To start with, you might see something you don't want to see. You might also become so fascinated with putting the puzzle together that you accumulate too much information, which might lead you to suspect something that's not realistic. For this reason, if you're extraordinarily involved with someone or something, please do distract yourself. You have trouble making a separation on an emotional level, so it can be really hard for you to think of anything other than The Other. Now, that can be a very good thing, if someone needs you, but is not so great if you become obsessed. Your mission is to provide yourself with challenges. Puzzles, riddles, and mysteries will all do just fine. You have antennae that are on full power 24/7, and it's often exhausting for you.

Now, speaking of exhausting, let's talk about those foolish people who think they can change you, which might be laughable if it weren't quite so ridiculous. Once you have made a decision, that's that. Period. End of story. The thing is, you make that perfectly clear, so anyone who is surprised at your resoluteness was obviously not paying attention and is therefore not worth your time.

Relationships

Sexy. Broody. Mysterious. That's how others see you, Scorpio, especially when they're attracted to you—which doesn't take a whole lot of work on your part. You are unquestionably the most sexual sign out there, but not too many others understand why. The thing is, you are a fixed water sign, which means your emotions are extremely strong—and you want the real thing. You don't care for air kisses, fist-bumping, or quick, meaningless hugs. When you make contact with a partner, it's because you're fascinated and you want to know absolutely everything about them. Of course, being physically intimate will most definitely achieve that aim, but there are many kinds of intimacy, as you well know, and you enjoy them all. A good, long midnight chat at the kitchen table will work just fine for you. You just can't settle for anything that's shallow. You realize that the tip of the iceberg is only 10 percent of what's really going on down there—okay, because that's exactly how you are—and you're not willing to settle for anything less than the whole deal. It takes a while to get to know you, but once someone is allowed through security, provided they stay loyal and honest and provide you with the depth in a relationship that you absolutely crave—well, to be perfectly honest, you'll fire-walk for them. There's just no one who's as loyal as you are when you care. As such, you can afford to be choosy, with regard to both friends and lovers. You're a catch, Scorpio. There's only one teeny, tiny little thing: you do tend to become a bit obsessive at times, and you often lie awake at night wondering what someone meant by what they said. Stop that. It's usually nothing, after all. Now, when it comes to long-term partnerships, your opposite sign, sensual Taurus, is often your best match—for obvious reasons. But you're so highly emotional that the other water signs, Cancer and Pisces, understand you best.

Your Career and Money

Here's the thing, Scorpio. You folks are perfectly comfortable with topics and activities that make most of us rather uneasy. That only makes sense, given that Pluto, the Lord of the Underworld, is your ruling planet. You're fascinated with the concept of process, and if it's a behind-the-scenes process, you love it even more. As such, you're often drawn to occupations that allow your intensity and core strength to do what most of us couldn't. You might be a tireless researcher, and sooner or later you will uncover something that no one else has—so keep at it. You may work in a position where sexuality is a comfortable thing, such as a sexual surrogate or sexual counselor. One way or another, if you deal with people while you're working, you will gather up information about them in four seconds that would take others four months. For that reason, you're an excellent counselor or therapist.

Money-wise, things can go one of two ways. First off, you can become so obsessed with something—and please, please don't ever allow that to be drugs or alcohol—that you really don't care what it costs or what you have to put off to pay for it. On the other hand, thanks to the influence of excessive Sagittarius on your solar second house of finances, you might tend to overspend on fun stuff. Regardless, you'll need to have someone else manage your finances. Although that may be your occupation, handling your own money may not be your specialty.

Your Lighter Side

What's fun for you, Scorpio? Well, outside of the obvious—you sexy thang—you do tend to enjoy figuring things out and solving mysteries. Novels by such authors as Clive Owens and Stephen King will keep you rapt for a good, long time during the day and well into the night as well. Once you're on board, you literally cannot put the book down. That goes double for movies, which you become totally wrapped up in. For that reason, you probably love the theater far better than watching at home with the lights on. You also love to dig, both physically, in the ground, as well as intellectually, through working at a project or problem until you have come to the very end.

Affirmation

I am empowered by my inner strength.

The Year Ahead for Scorpio

The really big astrological news for your sign is this, Scorpio: red-hot, passionate Mars will spend quite a bit of time in your sign and your solar first house of personality and appearance this year. In fact, he will spend four and a half months there, rather than two months, his usual stay. That said, on January 3, Mars will set off for your sign, activating all those qualities we love most about you. Your depth, keen gift of perception, and ability to sense trouble—no, smell it, actually—are all on the list. But lest we forget, you're a very sexy and very sexual creature, Scorpio, and Mars is a very passionate guy. Talk about a match made in heaven!

If you're back on the market for someone with the guts, courage, and intensity of spirit to be your lover, you might just find the shopping a lot easier to deal with now. To start with, Mars will amp up the fire in your personality, pushing you to pursue whatever or whomever you're fascinated with. Mars will stay on duty in your sign until March 5—his first trip this year through Scorpio. This time out, he will be interested in helping you get to know you, for better or worse. The good news is that no matter what you find, if you're not happy with it, you will have another shot at it, since Mars will retrograde back into your sign for a full month in June. In the meantime, pay careful attention to your finances and money matters. You might find that impulse spending is a problem that needs to be solved—and soon—or that someone who promised you financial help has most definitely not lived up to their word. If that's the case, Scorpio, what exactly are you waiting for? Do you have any idea how formidable you are when you're less than pleased? If that problem hasn't been solved by May 27, you'll have another shot at the title from then until June 29. Mars will be retrograde during that period, and retrogrades are all about the "re"—redoing, remodeling, rescheduling, re-whatevering. If you need a do-over, the Universe will be happy to provide you with it now.

The good news is that once Mars straightens out on June 29, you will finally be able to bring closure to a situation that you were beginning to think would never, ever end. The best news is that by August 2, you will be able to put something to rest that has made you lose sleep for years now. Now, let's talk about Jupiter, the Santa Claus of the heavens, who'll spend January 1 through September 9 in your solar eleventh house of friendships, group associations, and plans for the future. This is an excessive guy, Scorpio, and he's been on duty since last August, so at this point, you're no stranger to the concept of feeling betrayed. Your mission is to move on and trust another group or circle of friends with your oh-so-sensitive-but-oh-so-guarded heart.

What This Year's Eclipses Mean for You

There will be two sets of eclipses during 2016, Scorpio. Each consists of a Solar Eclipse—which brings the Sun and the Moon together in a super-charged New Moon—and a Lunar Eclipse, a Full Moon that's just as energetic. The eclipses occur in pairs every six months, two weeks apart.

This year, the first Solar Eclipse will arrive on March 8, all done up in romantic Pisces, your water-sign cousin. This meeting of the Sun and Moon will take place in your solar fifth house of lovers, playmates, and fun times, so if you've been hanging out with someone on a casual and/or platonic basis, that could be set to change one fine evening—right out of the blue. Since this house also rules creativity, you might suddenly develop the urge to learn an instrument or an artistic craft, and since another eclipse will occur here in September, that skill could turn into something much more than a hobby. Stay tuned...

On March 23, a Lunar Eclipse will occur, activating your solar sixth house of work and duties and your solar twelfth house of rest and rejuvenation. Now, this eclipse in itself points to the need for you to balance your work schedule with your play schedule, but since it will happen in Libra, the sign gifted with the ability to restore balance, chances are good you'll learn to juggle. On the other hand, you might also take up in secret with a coworker or higher-up. In that case, be very sure that if things don't work out, you two will still be able to see each other every day with absolutely no sniping.

On September 1, the second Solar Eclipse of the year will come along, all done up in precise, meticulous Virgo. Now, you get along just fine with Virgo energy, because you're super-perceptive and Virgo is a master of details. Together, these two signs can figure out absolutely everything—including the true motives of just about anyone. If a dear one isn't sure about a new lover, the three of you should probably get together for lunch—which will give you the chance to subtly conduct an interview.

Last but not least, a second eclipse will occur in Pisces on September 16, once again activating your solar fifth house of lovers, playmates, and fun times. This time out, however, rather than starting something up, you will probably be reaping the benefits. If a love affair has recently become just as emotional as it is physical, it might be time to make some serious decisions.

Saturn

If you haven't already, it's time to get yourself on a budget, Scorpio. Saturn, a very frugal kind of guy, is about to spend the entire coming year in your solar second house of money matters, and when he's in the neighborhood, splurging is frowned upon, to say the least. That said, he's wearing Sagittarius, the type of sign that believes "excess is best." You might feel a bit torn between opening a savings account and investing those savings on a five-star long-distance trip—but honestly, with this practical planet on duty, either one will go along well. Take your time and decide which would be the best for you. Now, the second house also rules possessions, and Saturn loves to straighten, organize, and trim down. Regardless of when you choose to do it, a major spring cleaning is in order, and probably a few trips to Goodwill, too. If you do any shopping, whatever you buy will necessarily have to be practical, and you'll want to get the warranty, too. The good news is you'll understand that money spent on quality goods is money invested in the future. Needless to say, quality will be ever so much more appealing to you than quantity. If you need to handle serious money matters, don't sign anything if Mercury is retrograde.

Uranus

Startling Uranus, who just so happens to proudly carry the title of "Mr. Totally Unexpected," has been on duty in your solar sixth house of work, health, and relationships with coworkers ever since March of 2012, Scorpio—so to say that your work situation has been a bit different or erratic ever since is an understatement. In fact, it has probably not been easy for you to work at all, especially if you're at the mercy of a higher-up or supervisor who seems bent on giving you a hard time. In this case, you will need to consider the fact that you might be sending out "please fire me" vibes without even realizing it. If unexpected situations keep coming up that force you to be less than the model employee, be honest with yourself—and then, if at all possible, begin the hunt for a way to earn your daily bread that is far more in keeping with your views, beliefs, and goals. Of course, with Uranus on duty in impulsive, hotheaded Aries, it's entirely possible that you might have already quit rather unceremoniously. If you were born between November 7 and 18, your Sun is also currently under the influence of an uncomfortable inconjunct from Uranus, in which case, all of the above will be a lot more intense—and putting up with restrictions on your daily freedom will be next to impossible. It might be time to investigate what it would take to strike out on your own and make your own career with your very own hours.

Neptune

Well! I'm willing to bet that the past five years have been pretty darn "interesting" for you in the department of lovers and playmates, Scorpio, which only stands to reason. Romantic Neptune has been making her way through your solar fifth house of love affairs for the duration—which means it's her playground, too. Now, she does tend to arrive with a whole lot of introductions in mind for you, so you definitely haven't been bored, but you might be a bit overwhelmed. The thing is, Neptune dissolves boundaries, and in a house this social, it's easy to draw in all kinds of people and experiences, some positive, some not so much. On the positive side, your love life has probably been fabulous! On the negative side, you may have "adopted" someone with problems without realizing exactly what you were getting yourself into. If you were born between October 29 and November 6, you're also receiving a trine from Neptune to your sexy little Sun, which means all that deep, intense sexual energy you own will be oozing right out of you. So in addition to drawing others in, you'll also be making it next to impossible for them to ever leave. Again, this can be terrific, if you're involved and happy about it. If you're not happy and you feel trapped, get busy. You're no stranger to the concept of clearing the deadwood from your life with great finality. Do yourself a favor and make it happen as soon as possible.

Pluto

Before we get started, Scorpio, we need to address the fact that this intense, no-nonsense, and often feared planet is your ruler. That means you're very good at handling the intensity of his visits—and that you always "reap" the best from them—if you'll pardon the pun. At any rate, now that Pluto is busy transforming things via authoritative Capricorn, he's focusing all his energy on your solar third house of communications, conversations, and short trips. Needless to say, you're due for some extremely heavy chats. Capricorn planets don't so much speak as they do announce. Fortunately, once again, his kind of news is news you'll be just fine with. You might have a bit of trouble with a sibling or neighbor who wants to control you—which would be quite comical if it weren't so irritating. Talk about an exercise in futility. All that said, if you were born between November 6 and 10, Pluto will send you the benefits of a lovely, energizing, stimulating sextile aspect to your Sun, providing you with a double dose of positive, comfortable transformation—okay, and great sex, too, if you're so inclined. Technically speaking, getting all these blessings from Pluto is cheating, especially to those of us who struggle with his visits. The very least you could do is to spare us the delightful details.

Scorpio | January

Relaxation and Recreation

Mars will enter your sign and your solar first house of personality and appearance on January 3, Scorpio, and the battles will begin. This is not to say that you will necessarily argue with anyone, but only that your encounters will be lively and quite passionate. Okay, and you might get mad once or twice. Still, as you well know, there's nothing more peaceful than the after-venting stage. Yes?

Lovers and Friends

With Jupiter holding his regal court in your solar eleventh house of friendships and like-minded others, you've probably been having quite the time of it lately. Invitations, offers, and more invitations. How exhausting—and how fun! Mercury will spend January 5 through January 25 moving in reverse, so getting around could be frustrating. Take your time. They're waiting for you.

Money and Success

On January 6, the Moon, serious Saturn, and Venus will get together in your solar second house of money matters, Scorpio, all of them in Sagittarius. You might want to be far more generous than is reasonably comfortable for you, regardless of the cost, if a loved one calls. You are willing to fire-walk for your loved ones, but please do think about your own needs, too.

Tricky Transits

On January 25, Mercury will turn direct, ready to rock and roll through your solar third house of conversations and communications. The thing is, the day this planet straightens his act out is often more problematic than his entire trip, so if you're trying to get from point A to point B without much success, it might be time to pull off the road and have some coffee.

Rewarding Days

5, 14, 18, 19, 29, 30

Challenging Days

3, 17, 20, 31

Scorpio | February

Relaxation and Recreation
On February 18, the Sun will set off for your solar fifth house of play-time, Scorpio, and you'll probably find that being around water is fun, but also necessary for your peace of mind. Makes sense, though. Water is your element, so it has always soothed you. On February 28, there'll be double those same feelings, so if you haven't yet made it to the beach, the lakeshore, or even the pool, better do it now.

Lovers and Friends
With ultra-sexy, ultra-passionate Mars on duty in your solar first house of personality and appearance, all done up in your sign, Scorpio—well, let's just say that this will be a month to remember. It might be that you have run into someone new who oozes sensuality almost as much and as skillfully as you do—and wouldn't that be lovely?

Money and Success
The New Moon on February 8 will occur in your solar fourth house of home and family matters, Scorpio, so if you've been thinking of adding on a room or converting a den into an office, this is a ter-rific time for it. Do yourself a favor and think outside the box while you're planning. Inventive measures may be called for.

Tricky Transits
The Sun in rebellious Aquarius will square off with Mars in your sign on February 7, Scorpio, and you might just find that someone very close to you is furious and just about ready to explode. The thing is, they may be mad at you for an unintended slight. Not to worry. Lovely Venus will help you talk them into sitting down and sorting things out.

Rewarding Days
3, 4, 9, 14, 25, 26, 29

Challenging Days
6, 7, 8, 22, 23, 27

Scorpio | March

Relaxation and Recreation

Well, Scorpio, you most certainly will have your share of adrenaline on or around March 14. It seems that on that day, chatty Mercury and loving Venus will band together to argue with red-hot Mars and serious Saturn—and honestly, there can be no winners in this battle. Keep all this in mind if someone tries to lure you into a no-win debate. Just walk away.

Lovers and Friends

You're probably getting used to having people come your way who are strays or outcasts, Scorpio—and maybe even animals in that same condition. Woozy Neptune has been on duty in your solar fifth house for some time now, encouraging you to take in strays and defend the underdog. That's all lovely, and we appreciate your efforts, but try not to let someone take advantage of you this month.

Money and Success

Serious Saturn has finally left your sign, Scorpio, and yes, that means he won't be in your neck of the woods for at least another twenty-eight years. Nice, yes? Well, the thing is, he's currently on duty in your solar second house of personal money matters, and as frugal as he is…well, it's definitely time to take your belt in a few notches.

Tricky Transits

Two eclipses are due this month, Scorpio. The first, on March 8, will plant a supercharged seed of new beginnings in your solar fifth house of lovers, playmates, and dealings with kids. If you've been trying to conceive, prepare for a happy bit of news. On March 23, however, the Lunar Eclipse will occur in partner-oriented Libra and your solar second house of finances, and you may need to collect on a debt.

Rewarding Days
6, 10, 11, 12, 15, 16

Challenging Days
4, 5, 8, 14, 20, 23

Scorpio | April

Relaxation and Recreation

The Full Moon will occur on April 22 in your very own sign, Scorpio, and your solar first house of personality and appearance. If you've been thinking about beginning a diet, quitting a bad habit, or getting on a strict exercise regime, this lunation will give you the energy and determination to keep at it until you reach your goals.

Lovers and Friends

From April 5 through April 29, the lovely lady Venus will spend her time in red-hot, impulsive Aries and your solar sixth house of work and relationships with coworkers. Now, this could certainly mean that if you've been trading glances with someone across the room—well, one of you might just be bold enough to cross that distance and introduce themselves. Oh, go ahead.

Money and Success

Mars will spend all of this month in Sagittarius and your solar second house, Scorpio, where matters pertaining to possessions and personal finances are handled. Now, he's an impulsive guy in an impulsive, excessive sign, so you probably won't exactly be a font of willpower when it comes to spending your hard-earned cash. Do try to avoid buying anything major on April 28.

Tricky Transits

Mercury's station on April 28 will occur in your solar seventh house of one-to-one relationships, Scorpio. Now, he'll be stationing to go retrograde through this house for the next three weeks, all done up in sensual, touch-loving Taurus, so if you've been missing someone who made your knees weak, you might just have a chance to reconnect.

Rewarding Days

2, 3, 5, 14, 29

Challenging Days

4, 6, 10, 15, 19, 27, 28

Scorpio | May

Relaxation and Recreation

The really big news for the month involves the Jupiter-Saturn square on May 26, which could be a bit troublesome for you when it comes to your personal finances. The thing is, Scorpio, if you have not yet put yourself on a budget, you might have to then. Don't look at it as a bad thing. Tuck your pennies aside for a rainy day.

Lovers and Friends

The Sun, Mercury, and Venus will take turns moving through your solar seventh house of relationships, Scorpio—and they'll be all done up in sensual Taurus. Now, this is the only sign—outside of yours, of course—with a reputation for skill in the most tender areas of life. If you're attached, you two won't be going out much.

Money and Success

Mercury will be moving retrograde through Taurus until May 22, and since this sign is known for being a money magnet, this wouldn't be the best time to invest, take out a loan, or go after a mortgage. If you need to handle any of those matters, try to wait until May 30, when Mercury and powerful Pluto will form an easy trine.

Tricky Transits

Passionate Mars will stop in his tracks to turn retrograde on May 27, Scorpio, and since he'll be in your sign and your solar first house of personality and appearance when it happens, you might feel a bit unsettled that day. Mars is your energy-pack, by the way, so don't be surprised if you tire out a bit more quickly than usual.

Rewarding Days

1, 2, 7, 9, 19, 30

Challenging Days

4, 5, 22, 26, 27

Scorpio | June

Relaxation and Recreation

Mars will spend the month in your sign and your solar first house of personality, Scorpio, turning up the heat on your already passionate personality. Now, there are all types of passion, so if you find yourself feeling cranky one day and amorous the next, not to worry. It's only normal. You might try to find an appropriate outlet for all this energy...

Lovers and Friends

Mars is all done up in your sexy sign, Scorpio, so that natural sexiness that oozes out of you on a regular basis will be running on high this month. That said, don't aim this energy at anyone you're not truly interested in. They'll be far too fascinated to notice. Your mission is to be fair.

Money and Success

A testy opposition between Venus and Saturn will fall across your solar axis of money matters on June 3, Scorpio. Now, Venus loves creature comforts and Saturn adores the no-frills approach to life. Obviously, these two aren't a match made in heaven, so if you feel torn between spending and saving, try to do a little of both. Moderation is the key.

Tricky Transits

The Full Moon on June 20 will combine forces with two tricky Mercury transits that same day to make financial conversations tough to understand, Scorpio. The thing is, this Moon will fall in your solar second house of personal finances, so there's definitely something about your money situation that she really wants you to see. It might be that certain someone who keeps promising to contribute but never has.

Rewarding Days

8, 12, 24, 25, 26, 27

Challenging Days

2, 4, 6, 9, 20, 22

Scorpio | July

Relaxation and Recreation

Loving Venus will get together with fortunate, optimistic Jupiter on July 1, Scorpio, setting the tone for what looks to be a wonderful month. If you take some time off, this would be a fine time to get out there and do some gardening or turn the sprinkler on for the kids. You'll enjoy being at home now, but you won't be lonely.

Lovers and Friends

With Jupiter on duty in your solar eleventh house of friendships, Scorpio, you've been pretty darn sociable for months now. If you're single, you could run into someone well rounded and versatile on July 8 or 9 who'll catch your attention, and hold it. If you're attached, it's prime time to have the family over for a cookout.

Money and Success

Serious Saturn has been on duty in your solar second house of money matters for over a year now, Scorpio—and he's quite the frugal guy. Now, this could mean that you've had to cut back on luxuries to accommodate added expenses, but it might also be that you've just now gotten your income stabilized and steady.

Tricky Transits

Venus will form several inconjuncts at the end of the month, Scorpio, and these aspects are notoriously tricky. The thing is, the two planets involved have nothing in common, so there's no comfortable way for them to communicate their needs to each other. If you're befuddled by someone's behavior and they won't explain themselves, let it go. At least for now.

Rewarding Days

1, 3, 8, 17, 20, 26

Challenging Days

2, 7, 10, 11, 21, 22

Scorpio | August

Relaxation and Recreation

There's never a bad time for you to be by the water, Scorpio, but this month, you'll feel especially refreshed and rejuvenated from a walk on the beach, a lakeside picnic, or a dip in the pool. That goes double for August 13 and 14, when stress and tension from work could make you feel drained or exhausted.

Lovers and Friends

Loving Venus will take off for Virgo and your solar eleventh house of friendships on August 5, Scorpio, where she'll stay until August 29. Now, during this time, you might be introduced to someone new by a friend of a friend—and boy, oh boy, will you be glad. Smile pretty and extend your hand.

Money and Success

With assertive, impulsive Mars and frugal, cautious Saturn on duty in your solar second house of money matters and personal finances, Scorpio, you're in a bit of a pickle. When Mars is around, we all become impulse shoppers, while Saturn, on the other hand, encourages us to save. They'll collide on August 24, so don't even bother trying to shop that day. It's not worth the stress.

Tricky Transits

Venus, Mercury, and Jupiter will get together from August 26 through August 28, Scorpio, and they'll be having their meeting in precise, meticulous Virgo, a sign that's ordinarily quite concerned with details. At the moment, however, expansive Jupiter is in the mood to see both the forest and the trees, and a conversation regarding a tough financial situation will work out quite well.

Rewarding Days
1, 5, 8, 22, 27, 28

Challenging Days
6, 7, 13, 24, 25

Scorpio | September

Relaxation and Recreation

After three long weeks moving retrograde, Mercury will turn direct on September 21 in your solar eleventh house of friendships, and suddenly, as if by magic, you'll be able to contact that person you've been just missing. It might not be for a day or two after, when Mercury starts to pick up speed, but you'll find them.

Lovers and Friends

Bighearted Jupiter will take off for relationship-loving Libra on September 9, Scorpio, putting everyone in the mood to partner up, both personally and professionally. That said, if you've just recently started seeing someone, it might soon be time to take your relationship to the next level. Fortunately, with Jupiter in your solar twelfth house of Privacy, Please, you'll have plenty of chances to slip away together.

Money and Success

If you're feeling lucky around September 16, you might want to invest in a lottery ticket, Scorpio. Fiery Mars in your solar second house will get together with unpredictable Uranus, who just loves surprises, so you might just have a nice one waiting for you when the numbers are announced.

Tricky Transits

The Solar Eclipse on September 1 will plant a seed in your solar eleventh house of friendships and groups, but Saturn will square off with it, and Saturn just loves to stall, delay, and block. You might not see what's begun just under the surface right away, but the Lunar Eclipse on September 16 will direct your attention to your solar fifth house of lovers—and bring along someone who's hard to miss.

Rewarding Days

6, 7, 19, 20, 23, 25

Challenging Days

10, 11, 12, 13, 15, 21

Scorpio | October

Relaxation and Recreation

For a while now, you've been far more interested in the mystical side of life, Scorpio, thanks to Neptune's presence in Pisces, an intuitive water sign like your own. If you haven't yet been able to find the right group, visit as many gatherings as you can from October 8 through October 11, when Mars in practical Capricorn will team up with Neptune to aim you in the direction of kindred spirits who share your core beliefs.

Lovers and Friends

Bright and early on October 1, loving Venus will get together with talkative Mercury, both of them all done up in your sexy sign, Scorpio, and on duty in your solar first house of personality and appearance. Now, this in itself is enough reason to find you on the receiving end of some wonderful attention, but let's add in the fact that they'll trine romantic Neptune, who's in your solar fifth house of love affairs. Yum!

Money and Success

On October 4 and 14, conversations about money matters will go quite smoothly, Scorpio, so if there's an issue you need to discuss with your partner, sit down and have a chat on one of those days. At the very least, you'll remove all doubt about what you expect from them. At best, you might find that they had no idea there was a problem and they want to help.

Tricky Transits

On October 23, dreamy Neptune will receive an inconjunct from Jupiter, who never fails to amp up the energy of the planets he visits. Now, in this case, you may find that you're in the mood to travel, most likely to the beach or the lake. If you can't arrange to take some time off, get yourself a tape of water sounds. It will soothe your soul. Promise.

Rewarding Days
4, 14, 17, 24, 27

Challenging Days
2, 12, 15, 25, 28

Scorpio | November

Relaxation and Recreation

As per usual, Scorpio, you'll want to spend your free time close to the water this month. You'll have plenty of opportunities to get there, too, as soon as November 1, when the Sun in your sign will form an easy trine with Neptune in your solar fifth house of playtime and recreation. Be sure to make time on November 19, when Neptune will station to turn direct and your intuition will be running on high.

Lovers and Friends

Getting back to November 19 and Neptune's station, Scorpio...lest we forget, Venus will sextile Neptune as she stations to turn direct. Now, this brings the Goddess of Love and the Goddess of Mystical Experiences together in Pisces, your romantic water-sign cousin. Since Venus is all done up in practical, realistic Capricorn, however, you won't need to worry about getting stars in your eyes and falling for the wrong person.

Money and Success

The Moon and Venus will get together on November 3 in your solar second house of money and possessions, Scorpio, and when these two join forces, treats, gifts, and goodies abound—especially since they'll both be in Sagittarius, a sign that does tend to be a bit on the extravagant side. If you feel the urge to splurge, try to limit yourself to one category.

Tricky Transits

Expansive Jupiter will square off with intense, sexy Pluto on November 24, Scorpio, and since Pluto is your ruling planet, you're going to really feel this transit, right down to your perceptive little toes. On the one hand, this team may inspire you to spend a huge hunk of time alone with someone delicious. On the other, you might find that someone you're quite fond of has relationship issues and needs to talk.

Rewarding Days

1, 2, 7, 18, 19, 20

Challenging Days

24, 25, 29, 30

Scorpio | December

Relaxation and Recreation

First of all, Scorpio, happy holidays! The Universe has scheduled an absolutely stellar month—no pun intended. It seems that just about all the energies hovering above are in the mood to party, pass out hugs, and smile fondly at loved ones. Yes, it's perfect timing, and yes, you're really going to enjoy the warm feelings—not to mention the mistletoe!

Lovers and Friends

Expect a call, text, or visit this month from someone you haven't seen in far too long, Scorpio. Now, you're quite emotional when it comes to the people you love, so prepare for happy tears to come to your eyes on or around December 10, when Mercury in practical Capricorn hooks up with dreamy, sentimental Neptune. This is the stuff that dreams come true are made of. Enjoy!

Money and Success

Finances may be a bit tight as the month begins, Scorpio, but it looks like a fortunate twist of fate will get you started on the new year with a boost in pay or a promotion. You'll have plenty of reason to celebrate and make merry, so be sure you have a corkscrew and a mistletoe bell in your purse, just for emergencies.

Tricky Transits

Do me a favor, Scorpio. If you're going to party on New Year's Eve, be safe. That means having a designated driver if you're out and about and you're planning to indulge. More importantly, don't do anything foolish or dangerous. Assertive Mars will collide with Neptune that night, and accidents are possible. Be sure you've got at least two options for a sober ride home.

Rewarding Days

All but two.

Challenging Days

19, 31

Scorpio Action Table

These dates reflect the best—but not the only—times for success and ease in these activities, according to your Sun sign.

	JAN	FEB	MAR	APR	MAY	JUN	JUL	AUG	SEP	OCT	NOV	DEC
Move	22, 23			13, 14					24, 25	21, 22		
Start a class			1, 2, 29, 30		22, 23, 24		15, 16	12, 13			2, 3	1, 2, 27, 28
Join a club	11, 12	8, 9			27, 28		21, 22			11, 12		
Ask for a raise			4, 5			2, 3, 4			1, 2		14, 15	
Look for work	27, 28	23, 24	21, 22, 23		25, 26		8, 9		12, 13			2, 3, 29, 30, 31
Get pro advice				17, 18, 19		11, 12		5, 6		26, 27		
Get a loan	4, 5		26, 27				13, 14, 15	9, 10, 11			27, 28	
See a doctor					16, 17				1, 2, 3			19, 20
Start a diet	24, 25			22, 23	21, 22	20, 21, 22		18, 19				
End relationship			23, 24				19, 20		16, 17	1, 2, 29, 30	29, 30	
Buy clothes		14, 15					1, 27, 28			17, 18		
Get a makeover		14, 15		9, 10		1, 2, 28, 29		23, 24			19, 20	11, 12
New romance			8, 9		6, 7				1, 2			
Vacation		3, 4		25, 26		18, 19, 20	16, 17, 18				29, 30	26, 27, 28

Sagittarius

The Archer
November 21 to December 21

Element: Fire

Quality: Mutable

Polarity: Yang/masculine

Planetary Ruler: Jupiter

Meditation: I can take time to explore my soul

Gemstone: Turquoise

Power Stones: Lapis lazuli, azurite, sodalite

Key Phrase: I understand

Glyph: Archer's arrow

Anatomy: Hips, thighs, sciatic nerve

Colors: Royal blue, purple

Animals: Fleet-footed animals

Myths/Legends: Athena, Chiron

House: Ninth

Opposite Sign: Gemini

Flower: Narcissus

Keyword: Optimism

The Sagittarius Personality

Your Strengths and Challenges

A long time ago, one of my very first astrology teachers told me that you Sagittarians are the favorites of the Gods because you amuse them. So first off, let's talk about laughter, which is as necessary to your soul as food is to your body. Yes, you certainly are a clown, and you'll stop at nothing to get a laugh. Your antics—even and maybe especially even in public—range from the outrageous to the downright hilarious. Most of us would be too embarrassed to do what you do, but you don't seem to own that emotion—especially if you're having fun and you've got an appreciative audience. You work very hard to see that a good time is had by all, and you're much appreciated for it. In fact, you're at the top of everyone's guest list, because if you're there, it's guaranteed to be a success. Oh, and when you throw a party yourself, you never have to worry about no-shows or anyone showing up empty-handed. You're famous for being quite the host.

There is a more serious side to you, though, and it tends to emerge whenever you're involved in a conversation about The Big Topics—politics, religion, and education, for example. You have some very definite ideas about how the world should be run, and it's often tough for you to understand how everyone couldn't possibly feel the same. That said, learning to allow others their own opinions is an important lesson. You can be honest and still be tactful and diplomatic.

Your ruling planet is Jupiter, who broadens and expands the energy of any sign or planet he contacts. Now, Jupiter's favorite words are *much*, *more*, and *many*. So what does this tell us? Well, you do tend to be pretty darn excessive. If one is good, two is better, so ten must be excellent. You're also famous for broadening your horizons on a regular basis. It might be taking a class or teaching one. It might be traveling, which you also think of as a learning experience. Just chatting with someone whose home is in another state or country works fine, too, especially if they're willing to regale you with interesting stories accompanied by a wonderful accent. Your mission is to collect as many new experiences as possible and share them with others.

Your Relationships

Talk about a good time! When you're happy, everyone is happy. You absolutely insist on it. You love to laugh and to make others laugh, so hanging out with you is always fun. Of course, your friends must necessarily be great fun, too—it's a prerequisite for the position. Yes, you're endlessly playful, but you're also quite loyal, often to a fault. Your innate optimism inspires you to always look for the good in others, which can make you quite an easy target. Your generosity is the stuff of astrological legend, and there's nothing you wouldn't do for a friend. You usually have a pack of regular companions—your private collection of kindred spirits—and you hang on to them forever, even if you need to travel long-distance to be with them. And speaking of traveling, you're only too happy to plan a group adventure, from ocean cruises to hiking trips.

Whether it's nature, bright city lights, or a warm, tropical beach, you'll always come up with just the right balance between rest and recreation. (You'd make a wonderful social director, by the way.)

When it comes to love, you often take your time signing up for anything permanent. Your personal freedom is extremely important to you, and you're not willing to give it up. You'd rather be single than be with the wrong person. Once you meet someone who can keep up with you, however, all bets are off. You'll do absolutely anything for them, and you usually earn the same loyalty in return.

Aries tend to catch your eye more than most other signs. You love their fire, their spontaneity, and their boldness—and they appreciate a partner who understands their fiery disposition. Your opposite sign, Gemini, makes for great friends and can be the perfect long-term partner. They're endlessly curious, playful, and restless. A lover under any sign can work out, however, as long as they don't try to tie you down—and as long as they don't bore you! That's a definite deal breaker.

Your Career and Money

If you had one wish, it would be to know everything about everything—every language, every skill, and everything about the world around you. For that reason, you're happiest when you're pursuing a field that constantly challenges you to keep learning. Books, of course, have always been very good friends, and while you might own a tablet, there's nothing like the feel—and smell—of a real book in your hands. Not surprisingly, many of you are drawn to work in libraries or bookstores—and you probably fantasize about what it might be like to be a professional student. Imagine it being your job to choose what you'd like to learn next—nirvana! Ah, well. If that's not possible, there are other equally satisfying alternatives. Teaching is the next best thing to being a student, and since many of you enjoy teaching adults, you're sure to glean more grist for the mill. English as a Second Language (ESL) is a perfect fit for you. All those accents! It's music to your ears. Plus, you're learning and teaching at the same time. Also nirvana!

Your fondness for animals might also mean you work in veterinary care on some level or for breeders or animal caregivers, and your insatiable wanderlust often lands you in the travel industry. You'll find that just about any job you stick with involves some type of traveling and lots of communicating. There's only one thing you just can't tolerate and won't put up with: boredom. Boredom is simply not an option.

Your Lighter Side

Laughter is your specialty, Sagittarius, and something you absolutely need on a daily basis, so surrounding yourself with lighthearted, positive friends is an absolute must. Of course, you're also quite philosophical—and heaven knows you have opinions—so chatting about The Big Topics is also great fun. There's nothing you love more than hopping on a plane, though, especially if you're exploring a new place. Plus, you get to hang out at the airport, chat with absolutely everyone who piques your interest, and do some serious people-watching. When you're back home, however, there's nothing that makes you happier than spending time with your pets. You're especially fond of dogs and horses, which only makes sense given that you're a four-legged creature yourself.

Affirmation

The best is yet to come.

The Year Ahead for Sagittarius

Your ruling planet, Jupiter, will spend the first eight months of the year in earthy, practical, and extremely well-organized Virgo, one of the signs that most loves dealing with details. Now, just the thought of paperwork and fine print and endless columns of numbers that won't add up right is ordinarily enough to send you off screaming into the woods, but chances are good that during Jupiter's time in this sign, you've come around a bit. Why, you might even have gotten yourself organized in the department of career matters and professional dealings. So during Jupiter's last few months in your solar tenth house of career and professional matters, you should probably expect that raise, bonus, or promotion to arrive—or at least be in the works. In the meantime, keep your nose to the grindstone and your work up to par. You'll learn very soon that patience really can pay off.

Now, on September 9, Jupiter will step off into Libra and your eleventh solar house of friendships and group affiliations, so if you've been thinking of investigating a new peer circle, this is the time to do it. Libra is pleasant, hospitable, and accommodating, so you can pretty much count on being welcome—even if you weren't already the life of the party and always at the top of any guest list. Of course, Libra's specialty is one-to-one relationships, and since Jupiter always broadens and expands the qualities of the sign he's inhabiting, you'll find that certain people will become even dearer to you. You'll also be willing to do anything you can to help them get themselves together, but please do stop short of putting yourself in a bad financial situation. You can't afford that now.

If you're currently attached, you'll truly enjoy each other's company more than ever now, and more than once over the coming year, you'll pat yourself on the back for making such a wise and wonderful choice. Relationships flourish with Jupiter here, provided they're built on mutual respect and lots of honesty—tempered with a heaping dollop of tact and diplomacy. Tending carefully to each other's feelings is important. Go out of your way to be kind and understanding, and do spoil each other whenever you can. If you're not happy and you feel that the situation isn't balanced or fair, you'll want out, and with unpredictable Uranus on duty in Aries, it won't take you long to make an escape. Be sure you're receiving as much as you're giving. You deserve it, and you're quality mate material—so you can afford to be picky.

If you're single, there's no better time to get out there and resume the hunt for the perfect soul mate. Mingle, mingle, and mingle some more. Make a list of all the qualities you're after in a mate, find the places someone of that sort might frequent, and get busy frequenting them yourself! The good news is that relationships that begin on solid footing during Jupiter in Libra tend to last forever.

What This Year's Eclipses Mean for You

Eclipses arrive in pairs, two weeks apart and roughly every six months. The first set scheduled for 2016 will begin on March 8 with a Solar Eclipse—basically, a supercharged New Moon. It will bring together the Sun and Moon in Pisces, planting a seed of new beginnings in your solar fourth house of home, family members, and domestic issues. Now, Pisces is a wistful, dreamy, and highly intuitive sign that feels absolutely everything, so you should expect to be quite sensitive around this time. Try not to take things too personally. Do what you do best: try to understand the motivation behind the behavior. This is a terrific time to start up a new spiritual regime. Consider meditation or yoga. Feed your soul, and make your home a sanctuary.

The second eclipse will arrive on March 23 and will occur in Libra and your solar eleventh house of group affiliations and peer circles—and the news certainly could be worse. Libra is expert at restoring balance in general, but primarily in one-to-one relationships, so if you've been at odds with a dear one, this is the perfect time to either extend or accept an olive branch. On the other hand, since this is a Lunar Eclipse (Full Moon) and the culmination of a cycle, you might just realize that you're ready for new friends that share more of your goals for the future and expectations of the present. Kindred spirits will be available, so don't be afraid to get out there and mingle.

The second set of eclipses will occur in September, calling your attention to your professional life. On September 1, a Solar Eclipse in Virgo will bring the Sun and Moon together in your solar tenth house of career matters, affording you the chance to make a whole new start in a field that's more in keeping with your beliefs. The spiritual dance you began back in March will blossom, and you'll have no patience with anyone who is critical, negative, or nitpicky. You might begin training for an entirely different career, or start taking classes to obtain a certificate or add to your resumé. A career in Eastern medicine or alternative therapies such as massage, herbal remedies, or yoga might pique your interest.

On September 16, the second Lunar Eclipse of the year will set up shop in Pisces, activating your axis of personal-versus-professional matters. If you feel as if you're in the middle of a tug of war between authority figures and family members, you're probably right. There's only one thing to do: learn to juggle. Make it clear to higher-ups that you're doing your best, and to family members that this is your job, not just your hobby, and you have to do the work to be paid. Let them all know that you're dancing as fast as you can. This lunation is also in ultrasensitive, intuitive Pisces, so if you feel a bit of déjà vu, it may be that these circumstances are something you've dealt with before, and many times over. So what's the lesson to be learned?

Saturn

Saturn will spend the year in your sign, Sagittarius, and your solar first house of personality and appearance. Now, Saturn is a very serious energy, and your sign usually isn't, so this doesn't initially sound like a match made in heaven. But if you've got to get organized, Saturn will be a terrific help, providing you with the self-discipline and, yes, even patience to stick with a project until it's done, and done well. That said, if you don't cooperate and continue to ignore potential pitfalls, you might have a problem with his visit. It's time to trim the fat, cut out what's unnecessarily excessive, and live within your means—in all departments. In the process, you might actually find that you're truly enjoying the routine you've newly fashioned for yourself, and that you're far more efficient and productive—which means less time at work and more time for play. See how this works? Saturn is known to be a strict taskmaster, but only if he feels we're moving too fast or becoming too scattered. Your mission is to cooperate—and give yourself a well-deserved pat on the back, too! Of course, Saturn also represents authority figures and higher-ups, so you might begin to feel a bit stifled or restrained on the job, in which case you should start looking around for something that's more in keeping with your beliefs and personality and far less suffocating to your spirit.

Uranus

This surprising, unpredictable guy is set to spend yet another year in red-hot Aries, your fire-sign cousin—which puts him right smack dab in the middle of your solar fifth house of lovers, playmates, and recreational pursuits. Now, Uranus's mission is to call attention to any ruts you've fallen into without noticing, and to jolt you out of them. Sometimes he's a bit drastic in his methods, but when all is said and done, the sudden changes he ushers into your life will turn out to be the best things that could possibly have happened. So if you're feeling the need to pursue a different hobby or meet up with interesting, unusual new play-mates, don't even try to resist. You might also expect some extremely pleasant surprises via your children, and your creativity will be running on high. Very high. Be sure to keep a notepad with you at all times. The creative inspiration of Uranus is fleeting and easy to forget—especially since it's going to happen all the time. Write it down! If you were born between December 6 and 18, you'll feel electricity and possibly tension in the air around you, but since Aries is a kindred spirit to your sign, the energy will probably be more energizing and exhilarating than stressful. Either way, your mission is to pack light, because you won't be the same person at the end of this journey. It's all about exploring, adventuring, and experimenting. Be spontaneous!

Neptune

The lovely lady Neptune will continue her trek through your solar fourth house, where issues of home and family are dealt with, and since Neptune turns up the sensitivity in our hearts, you should expect another emotional year ahead. This house is also where we keep our stash of memories, especially those from childhood, and Neptune is an extremely nostalgic energy, especially now that she is all done up in Pisces, the sign through which she operates most clearly. Needless to say, you might be doing a bit of sighing and staring out the window, and concentration could be a bit tough at times. The thing is, Neptune is urging you to tap into your innermost spiritual side, find out what really makes you tick, and make it your business to surround yourself with only positive influences. You might need to change peer groups so you can find kindred spirits who more closely share your beliefs and goals for the future, but it will all work out for the best. Avoid drastic moves in domestic matters. Neptune has a penchant for fogging up the truth, so in times of confusion, seeking out the advice of a trusted friend or professional will always be your best bet. If you were born between November 27 and December 5, you'll feel this dreamy energy more than the rest in your sign. Your mission is to avoid temporary escape hatches to soothe your soul. Discover what will make your soul happy in the long run, and go after it.

Pluto

If you were born between December 6 and 8, you will be enjoying a visit by semisextile from intense Pluto this year, from his spot in your solar second house of money matters and personal finances. Now, Pluto is in even-handed, practical Capricorn at the moment, so even if this all-or-nothing energy brings along drastic financial changes, you'll be able to understand the necessity for those changes, and you'll be willing to let go of what's not working and isn't truly necessary. You're not known for being especially frugal—to say the very least, Sagittarius—but once the light goes on and you see how much easier your life would be if you cut back on expenses and unnecessary purchases, it will definitely come much easier to you. Pluto will insist that you let go of something you valued highly in the past, and he's not the kind of energy that takes no for an answer. Go along willingly and assist the process. It's only loss if you refuse to let it go. This energy is perfect for creating a budget and living within your means, which might mean working less and enjoying life a lot more. Clear the decks of whatever isn't working. Your values are subtly shifting—but in a very big way.

Sagittarius | January

Relaxation and Recreation

It is hard to imagine you having much time to relax during January, Sagittarius—much less that you might actually want it. With unpredictable Uranus in Aries enjoying easy sign-trine visitations from Venus, Saturn, and the emotional Moon, it will be tough for you to resist the urge to play, especially if you have new playmates with interesting stories to tell. Be on the lookout around January 6 for someone a bit older or younger than yourself.

Lovers and Friends

You've never had a problem making friends, Sagittarius, but you've also never had a problem keeping them on a long-term basis. That said, right around January 12 and 17, charming Venus in your sign will be more than happy to lure all kinds of interesting new others your way—and yes, they will probably have accents that sound like music.

Money and Success

If you're out negotiating for a loan or trying to resolve an inheritance, do yourself a huge favor and put it off until well after January 5, when a sky full of warring energies will make it very tough for you to make friends and influence people. The main thing is that Mercury will turn retrograde for the next three weeks, making it tough to fully communicate your needs. Hang tight.

Tricky Transits

With Mars in your solar twelfth house of secrets and Privacy, Please as of January 3, you might be spending a lot of time behind closed doors, especially if you're infatuated, in love or in lust. Mars will enter sexy, intense Scorpio that day, and Scorpio planets find it very hard to stop doing whatever feels excellent—and so do you. Have a safe word for friends. Have them call and see if you might not need a breather.

Rewarding Days

6, 12, 15, 23, 24

Challenging Days

4, 5, 7, 17, 20, 29, 31

Sagittarius | February

Relaxation and Recreation

You'll have several chances to kick back, chill out, and be sweet to your partner/lover or best friend this month, Sagg, but if you want to do it guilt-free, February 8, 9, and 10 would be best. On those days, loving Venus in Capricorn will get together with your ruling planet, outgoing Jupiter, and when The Benefics combine forces in earth signs, it's time to go all out and please your senses.

Lovers and Friends

Passionate Mars will stay on duty in ultra-sexy Scorpio and your solar twelfth house of secrets for the entire month, Sagittarius, so if you're doing something you'd like to keep under wraps or doing the same for a friend, you might be able to pull it off. As of the 5th of next month, however, not so much.

Money and Success

Venus rules not just love but also your personal monetary issues, Sagg, so on February 5, when she meets up with intense Pluto, you might find that what you need to move forward with a financial plan is well within your reach, provided you're willing to go after it—with all the proper paperwork completed this time, please.

Tricky Transits

Right around February 6, you'll find it especially easy to communicate with your nearest and dearest, even if they've just given you the surprise of your life. This goes double for lovers, siblings, and kids, who have probably been holding on to a secret for quite some time now. Stop snooping and let them wow you!

Rewarding Days
2, 3, 5, 6, 9, 14, 29

Challenging Days
1, 7, 8, 22, 28

Sagittarius | March

Relaxation and Recreation

With red-hot Mars set to take off for your sign on March 5, you'll have plenty of energy. In fact, you'll probably find yourself craving adrenaline, action, and adventure. Well, hang on for a little while, and you'll certainly have it. Mars will get together with several planets in fire signs toward the end of the month, and exciting invitations will abound!

Lovers and Friends

You're of the opinion that life is really just a series of extended vacations, so finding playmates is never hard for you, Sagittarius. But this month you're due to come across some really unusual types who might just show you a thing or two about enjoying life. Look to March 2 for someone really different to cross your path.

Money and Success

A meeting with an advisor on March 1 will get your month off to a terrific start. If you're thinking of investing, have someone who knows what they're doing go over the paperwork. Your ruling planet, Jupiter, has been in your solar tenth house of career matters for months now, and since you just so happen to be his favorite, he might just bring you some amazing news on March 16.

Tricky Transits

March 30 and 31 could be a bit problematic, especially if someone close to you has a rather fiery temperament. You're usually quite good at smoothing things over, either with humor or a philosophical point of view, or both. If they seem more volatile than usual, just stay out of it. Not your circus, not your monkeys.

Rewarding Days

1, 2, 3, 16, 19, 20, 26, 28

Challenging Days

7, 8, 22, 23, 30, 31

Sagittarius | April

Relaxation and Recreation

You might not get much sleep this month, Sagittarius, but you'll be doing a whole lot of smiling. Venus, Mercury, and the Sun himself will be all done up in their impulsive Aries outfits, which puts them in your solar fifth house of fun times. Your usual playmates will be a lot more adventurous, and you won't argue with anything they suggest. Careful!

Lovers and Friends

If you're thinking of settling down—yes, with just one person—you might be especially keen on the idea around April 5. Loving Venus will dash off into impulsive Aries, and Mercury will step into sensual Taurus. Now, this fixed earth sign (Taurus) plays for keeps, but not to worry. That same day, the Sun will form an easy trine with practical Saturn in your sign. Trust your gut.

Money and Success

Mercury will be in quality-loving Taurus from April 5 of this month through June 12, so material comforts will be on your mind—along with how to make the money you need to enjoy them. If finances get tricky around April 28, it's not just you. It's Mercury retrograde. Don't make any drastic moves for at least three weeks—and don't be rushed by anyone!

Tricky Transits

Oddly enough, the trickiest day of the month for you will probably be April Fools' Day. The emotional Moon will be in unpredictable Aquarius and your solar third house of conversation and communication, so you should expect at least one startling encounter. Oh, and Mercury will get together with quirky Uranus. Fortunately, you happen to adore surprises, so fasten your seat belt and enjoy the ride!

Rewarding Days

1, 2, 3, 5, 9, 12, 18, 30

Challenging Days

4, 6, 15, 16, 19, 27

Sagittarius | May

Relaxation and Recreation

Several planets in earthy, comfort-loving Taurus will hold court this month, and while you've never needed any excuse to indulge a bit every now and then, you'll develop a taste for the finer things in life—rich food, fine wine, and a few designer items, for example. Fortunately, you've probably been working hard, so a few days of hedonism are definitely in order. Enjoy!

Lovers and Friends

During the first half of the month, relaxing with dear ones in a quiet, peaceful environment will do your heart good—and all those calm, relaxed planets in Taurus will be happy to help with the ambiance. Once the Sun dashes off into Gemini on May 20, however, all bets are off—especially around May 24, when loving Venus joins him. Expect playmates galore and all kinds of new activities.

Money and Success

The heavens are full of earth energies, Sagittarius, which tend to concern themselves primarily with life on the material plane—and your ruling planet, Jupiter, is one of them. He'll pass out easy, prosperous trines on May 3 and 10, so you should expect to be in the right place at the right time to meet others who can put you right where you want to be, financially speaking. Listen up!

Tricky Transits

Loving Venus and passionate Mars will face off on May 24, Sagittarius, activating your solar relationship axis. These two planets have been lovers forever, but in this aspect, things have been known to heat up a bit. Now, this can go one of two ways. First off, you and someone dear to you may be doing a bit of bickering—which, of course, Mars is always up for. But there really are better ways to get some adrenaline flowing...

Rewarding Days

1, 2, 9, 10, 13, 28, 30

Challenging Days

4, 5, 22, 23, 24, 26

Sagittarius | June

Relaxation and Recreation

Ready or not, Sagittarius, the Sun, Venus, and Mercury will take turns getting together with electric, unpredictable Uranus in impulsive Aries and your solar fifth house of lovers and playmates. Talk about a good time! Spontaneity is the only way to go if you don't want to miss anything—and when have you ever? If you're attached, a weekend stay at an elegant hotel might be nice. Get a hot tub!

Lovers and Friends

Romance is on the agenda for you, Sagittarius—big time. Loving Venus will continue on her trip through fun-loving Gemini and your solar seventh house of relationships. And she has company, too—the Sun and chatty Mercury, for starters. Then on June 4, the New Moon will join in the fun. Well! If you're shopping for a new flame, think of this as a buffet.

Money and Success

On June 30, watch out for a potentially testy opposition between Venus, who rules not just love but also money, and intense Pluto, who tends to be a bit on the jealous and possessive side. They will activate your axis of finances on the June 30, so a financial tug of war is entirely possible. You'll see the signs around June 17, so pay attention and nip the situation in the bud.

Tricky Transits

You may have a bit of trouble getting your point across to your partner around June 6 and 14, but not to worry. There are all kinds of ways to communicate, so if words fail you, consider music—or maybe some good old-fashioned silence. Be sure you have your facts straight before you say anything you might regret.

Rewarding Days
11, 12, 13, 25, 26, 27

Challenging Days
2, 3, 6, 14, 15, 20

Sagittarius | July

Relaxation and Recreation

Early on this month, your idea of a good time will probably be hanging out at home with the ones you love. Think pool parties, barbeques and cozying up to watch a movie with the lights out. The Sun, Mercury, and Venus will pass through warm and fuzzy Cancer, urging you to slow down and breathe. Once July 12 arrives, however, a parade of Leo planets will begin, and the party will be on!

Lovers and Friends

Your ruling planet, generous Jupiter, has a delightful month set up for you. The fun starts on July 1, when The Big J will pass out a nice, juicy sextile to Venus, the goddess of love and money. You might not get rich overnight, but you'll certainly know you're loved by your family and close friends—which is even better, right?

Money and Success

Your solar axis of money matters will be quite active this month, Sagittarius, courtesy of several planets in Cancer who'll face off with intense, determined Pluto. Now, Pluto has been on duty in your second solar house of finances and values for some time now, so you might not notice him anymore, but those Cancer energies will rattle his cage. Expect power struggles, and expect to win them easily!

Tricky Transits

A family member might have a bit of trouble making ends meet around July 2, and if they haven't found a way to work things out around July 7, you'll probably want to step in and help them out. Your generosity is famous, but if you feel that you're being taken advantage of, make this the last time. Really.

Rewarding Days

1, 3, 18, 20, 31

Challenging Days

2, 10, 11, 13, 19, 21

Sagittarius | August

Relaxation and Recreation

The Sun is in fiery, adventurous Leo and your solar ninth house, where travel and education are handled—both of which happen to be among your specialties, Sagittarius. Needless to say, it won't take much to talk you into a vacation. If the dates aren't set in stone, try to take off around August 1 or 2, when stable Saturn and energetic Mars will get you off to a good start.

Lovers and Friends

Loving Venus will get together with dreamy Neptune on August 14, so if you're single and you meet someone who's just perfect, take a deep breath and step back. Give it a few days before you decide you're in love. In the meantime, use the energy of an easy trine between the Sun and Uranus on August 16 to play, observe, and ask questions.

Money and Success

Conversations about money, possessions, and other resources could be tricky on August 6 and 13, Sagittarius, so if you're not sure what's really going on, don't make any decisions or sign anything official. By August 10, you'll have managed to dig up some answers, and you'll be better equipped to choose. If a higher-up gives you a hard time, don't fuss. Rise to the occasion and excel at your work.

Tricky Transits

You've never been fond of details, Sagittarius, but you'll need to handle quite a few this month, and resistance is futile. An elder or authority figure will insist. Now, you don't take well to being told what to do, but every now and then, it's necessary. This is one of those times. Not to worry. Jupiter and Venus will straighten things out on August 27.

Rewarding Days

1, 2, 10, 14, 18, 27, 29

Challenging Days

5, 6, 13, 19, 24, 25

Sagittarius | September

Relaxation and Recreation
You'll be a part of the group and, more importantly, the fun when Venus touches base with both unpredictable Uranus and red-hot Mars on September 18 and 19. An old lover could show up at a party or other gathering around that time, too.

Lovers and Friends
Count on a whole lot of invitations this month. What a great time to introduce your partner to your friends. If you're single, not to worry. Venus in this sign will offer up all kinds of invitations and opportunities to mingle with pleasant, interesting others. One of them might strike your fancy around September 18, 19, 25, or 30.

Money and Success
The New Moon on September 30, Sagittarius, will be a whopper. Whatever changes were set in motion by the Solar Eclipse on September 1 in your solar tenth house of career matters will come to fruition now. The good news is that with generous Jupiter, your ruler, currently on duty in charming Libra, where the New Moon will occur, there's really nothing to worry about. All will end well.

Tricky Transits
Eclipses inspire great big changes, so if you have been mulling over the right time to take action, look to September 1 for the Solar Eclipse in Virgo for new information about your chosen career field. The Lunar Eclipse on September 16 could cause a bit of a stir on the home front, so be prepared for some confusion.

Rewarding Days
7, 9, 18, 19, 22, 25

Challenging Days
1, 2, 10, 11, 12, 13

Sagittarius | October

Relaxation and Recreation

As far as relaxing goes, Sagittarius, you might not have a lot of time for it, but your social life will be so entertaining, you won't mind being a little bit tired. Jupiter, your ruler, is out to introduce you to all kinds of new people, and you'll spend quite a lot of time in happy, comfortable group situations.

Lovers and Friends

What a great month to be you! Between Jupiter in partner-loving Libra and Venus in your sign and your solar first house of personality and appearance, your popularity will be off the charts. If you're single, bet that doesn't last much longer. If a sibling is sure they've found your soul mate, let them fix you up. You never know...

Money and Success

Arguments over financial issues could come up around October 18 or 19, and this time around, you'll have to deal with them. If you've been carrying the entire burden on your own, it's time to put an end to that nonsense. You need to stop supporting anyone other than yourself. Invest in a lottery ticket on October 26.

Tricky Transits

Telling you to exercise moderation is an exercise in futility, but you should know that too much of a good thing could put you under the weather around October 7 or 11 and again around October 25. Take a levelheaded friend along who knows how to pry "just one more" of anything out of your excessive little hands.

Rewarding Days

1, 4, 5, 11, 26, 29

Challenging Days

2, 7, 18, 19, 25, 28

Sagittarius | November

Relaxation and Recreation

Travel will be great fun for you this month, Sagittarius—yes, even more than usual. The heavens will host several planets in your sign and your solar first house of personality and appearance, and with your ruler, Jupiter, in the mood to mingle, group adventures will be best. A conversation with the owner of a delightful accent around November 22 could lead to something wonderful.

Lovers and Friends

Long-distance love could be on the agenda for you this month, but not to worry. If anyone can pull this tough assignment off, it's you. Besides, people move across the country all the time—and across the ocean, too. Don't hold back because the geography is challenging. This is an experience you shouldn't miss out on.

Money and Success

Let your gut feelings guide your financial decisions around November 3, 4, and 5, Sagittarius, when loving Venus will make contact with intuitive Neptune. That same day, Uranus could bring along a job offer you were never expecting that will allow you far more personal freedom—which, after all, is one of the things that you live for and absolutely must have.

Tricky Transits

Venus and Pluto will get together in businesslike Capricorn and your solar second house of money matters and personal finances on November 25, so if you have an appointment to talk with a professional about a loan, inheritance, or joint financial dispute, get your paperwork ready early on. You can win this thing if you stay organized and think practically.

Rewarding Days

3, 4, 5, 15, 22, 23

Challenging Days

6, 17, 18, 24, 25, 30

Sagittarius | December

Relaxation and Recreation
Your holidays look just terrific, Sagittarius, thanks to the generous, positive influence of Jupiter, your very own patron planet, but the excitement will begin bright and early on December 1. It might be that someone very far from you has found a way to come to you, or that you've found a way to get to them. Enjoy!

Lovers and Friends
Expect to be pretty darn spoiled this month, Sagittarius—and not just because of your birthday or the holidays. Someone out there will make quite a display of their feelings for you, and your heart will be full and warm. If you're out to surprise your partner, choose December 25. Loving Venus will see to it that you receive a truly lovely "reward."

Money and Success
Forget about the budget you swore you'd stick to this year, Sagittarius. A large-ticket item you're positive someone close to you would adore might be on sale or available only for a brief time, and you'll grab it. Of course, you might also receive something lavish and astonishing yourself. Remember, though, that your company and your love are the best gifts of all.

Tricky Transits
With the possible exception of a friend in a bad spot on December 10 or an authority figure who reads you wrong on December 28 or 29, this looks to be a terrific month. All those planets in your sign will take turns forming easy trines with unpredictable Uranus in your solar fifth house of lovers, playmates, and dealing with kids, so happy surprises will be on the agenda.

Rewarding Days
1, 3, 6, 9, 11, 12, 24, 25, 26, 27

Challenging Days
28, 29

Sagittarius Action Table

These dates reflect the best—but not the only—times for success and ease in these activities, according to your Sun sign.

	JAN	FEB	MAR	APR	MAY	JUN	JUL	AUG	SEP	OCT	NOV	DEC
Move	7, 8					7, 8		1, 2, 28, 29			18, 19	
Start a class	11, 12		1, 2, 29, 30	3, 4			16, 17, 18		1, 2, 3			1, 27, 28
Join a club		7, 8, 9			1, 27, 28					11, 12		
Ask for a raise	18, 19		8, 9			21, 22, 23		17, 18	11, 12			
Look for work	9, 10			1, 2, 27, 28	8, 9, 10		18, 19	15, 16		8, 9, 10	16, 17	
Get pro advice		23, 24				10, 11, 12					22, 23	
Get a loan			27, 28, 29		20, 21		13, 14					23, 24, 25
See a doctor	27, 28			17, 18				5, 6		26, 27		
Start a diet					21, 22				16			
End relationship		28, 29, 30	23, 24				19, 20		16, 17, 18			
Buy clothes			12, 13, 14		6, 7, 13, 14			3, 4, 23, 24			14, 15, 20, 21	
Get a makeover	24, 25		8, 9			3, 4, 9, 10						11, 12, 13, 17, 18
New romance			24, 25				6, 7			13, 14, 23, 24		
Vacation		3, 4, 5		25, 26, 27				12, 13			29, 30	

Capricorn

The Goat
December 21 to January 20

♑

Element: Earth

Quality: Cardinal

Polarity: Yin/feminine

Planetary Ruler: Saturn

Meditation: I know the strength
of my soul

Gemstone: Garnet

Power Stones: Peridot, onyx
diamond, quartz,
black obsidian

Key Phrase: I use

Glyph: Head of goat

Anatomy: Skeleton,
knees, skin

Colors: Black, forest green

Animals: Goats, thick-shelled
animals

Myths/Legends: Chronos,
Vesta, Pan

House: Tenth

Opposite Sign: Cancer

Flower: Carnation

Keyword: Ambitious

The Capricorn Personality

Your Strengths and Challenges

Unbeknownst to most, you're not at all afraid to let your hair down when the time is right, Capricorn—but of course, the time isn't right until you've paid your dues and you've earned some fun. Your work ethic is so strong that even if you're successfully tempted and you leave something undone and try to enjoy a treat, it just won't happen. It's the guilt. In your mind, you can't play until you pay, so there's a lot of bargaining that goes on in there, well behind the scenes. *If I do this, I'll give myself this. If I do that, I'll have a taste of that.* You see? Basically, you are of the belief that time off, relaxation, and playtime are earned commodities, which makes you a simply wonderful human being. It also makes you far more appreciative of R&R than most of us. When you actually kick back and have some fun, it's because you did what it took to have some time off.

Now, this could mean that you're quite fond of bribes, in which case, you should make them all positive—as in positive reinforcements. We understand your motivation and applaud it. The thing is, every now and again, good things happen to good people and we're allowed to shake off responsibilities and just enjoy being us. That doesn't happen much for you, since you're such a strict taskmaster, but when it does, stand back and buckle up, because you're certainly not boring. You're simply wise enough to understand that there is a delicate balance in energies going on at all times, and if you want to master those energies, you need to follow the rules. This also doesn't mean that you will break a few rules every now and then, only that you have the rules down pat. So if anyone is all-out qualified to break them, it's most certainly you. No matter what your age, you end up being the hip "older one" or "authority figure" in the crowd—and that definitely has its perks. The thing is, if you're too focused on the end result and not the process, you'll miss a whole lot of what life has to offer. Do yourself a favor and sit still every now and then. Outside, please. After all, you're an earth sign. Don't forget to renew your connection with our planet every now and then. And no phones allowed!

Your Relationships

Think of all the things you'd ever want in a best friend, business partner, or romantic partner, Capricorn, and what you'd end up with is a list of everything your sign is known to be: reliable, practical, trustworthy, and hardworking—all qualities we see far too rarely and prize greatly. Not a bad resumé so far, but let's add a few more admirable adjectives that would also sell well on eBay. Ambitious, for example. Lover of permanence and quality versus quickies and quantity—oh, and master/mistress of preparation, hands down. All that together with all those other lists of terrific qualities you come by naturally make it easy to understand why we love and cherish you so very much.

Now, all that admiration is lovely and well deserved, but it doesn't necessarily mean that someone will make it through the well-guarded door to your inner circle. You have quite the admittance form to get there. Filling it out inside your head is what you consider first dates to be most useful for. When you sign up, it's because the person has made you feel safe and secure with them—not to mention totally confident that they'll never embarrass you, which, according to a recent poll of Capricorns, is ranked worse than death. Yep, that whole embarrassment thing is a deal-breaker. You're very, very conscious of what's socially acceptable and what's not, and never the twain shall meet.

Once we're lucky enough and have proven ourselves to be worthy enough to have you in our lives, whether as a friend or lover, in your mind, it's for keeps, so as per your rather cautious nature, you do a good deal of homework before you submit your final answer.

Like is drawn to like, Capricorn, so the other two earth signs (Taurus and Virgo) are always welcome in your world. The thing is, Taurus gets a bit too bogged down for your tastes, since you're a fast-moving cardinal sign, and Virgo isn't all that good at looking over the big picture. That said, when it comes to partnering up, Cancer is often your best choice. These home-loving souls are more than happy to tend to the home fires while you're off conquering the world. It's the best of both worlds.

Your Career and Money

Career matters are extremely important to you, Capricorn, mostly because it's not just your profession that's on the line, it's also your reputation. You're very good at your chosen path. That said, when you sign up for a job that's just a job—a way to earn your daily bread, that is, which is one of the most important components of your self-esteem—you treat it with all the attention and affection that you'd give to any other project you were hell-bent on tackling. This year, however, as of September, you should expect to be constantly tied up in negotiations—and to be constantly and consistently very good at achieving balance where others said it absolutely couldn't be done.

You do actually allow yourself to spend a bit on yourself, rather than your partner, but it doesn't happen all that often. If the mood strikes you, go for it! It's time to please you first—before anyone or anything else.

Your Lighter Side

What's fun for you? Building, building, and building—and I mean from the ground up. If you're at work on a project to restore, renew, or expand your home, you will be one of those extremely hands-on types. If all is well with your much-cherished and extremely well-guarded home, you might decide to have some fun. In that case, you'll pull out the jigsaw puzzles and have at it. You also have a certain silliness when you're out playing that's not often seen by many, mainly because you tend to feel embarrassed about it the next day. Don't let that hold you back. Relax and have fun!

Affirmation
The structure my life is built upon is unshakable.

The Year Ahead for Capricorn

You probably did a bit of long-distance traveling over the last half of 2015, Capricorn, but if you haven't yet, prepare yourself. It seems that Jupiter—who never does anything "just a little"—has taken up residence in your solar ninth house, and he'll stay put there until September 9. Now, this house has everything to do with broadening our horizons, and travel is certainly a terrific, exciting, and enjoyable way to do that, but there are other options. Higher learning, for example. You might have already signed up for classes to improve your resumé or learn an entirely new skill, but if you haven't, think about it now. With Jupiter all done up in precise, detail-oriented Virgo, you'll have the patience to sit still and focus. The best of all worlds? Taking classes in another state or even another country. Talk about eye-opening experiences!

Of course, once Jupiter leaves Virgo behind for partner-oriented Libra on September 9, he'll be doing some traveling of his own, off to spend a year in your solar tenth house of career matters and dealings with authority figures. If you took those classes we talked about, you'll be glad you did. Jupiter opens doors and offers opportunities, and in this house, he's hard to beat. If you're ready to start your own business, consider taking on a partner, but be sure they're every bit as committed to success as you are.

Now let's talk about Mars, who'll spend all but the last three months of this year in Scorpio and Sagittarius. He'll set off for Scorpio and your solar eleventh house of group affiliations and goals for the future on January 3, putting all the red-hot energy of this assertive, ambitious kind of guy at your disposal. If anyone can help you push ahead with your plans for the future, it's Mars. An added bonus is that Scorpio planets are extremely perceptive, so you'll be able to spot the right people to associate with—the ones who've already made it in the field you've chosen.

Mars's trek through Sagittarius will begin on March 6, as he storms the borders of your solar twelfth house of alone time and Privacy, Please. You may need to do some work all on your own to iron out the kinks in a plan. Mars's retrograde trip, from April 17 to June 30, will be quite helpful in this department, giving you plenty of energy—and plenty of enthusiasm, a quality Sagittarius planets never, ever run short on. The twelfth house has everything to do with rejuvenation and respite, however, so if you feel exhausted, reserve some quality time alone and recharge your batteries.

What This Year's Eclipses Mean for You

As per usual for the Universe, things in Eclipse-Land are quite organized and quite regular. Eclipses have a very strict schedule. They occur in pairs, every six months, over a two-week period. Lunar Eclipses put the Sun and Moon opposite one another, so basically what we end up with is a supercharged Full Moon. Likewise, when the Sun and Moon come together every month, we call it a New Moon and recognize its potential to seed new growth—but once every six months a Lunar Eclipse occurs, and whatever is planted then will come to fruition quickly.

At any rate, the first Solar Eclipse of the year will occur in Pisces on March 8 in your solar third house of conversations and communications.

Now, your sign is nothing if not practical and organized, not to mention quite tied to reality. So if you feel a bit woozy that day and for a week or so afterward, not to worry. You're not losing your edge, you're just experiencing the effects of Pisces energy, which much prefers feelings to facts. Pay attention to the direction in which your antennae are twitching. This could be a very strong hint that when it's time to make decisions, it's also time to incorporate the messages your gut throws your way. The rules and regulations you love and have come to rely on are tried and true—but as you already know, nothing is simply black and white. Pave the way for gray.

On March 23, the Lunar Eclipse will light up the sign of Libra, which just so happens to be the ruler of your solar tenth house of career matters and dealings with authority figures. Since Libra is so gosh-darn accommodating and well liked, no matter what you need to talk over or negotiate with a higher-up, set up the meeting around this date. Your career and professional life, as well as your public reputation, are very important to you, so if anything suddenly comes to light that you find less than flattering, your mission is to sit tight and refuse to comment. Everything will blow over eventually. Sit tight until it does.

The last set of eclipses will begin on September 1 with a Solar Eclipse in Virgo. Now, this will set something in motion that involves a loved one you have not seen in way too long. If you're in the mood to be a bit excessive—which doesn't happen all that often—you might want to send them a plane ticket or buy yourself whatever kind of ticket will get you to them ASAP.

On September 16, the second Lunar Eclipse of the year will occur, all done up in intuitive Pisces, the sign that much prefers feelings over facts, especially with regard to the decision-making process. Once again, just like last March, you will allow your feelings to affect your conscious choices.

Saturn

Saturn is your planetary ruler, Capricorn, so you tend to have an easier time with his visits than many of us do. The thing is, he's marching through your solar twelfth house of secrets, private matters, and alone time—which could be problematic for anyone, you included. The good news is that he's in a somewhat lighter frame of mind thanks to his transit through funny, fortunate Sagittarius, but you'll still need to watch out for a tendency to think heavy thoughts—and no hibernating in the dark, either! On the other hand, if you're running on empty, emotionally speaking, then time alone to relax, recharge, and renew your spirit will be absolutely mandatory, so please do take it. If you're spending too much time on your own and you're not happy, it's time to speak with a professional about it. With Saturn here, you can rest assured that you'll find the help you need. Now, this house also has a lot to do with what we tend to do when we're all by ourselves. Saturn on duty here certainly could translate into working at home alone or handling a big project that only you are qualified to do. Either way, you'll invest absolutely everything you've got into being thorough, efficient, and timely. Of course, in the long run, all that effort will earn you big points with higher-ups or patrons of your work.

Uranus

Ever since March of 2012, your carefully arranged schedule has been the victim of shocking Uranus, Capricorn. Now, he's on duty in assertive, aggressive Aries and your solar fourth house of home, family, and emotional matters, so a family member—a child or an elder, it seems—has probably been in need of a whole lot more of your time, and when the phone rings, you have needed to dash out the door to handle a situation for them. Needless to say, this has brought a seriously erratic tone to your daily life, especially since Pluto in your sign and your solar first house of personality and appearance has been doing his best to keep you on a rather strict diet of rules and regulations. If you feel pulled in two directions, you are absolutely right, and you absolutely need relief from the situation—or situations. If you were born between January 6 and 16, this highly unpredictable energy is also in a square aspect to your Sun, which means you are in the midst of extreme, fast-moving changes you might not realize are happening for a few years down the road. The thing is, squares insist on action, Uranus insists on change, and Aries insists on adrenaline. Apply all those demands to the condition of your well-structured, well-organized Sun, and you'll be able to understand what's going on. Your mission is to cooperate. Let change happen when it will, and try your best to enjoy it.

Neptune

Your solar third house is currently hosting intuitive Neptune, and since this house has everything to do with communication, thoughts, and conversations, your decision-making process has probably changed quite a bit, Capricorn. Now, ordinarily you rely pretty much entirely on facts and figures when you need to figure something out. Now that your mind has been Neptunized, however, you're probably also far more in touch with your intuitive side, so that will become a bit part of the process. The good news is that combining intellect and emotions in a positive way just can't be a bad thing. You'll learn more on a daily basis by simply wandering down the street than you could ever have imagined. If you were born between December 27 and January 5, Capricorn, you're also currently enjoying an exciting, stimulating sextile aspect from Neptune to your Sun—which means your creativity is running on ultra-super-high. Because this involves your solar third house of thoughts, the insights you're having are probably hard to believe, so be sure to jot them down. Likewise, your dreams will be quite prophetic, so if you aren't already journaling, get right on that. You'll probably be in the mood to read up on metaphysical or spiritual topics, and understanding it all will come easily. Think of it as being temporarily endowed with several superpowers, including the ability to read minds without much effort.

Pluto

Your solar first house of personality and appearance has been playing host to Pluto since way back in 2008—which means that at this point, you're somewhat of an expert on the subject. Oh, and let's not forget that Saturn, your ruling planet, just finished up a two-and-a-half-year stint in Pluto's sign, Scorpio, last September. Whew! Obviously, you've had an awful lot of intensity in your life over recent years, and you're probably ready for a break in the action or at least a lessening of the responsibilities you've been enduring (and rising to meet quite admirably, by the way). The good news is that after all this time, Pluto in your authoritative sign has probably taught you the joys and delights of delegating duties. Talk about a boon! He's also been there long enough to infuse you with his detective-like ability to spot things that most, if not all, of us miss—including picking the right person to fill in for you so you won't have to worry. If you were born between January 5 and 9, Pluto will also form an exciting, stimulating, and extremely helpful sextile aspect to your Sun. This is one of those transits people would pay big bucks for, by the way, because absolutely everything you want will be entirely possible to achieve. Use this temporary gift of superpowers wisely.

Capricorn | January

Relaxation and Recreation

Urgent business of either a professional or family-oriented nature will come about around January 5, Capricorn, and you may not have time to let everyone know about your plans before you leave. If you can't reach the one person who'll be able to take care of things in your absence, keep trying. In just a few hours, all will be well and well taken care of in your world.

Lovers and Friends

The Sun will storm off into your solar second house of personal finances on January 20, Capricorn, followed in short order by chatty Mercury and startling Uranus, both of whom have never been especially patient. If you have been very nice about waiting for a debt that needs to be repaid, this may be the day when you decide that it's high time you're repaid—or you'll know the reason why.

Money and Success

With Mercury and the Sun in erratic, unpredictable Aquarius and set to make their way through your solar second house of personal finances, you may not be able to count on much, financially speaking, Capricorn—which means you'll be awfully glad about that secret stash you put aside specifically for times like these.

Tricky Transits

Venus will square off with Jupiter on January 17, creating several possible scenarios. The most popular choice seems to be a temporary fondness for excess and all the delightfully hedonistic feelings that go along with enjoying every bite of that rich, lovely dinner and every note of that lush, lovely music that's on in the background. It's time to spoil yourself.

Rewarding Days

12, 13, 14, 15, 18, 30

Challenging Days

5, 6, 7, 17, 20, 25

Capricorn | February

Relaxation and Recreation

There's nothing better, in your mind, than when a plan comes together exactly as you pictured it, Capricorn. That said, you should know that all your plans are subject to sudden change around February 6 and 7, so try not to get too attached to your schedule. Oh, and your Valentine's Day ideas will go along quite swimmingly, so go forward with your master plan for romance.

Lovers and Friends

Fiery, passionate, impulsive Mars will spend the month in your solar eleventh house, all done up in sexy, intense Scorpio—so someone you have always thought of as strictly a friend may suddenly pique your interest for reasons that have nothing to do with being friends. Even if you've never talked about how attracted you are to each another, one of you may finally give some rather obvious hints.

Money and Success

On February 5, Capricorn, the lovely lady Venus—who holds both love and money under her jurisdiction—will collide with intense, determined Pluto. Now, they'll both be in your sign and your solar first house of personality and appearance at the time, so if you have financial issues to settle, you'll arrive with a "just-the-facts-ma'am" attitude that will work perfectly in your favor.

Tricky Transits

Mercury will get into an uneasy inconjunct aspect with Jupiter on February 27, Capricorn, and since he's the God of Communication, things could get a bit hairy around that time. A certain someone you've been trying to reach with your words may not seem to understand your point at all. Don't beat yourself up. Take a day and try again. Bet it works out fine this time.

Rewarding Days
3, 8, 9, 14, 16, 25

Challenging Days
6, 7, 10, 22, 23, 27

Capricorn | March

Relaxation and Recreation

It might not be easy for you to relax this month, Capricorn, but thanks to the Solar Eclipse in Pisces on March 8, you'll be more than ready to speak your mind without filtering anything out via a two-second delay. Of course, Pisces planets love to party, so you sure will be able to have some serious fun—which, after all, will keep you happy and spiritually well fed.

Lovers and Friends

On March 14, your ruling planet, serious Saturn, will get into an edgy battle with Venus and Mercury. Now, fiery Mars will be on Saturn's team, so if an offense has been committed, sweet words just won't cut it. If one of you really wants to make up and make nice, it will require an all-out admitting that yes, you were wrong.

Money and Success

Venus and Mercury will make their way through your solar third house of communications, all done up in woozy, dreamy Pisces. Now, this could be tough to deal with if you're trying to balance your monthly bills. After all, paperwork has never been one of Neptune's specialties, and she owns Pisces. If you're trying to change careers—toward something more in line with your beliefs—you'll have yourself the perfect planetary envoy.

Tricky Transits

Two eclipses will occur this month, and while neither of them will be in your sign, their effects will still be quite potent—and probably quite unexpected. On March 23, for example, the Lunar Eclipse will arrive, ready to shake things up in your solar tenth house of career matters and dealings with authority figures. No matter how sweetly and attractively they phrase it, don't allow yourself to be taken advantage of.

Rewarding Days
10, 11, 12, 15, 16, 17

Challenging Days
3, 4, 5, 8, 14, 23, 30, 31

Capricorn | April

Relaxation and Recreation

A New Moon in Aries and your solar fourth house of home and family matters will occur on April 7, Capricorn, and since you have never been fond of acting impulsively, especially with regard to your personal life, whatever seed this Moon plants will likely be surprising to you when it pops its little head up. No, you're not necessarily going to be a parent or grandparent—but wouldn't that be terrific?

Lovers and Friends

The Sun and Mercury will spend some time in Taurus and your solar fifth house of lovers and playmates, Capricorn, but as of April 29, the lovely lady Venus will be in the house—all done up in her favorite sign. Now, Venus in Taurus is a very powerful kind of lady, so if you're interested in someone and you aim this magnetic energy in their direction—well, let's just say that "resistance is futile" might just be your battle cry.

Money and Success

The Moon in Aquarius—who just adores independence—will make her way through your solar second house of personal finances and money matters around April 2 and then again as of April 30. If you've been trying to get a major hurdle out of your way, Capricorn, these are the times to get your funding without encountering any unnecessary stalls.

Tricky Transits

On April 27, Mars in Sagittarius will get into an uneasy inconjunct aspect with the Sun in Taurus and your solar fifth house of lovers, Capricorn. Now, this puts your solar fifth house at odds with your solar twelfth house of alone time and Privacy Please, so getting together with someone delicious might not be an easy feat. Tell you what, though—once you two close the door, it will all be worth it.

Rewarding Days

5, 12, 14, 17, 29

Challenging Days

4, 6, 10, 15, 27, 28

Capricorn | May

Relaxation and Recreation

What a great month to be you, Capricorn! The heavens are fairly bursting with solid earth signs like your own, and fully committed to seeing to it that you enjoy your share of creature comforts. Now, May 26 could be tricky, so if you feel a bit stressed around that time, get into a hot tub or have a massage.

Lovers and Friends

A parade of earthy, sensual planets in Taurus will make its way through your solar fifth house of lovers and playmates this month, Capricorn, and since one of them is Venus—well, you may not be able to relax all that much, but you'll certainly enjoy some wonderfully warm evenings wrapped in the arms of your sweetheart. Nice.

Money and Success

With all those Taurus planets in your solar fifth house of speculation this month, Capricorn, you can count on feeling stable and solidly grounded—not to mention lucky. Taurus planets are money magnets, to start with, but since they'll all take turns forming easy trines with generous Jupiter, you're looking at a bit of a windfall.

Tricky Transits

Mars will retrograde back into Scorpio on May 27, Capricorn, ready to retrace his steps through this sexy, intense sign. Now, this will put him in your solar eleventh house of friendships, so if you run into someone you haven't seen in a very long while, you two might make a really lovely connection.

Rewarding Days
12, 10, 12, 19, 30

Challenging Days
4, 5, 21, 22, 27

Capricorn | June

Relaxation and Recreation

A pack of planets moving through Gemini and your solar sixth house of work will keep you on your toes this month, Capricorn, particularly from June 1 through June 6. The good news is that no matter what you're given to do, you'll be able to do it well and quickly—and if you need to multitask, that will come easily to you.

Lovers and Friends

Mercury in Taurus and your solar fifth house of lovers will get into a face-off with Mars in Scorpio, who's passing through your solar eleventh house of friendships. Now, contrary to popular opinion, oppositions aren't necessarily difficult, and that goes double for this one—after all, Taurus and Scorpio are the two signs most famous for their abilities in the boudoir.

Money and Success

You'll be busy this month, Capricorn, and you may not have much time to yourself, but this is your chance to make a name for yourself in your chosen field, if you haven't already. A pack of talkative Gemini planets will be more than happy to help you chat up absolutely anyone who can point you in the right direction.

Tricky Transits

On June 22, Mercury will square off with Jupiter, an energetic aspect linking two very energetic energies. If you've got errands to run, do them now, and they'll go quickly and efficiently. If you're thinking of taking a trip, wait until the 1st of next month to set your plans in stone.

Rewarding Days
8, 12, 13, 22, 26, 27

Challenging Days
1, 2, 3, 20, 29, 30

Capricorn | July

Relaxation and Recreation

A pack of planets in home and family-oriented Cancer will pass through your solar seventh house of relationships this month, Capricorn, all of them intent on keeping you busy, puttering around your nest with your significant other. This is a great time to garden or spruce things up with a fresh coat of paint.

Lovers and Friends

The New Moon on July 4 will plant a seed in your solar seventh house of one-to-one relationships, Capricorn, so if you're single, pay careful attention to anyone you run into who strikes your fancy. You may not actually get together until the Full Moon on July 18, but then, having to wait makes things more exciting, right?

Money and Success

Venus will form an easy, cooperative trine with reliable Saturn on July 20, from her spot in your solar eighth house of joint finances, loans, and inheritances. If you need to borrow money, apply today, when this sturdy team will help you to put your best foot forward.

Tricky Transits

Mercury will square off with Mars on July 29, Capricorn, a testy aspect that might very well inspire a bit of bickering, if not an all-out argument. Either way, you can choose not to participate. Mars in Scorpio is a passionate energy, as is Mercury in Leo. Bet you can think of something better to do with all that energy.

Rewarding Days

1, 3, 5, 6, 20, 26

Challenging Days

2, 10, 11, 13, 21

Capricorn | August

Relaxation and Recreation

Your solar ninth house will be a very busy place on August 22, as the Sun sets off for Virgo, your practical, hardworking earth-sign cousin. Now, the ninth house is associated with new experiences, so if you're bored with the usual routine, give yourself the day off and go exploring with a friend.

Lovers and Friends

If you're angry with your sweetheart around August 13, Capricorn, try not to say anything you'll regret. Venus will square off with Saturn that day, just as he's stationing, so your words will carry a lot of weight. If you're done with your current relationship, on the other hand, this may be the day you choose to say goodbye.

Money and Success

The Full Moon on August 18 will light up your solar second house of personal finances, Capricorn. She'll be wearing Aquarius, a sign that can always be counted on to think outside the box—so if you're trying to come up with a plan for a new business or a new way to earn your daily bread, she's your gal.

Tricky Transits

Mercury will station to turn retrograde on August 30, Capricorn, all done up in Virgo and your solar ninth house of travel. If you're on the road that day, be sure to inspect your vehicle carefully before you leave, and make sure you have your GPS with you—or good directions, at the very least.

Rewarding Days
1, 5, 10, 16, 27, 28

Challenging Days
6, 7, 14, 19, 24, 25

Capricorn | September

Relaxation and Recreation

If you're traveling this month, Capricorn, you should know that Mercury will be retrograde until September 21, so you might run into a few delays. Before you get cranky, though, think about where you are and what you're looking at that you would never have experienced if you had whizzed on by.

Lovers and Friends

The Lunar Eclipse will arrive on September 16, Capricorn, all done up in romantic Pisces. This lunation will occur in your solar third house of conversations and communications, so if you're single, by all means do allow a sibling or neighbor to introduce you to someone they're sure is just perfect for you—no matter what happened last time.

Money and Success

The Sun will get together with generous, benevolent Jupiter on September 25, Capricorn, and they've chosen to meet in your solar tenth house of career matters. Now, since they're in partnership-loving Libra, you might decide to take on a partner at work or to start your own business with someone. Be sure they're just as committed to making it a success as you are.

Tricky Transits

On September 10, practical Saturn will square off with dreamy Neptune, who prefers fiction and fantasy to anything even remotely resembling reality. Now, this pair obviously isn't a match made in heaven, but there's a method to their madness. It's time to wake up and smell the coffee. If someone always assumes you'll pick up the tab, you might want to ask yourself why you're putting up with it.

Rewarding Days

6, 7, 19, 20, 23, 30

Challenging Days

15, 17, 18, 21

Capricorn | October

Relaxation and Recreation

Your ruling planet, Saturn, will get into an easy sextile with restless Mercury on October 14, Capricorn, so if you wake up in the mood to play hooky and have some fun, go for it. Bet you'll have company, too. No fair feeling guilty, either. When was the last time you took an entire day to simply enjoy life? You deserve this.

Lovers and Friends

Your month will start off on an extremely romantic note, Capricorn, thanks to the combined efforts of Venus, Mercury, and Neptune, all of which are in sensitive water signs. Now, Venus and Mercury are all done up in sexy Scorpio and on duty in your solar eleventh house of groups, so if you're still waiting for your soul mate, it might be time to get out there and resume the hunt.

Money and Success

Venus rules money as well as love, Capricorn, and she's set to meet up with your ruling planet, Saturn, on October 29. Now, two possible scenarios come to mind immediately. First, you might want to invest your hard-earned money in a large purchase or a bank account. On the other hand, if you have been playing loose and free with your plastic, the bill may come due now.

Tricky Transits

Well, Capricorn, on October 19, you'll have to be especially careful to watch your temper. It seems that aggressive Mars will get together in your sign and your solar first house of personality with intense Pluto, a combination that can turn anger to rage in a quick minute. On the other hand, they can also turn a minor attraction into a major passion. Hey, I know which one I'd choose.

Rewarding Days

1, 11, 14, 26, 27

Challenging Days

2, 5, 9, 12, 23, 25

Capricorn | November

Relaxation and Recreation

The Full Moon on November 14 will set up shop in your solar fifth house of playtime and playmates, all done up in sensual, earthy Taurus. Now, this is some pretty darn wonderful news, whether you're single or attached. You single folks can count on having a lovely physical experience with someone quite dear to your heart. If you're taken, you two will rekindle the spark that brought you together—big time.

Lovers and Friends

Romance will be on your agenda in a big way on November 19, as Neptune stations to turn direct and forms a sextile to Venus in your sign and your solar first house of personality and appearance. Now, lest you worry that this is way too much sentimentality for you, keep in mind that in your sign, Venus is a very practical kind of gal, so while romance will be sweet, you'll still have your feet rooted firmly to the ground.

Money and Success

With impulsive Mars in equally impulsive Aquarius set to invade your solar second house of money matters and spending habits, you might want to have someone hold any credit cards you don't want to use, Capricorn. Yes, you're usually quite responsible with money, but when this spark plug is in the area, even you can be tempted.

Tricky Transits

The Sun, Venus, and Mercury will take turns passing through your solar eleventh house of friendships this month, Capricorn. Now, they'll be all done up in sexy Scorpio—and one never knows what might happen between you and a certain someone you've only thought of platonically for the longest time. If you think there might be something more between you, take it out for a test ride.

Rewarding Days

1, 2, 5, 21, 22, 23

Challenging Days

6, 24, 25, 29, 30

Capricorn | December

Relaxation and Recreation

Happy holidays, Capricorn—and what a month the Universe has arranged for you! Bright and early on December 1, Mars in Aquarius will get into an easy, comfy trine with Jupiter in sociable, loving Libra. Now, Jupiter expands the qualities of the sign he's wearing and the planets he touches, so camaraderie will come easily and everyone will be welcomed into the fold at your place. Party on!

Lovers and Friends

Venus will set off on December 7 for friendly Aquarius, the sign that most loves to be in the company of kindred spirits. Of course, in this sign, Venus will sparkle most brightly when you're with familiar loved ones—but hold on just a second. Aquarius planets are quite fond of the unusual and unexpected, so you can expect all kinds of surprise visits and drop-ins from folks you doubted you'd see again for a very long while. Enjoy!

Money and Success

If you're in line for a promotion, Capricorn, your ruling planet, Saturn, will see to it that you're considered, at the very least. Of course, anyone who wouldn't hire you should have their head examined. You're hardworking, affable, and thorough. What's not to love? Prepare to welcome in the new year with a bigger paycheck. Congrats!

Tricky Transits

On December 19, Mercury will stop in his tracks to turn retrograde in your sign, so if you're out and about, traveling to a holiday gathering, you might want to allow yourself some extra time to get there, just in case. And then, on December 31, Mars will collide with Neptune in woozy Pisces, making it all too easy to overindulge. No fair driving. It's Amateur Night.

Rewarding Days

Just about all of them, really.

Challenging Days

19, 31

Capricorn Action Table

These dates reflect the best—but not the only—times for success and ease in these activities, according to your Sun sign.

	JAN	FEB	MAR	APR	MAY	JUN	JUL	AUG	SEP	OCT	NOV	DEC
Move	9, 10			13, 14		5, 6, 7			21, 22			15, 16
Start a class	11, 12		6, 7		27, 28, 29		16, 17			6, 7		
Join a club		7, 8, 9		3, 4, 5		23, 24		17, 18, 19			7, 8	
Ask for a raise			3, 4		6, 7, 25, 26		27, 28			17, 18		11, 12
Look for work	20, 21		14, 15			11, 12, 13			11, 12		5, 6, 7	
Get pro advice		23, 24		17, 18				5, 6, 7	1, 28, 29			
Get a loan	4, 5, 6				20, 21					3, 4, 5, 31		24, 25, 26
See a doctor			21, 22				8, 9		28, 29, 30			
Start a diet		22, 23		22, 23				18, 19			29, 30	
End relationship	24, 25		23, 24			14, 15, 16			16, 17, 18			
Buy clothes				9, 10, 11			6, 7, 8			17, 18, 28, 29		
Get a makeover		14, 15	12, 13		6, 7, 8			3, 4, 5, 23, 24			14, 15	17, 18
New romance	2, 3, 29, 30			20, 21			11, 12				24, 25	
Vacation		4, 5, 6			22, 23, 24				6, 7, 8			

Aquarius

The Water Bearer
January 20 to February 19

Element: Air

Quality: Fixed

Polarity: Yang/masculine

Planetary Ruler: Uranus

Meditation: I am a wellspring of creativity

Gemstone: Amethyst

Power Stones: Aquamarine, black pearl, chrysocolla

Key Phrase: I know

Glyph: Currents of energy

Anatomy: Ankles, circulatory system

Colors: Iridescent blues, violet

Animals: Exotic birds

Myths/Legends: Ninhursag, John the Baptist, Deucalion

House: Eleventh

Opposite Sign: Leo

Flower: Orchid

Keyword: Unconventional

The Aquarius Personality

Your Strengths and Challenges

You're a people-watcher, Aquarius. The thing is, you folks often feel as if you're from another planet, so it's fun to see what the humans are up to now. Of course, this could be where your reputation for being detached comes from—because when you're concentrating on someone, you're so totally involved on an intellectual level that you look a bit like a statue. This doesn't mean you really are cold, however. In fact, if someone happens to be downtrodden or an outcast, you're the very best friend the astrological market has to offer. You're also pretty darn good at coming up with solutions to the problems of others. You think outside the box, so you naturally consider more options—many of which are quite unconventional, and all of which are downright brilliant.

Your ruling planet is electric Uranus, the planet in charge of mass communication. This tidbit certainly does explain a lot. Take, for example, your fondness for computers—and your love affair with the Web. You also feel kinship with computers, so much so that I'm willing to bet at least one someone insists that you leave it at home when you're together. Same thing goes for your phone, and any electronic device, for that matter. You usually have the latest model, and well before the rest of us. Gadgets in general fascinate you. You might even have invented one or two yourself. You're equally fascinated with the state of the world, and you have an awful lot to say about it. You've never been famous for holding your tongue, but no one who knows you would ever want that to happen, anyway. You inspire us with your unique approach, so please do keep telling us all about it. Your car bumper is probably plastered with bumper stickers, and they're odd ones, too. Anyone who accuses you of being "normal" or "just like everyone else" had better hit the ground running. How insulting! You're also quite the rebel. In fact, you'll need to be careful of a tendency to rebel just for the sake of rebelling. Now, when you find something that's unfair, unjust, or outright wrong—in your not-so-humble opinion—the war of words is on. Keep up the good work.

Your Relationships

The term "significant other" seems to have been created especially for you, Aquarius. It has a slightly detached sound to it and allows for a variety of possibilities. And speaking of possibilities, you are not usually prejudiced against anyone or anything, so you tend to have relationships with all kinds of people, both platonic and romantic. In fact, you probably pride yourself on your collection of friends, a motley crew of all ages, races, and sexual leanings. They will all share a very important common denominator in your eyes—the fact that they, too, feel as if they are not from this planet. This circle becomes your tribe, and you're quite devoted to it.

Anyone who's "interesting" can easily earn a place in your heart. If they regularly attend Burning Man or are quite opinionated—even if you do not agree—so much the better. You'll be fascinated, and in your cerebral book, that's mandatory. The brain must be engaged before the heart, and libido can follow—but it's no easy task. Anyone who earns a lasting place in your life has been complimented greatly. They're true individuals and free thinkers. They should also feel pretty darn proud of themselves.

You need a partner who will double as your best friend. That's the number-one prerequisite to landing you. You also need someone who knows how to hold on with an open hand. Any hint of extreme jealousy or possessiveness, and you're outta there. Personal freedom and independence are far too sacred to you to allow anyone to tie you down. One whiff of pressure on the subject of being monogamous is enough to scare you off for good. It's not that you can't be monogamous. You simply need to find someone as open-minded and restless as yourself.

For that reason, you tend to do well with Gemini and Sagittarius. Gemini is an air sign like your own that is every bit as much in love with computers and gadgets, so you'll never be bored—the one thing that neither of you can tolerate. Sagittarius is freewheeling and freedom-loving, too, and loves to learn, so they're full of interesting facts—and also can't stand to be bored. You might make good friends with Libra, but in a relationship, they tend to be a bit too focused for your taste.

Your Career and Money

Your nonstop determination to remind everyone that you're not like anyone else extends into your work, Aquarius. If it's an occupation so different that your chances of meeting someone in that line of work are next to nothing, so much the better. You're in. The more unusual, the better, too. Astronaut. Astrologer. Deep-sea diver. Your work needs to be endlessly fascinating to hold your interest. If it's not—if there's any hint of boredom—well, that's a deal breaker. You'll be on your merry way in no time flat, often without any warning or any notice. You've probably quit jobs on the way there, because the thought of going through that again was just too much for you. Of course, if you have a "normal" job, as long as you're allowed a whole lot of freedom to make your own schedule and set your own hours, you're good to go. Computers, of course, are always a welcome addition to your day, so working on one would suit you just fine. Your main goal is to be completely self-employed and self-reliant, so start saving your pennies for a down payment on your own business. Oh, and if you're considering taking on a partner, be sure you choose carefully. After all, you don't want to be saddled by someone who isn't as devoted to the project as you are.

Your Lighter Side

What's fun, Aquarius? Well, at the risk of sounding like a broken record, one word: computers. Well, actually, two more words: and phones. You are just about surgically attached to yours, and you have all the latest apps and the highest Internet speed. I really can't imagine what you folks did before the Web was invented, but I'll bet it wasn't nearly as much fun as hopping online to visit with your cerebral tribe. You love social media sites and how-to sites, but you need to watch for a tendency to alienate others by insisting that they share your opinions. Remember, we're all different. That's what makes it such a beautiful world.

Affirmation
I cherish my uniqueness.

The Year Ahead for Aquarius

Red-hot Mars will spend an unusually long time in Scorpio and Sagittarius this year, Aquarius, which will put him in your tenth and eleventh solar houses. As of January 3, Mars will be in intense, sexy Scorpio and your solar tenth house of career, profession, and dealings with authority figures. That said, if you suddenly find yourself attracted to someone who is a higher-up or your direct boss, it wouldn't be surprising, but before you sign up for anything romantic, be sure you can still work together if things don't work out as planned. If all systems are go—well, enjoy yourself. Since you're in the same field, chances are good that you two will share quite a few of the same opinions, which of course is absolutely mandatory in your book.

Mars will move through your solar eleventh house from March 5 through May 27, and the party will most definitely be on. Talk about a good time! This house is where we handle friendships, group affiliations, and gatherings of like-minded others—and in Sagittarius, there's sure to be an amazing variety of individuals to play with. Sagittarius planets also love to play and have a terrific sense of humor, so you can expect lots of laughter and fun. Now, since Mars will spend a month moving retrograde through this sign, he'll be looking over his shoulder, and you'll probably end up looking for a certain someone you haven't seen in far too long. Don't just sit there. Open up your computer and find them. As Mars travels through this house in August and September—moving forward this time around—you two might just do some traveling together, or traveling to get to each other. What fun!

Now let's talk about Jupiter, who'll be in meticulous Virgo and your solar eighth house all year until September 9. This is quite a sign/planet combination. Jupiter adores the big picture and Virgo adores details. They can balance each other out or irritate each other into submission. It either works well or doesn't work at all—but now that you know it's happening, here are some tips. First off, the eighth house has everything to do with intimacy and shared resources, so if you're attached, try not to be too critical of your lover/partner—and don't allow them to pick on you, either. If you're in the middle of a financial deal or trying to get through the paperwork associated with a loan or inheritance, however, you'll be well armed to handle it.

Now, Jupiter will set off for your solar ninth house on September 9, and this house has everything to do with travel, far-off places and people, and long-distance relationships. Between Jupiter in the ninth house and Mars in Sagittarius, it certainly sounds like someone's going to be spending a bit of time in the air. You might also decide to start a yearlong course of study, which is a terrific idea.

What This Year's Eclipses Mean for You

Every six months, a New Moon and a Full Moon make astrological headlines, Aquarius. They turn themselves into eclipses, and instead of just asking nicely for change, they cross their arms and demand it. On March 8, the first Solar Eclipse of the year will occur in your solar second house of personal finances and money matters. This supercharged New Moon will bring the Sun and Moon together in Pisces, a spiritual sign that much prefers feelings over facts. You'll have to be careful not to lose your money—literally, by misplacing it, but also through making the wrong financial choices. If you're about to make a major purchase, just this once, please do get the warranty, and please don't overextend yourself through monthly payments that are more than you can handle. If there isn't already a spiritual or metaphysical component to the way you earn your daily bread, you'll want that to change.

On March 23, the first Lunar Eclipse will occur, all done up in partner-oriented Libra and your solar ninth house of far-off loved ones. If you've been involved in a long-distance relationship, chances are you'll want to end that nonsense. You or your partner might suddenly decide to move, or you might just as suddenly end the relationship. On the other hand, someone with a dynamite accent could come along and pique your interest. Pay attention. They have something to teach you. And speaking of learning, this house is also where educational matters are handled, so if things aren't working out well for you in your current field, it might be time to pursue a new one. Computers, perhaps?

On September 1, a second Solar Eclipse will occur, this time in practical Virgo and your solar eighth house of loans, inheritances, and joint money matters. Get ready for some paperwork, either to put a rapid-fire end to a problematic partnership or to start a business of your own. Cross all your t's and dot all your i's, because eclipses play for keeps. This house also rules intimate relationships, so be careful of the Virgoan tendency to pick and criticize your dear ones. You might drive someone away without realizing it.

The last Lunar Eclipse of the year will occur on September 16, a supercharged Full Moon in Pisces that might just bring back memories. Remember, a Solar Eclipse occurred in this same sign and house last March. Once again, money matters could be tricky, especially if something comes to light regarding a financial partner that causes you to trust them a whole lot less. In that case, you'll want to split with them immediately, but don't be in such a rush that you fail to go over your books and records carefully. Better still, get a professional to do it for you.

Saturn

Saturn will spend the year in your solar eleventh house of friendships and group affiliations, Aquarius, and remember, he never fails to bring added responsibilities with him. He's also quite fond of wielding authority. That said, if he pushes you to take over the reins of a group you already belong to, it won't exactly be a hardship for you. Let's face it. You're quite opinionated and you have some very definite thoughts on how the world should be run. Put two and two together, and this could be a match made in heaven. You will need to be on guard against a tendency to take over even if it's not your job and you haven't been asked—and heaven help anyone who tries to tell you what to do and when to do it, because you won't take kindly to it. If they insist? Well, they'll soon learn that this sort of thing has an amazing effect on you. When you hear "should," "don't," or "can't," it sounds very much like an irresistible invitation to do just that. In this case, you'll want to righteously rebel, right in front of the entire group. Now, the eleventh house also has a lot to do with our goals for the future, and the company we keep has a lot to do with our goals. Make sure you're spending your time with the type of people who are on the same evolutionary page and share your value system, too.

Uranus

Your ruling planet is Uranus, which certainly explains a lot. This guy is very, very fond of surprises, from sudden U-turns in traffic to winning the lottery to hearing, seeing, or saying the very last thing on earth that could ever be expected. So let's talk about the fact that he's currently on duty in your solar third house of conversations and communications, all done up in Aries. Now, this is an impulsive, impatient sign, which suits Uranus just fine—which means it suits you just fine, too. The thing is, while you're busy emoting, expressing your views to anyone and everyone who'll listen, and trying to win them over to your team, you might not realize that your efforts are having the reverse effect. Think of how you feel when someone is determined to change your mind on a subject you feel very strongly about. Now think about the effects your words are having on others. At the very least, you might want to soften your approach. If you were born between February 4 and 14, you are also currently enjoying a stimulating, refreshing sextile from Uranus to your Sun, and with Uranus's electricity coursing through your veins, you're probably having a fine time of it, shocking others and making sure everyone knows that you are totally unique and unlike anyone else. That's all well and good—and by the way, when this transit is finished, you'll have far more personal freedom and far less heavy authority in your life. Take charge, and make changes where they're needed, even if it upsets someone else's applecart. You and only you are in charge of making yourself happy.

Neptune

For the past five years, Neptune has been making her way through your solar second house of personal finances, Aquarius—and what a ride it's been! On the positive side, Neptune's fondness for bringing the spiritual side of life to us could mean that you've recently begun to earn a rather comfy income from a profession involving metaphysics, or as a spiritual advisor. Then, too, art and music are under her jurisdiction, so that type of work might also be on your agenda, if it's not already. The tough part of this transit might involve losing money—literally, as in losing your wallet at the ball game. Credit cards are particularly dangerous when Neptune is in this house, since this planet specializes in illusions—for example, the illusion that trading a piece of plastic for what you want won't eventually end up costing you far more than it should. If you were born between January 27 and February 1, your Sun is also receiving Neptune's direct attention via a semisextile. Now, this aspect isn't known for being especially potent until it's exact, and the effects don't seem to last as long, but then, it doesn't take long to make or break a financial situation. Do yourself a favor and see to it that you're using your intuition when deciding how much to spend, or better still, take along a chaperone when you shop—preferably a friend who's not afraid to pry the plastic out of your hand before it's too late.

Pluto

This intense, brooding energy has been stationed in your solar twelfth house since back in 2008, Aquarius, which probably does explain a lot. You are and always will be quite rebellious, assertive, and fixed in your views and always willing to take to the road if kindred spirits might be in the area. Your lifelong mission is to explain The Right Thing to Do to the masses. That said, it's not hard to imagine you hitting the road a whole lot less often lately, since much of your energy has been focused on more private matters—say, the fact that you've been dealing with a loss, and doing your best to recover from it. As per usual, you handle emotional issues quite easily and placidly—on the outside. On the inside, however, there's a hurricane of feelings raging. It's cool. You're quite aware that looking relaxed and confident will come to mean feeling relaxed and confident. If you were born between February 4 and 7, all this goes double for you, but you'll have to pay attention to even the tiniest of signs, omens, and celestial pokes—a skill that just so happens to be on your list of specialties. No fair gloating at the rest of us who are suffering!

Aquarius | January

Relaxation and Recreation

Happy New Year, Aquarius! And what a year it's going to be. The fun starts bright and early on January 1, when Mercury edges into your sign and your solar first house of appearance. Now, this planet will stop in his tracks to move retrograde just a few days later, so if you're ready to do some traveling, try to plan for it around January 5 or 25.

Lovers and Friends

The lovely lady Venus will stay on duty in fiery, funny Sagittarius until January 23, and since this puts her magnetic energy in your solar eleventh house of friendships and groups, you certainly won't be lonely. You might even attract the admiring attention of a friend of a friend. Maybe someone from out of state?

Money and Success

Jupiter will stop to turn retrograde in your solar eighth house of joint resources, loans, and inheritances on January 7, Aquarius, so if you're in the market for a mortgage or loan, try to avoid applying around that time. You'll be better off waiting until after Mercury turns direct on January 25, anyway.

Tricky Transits

On January 20, the Sun will move into your sign, Aquarius, and the party will be on. It might be a surprise party, too, because on that same day, Mercury will square off with your ruling planet, startling Uranus, who's always been a big fan of surprise endings and U-turns. At the very least, some surprising news is en route.

Rewarding Days

12, 13, 14, 18, 30

Challenging Days

3, 5, 7, 20, 25, 31

Aquarius | February

Relaxation and Recreation
More surprises? Oh, you bet. Fortunately, Aquarius, as the private property of Uranus, not much rattles you, and you're very fond of the unpredictable, so you'll enjoy them all. On February 6, in fact, you might cross paths with someone delightful from another state, coast, or country—and if you take a fancy to them, this thing will move fast.

Lovers and Friends
Venus will slip into your sign on February 16, Aquarius, so if you're not already seeing someone, she'll draw some admirers your way. And since she'll will be in your sign, you can count on every one of them being quite "interesting," your favorite quality. On February 29—an unusual day—Venus might even inspire you to settle down. A little. For now.

Money and Success
February 29 looks to be a lucky day, too, Aquarius—for both love and finances. Venus will get into an energizing sextile with Saturn, so authority figures will be more than willing to listen to your ideas—which, of course, you just love—and sign you up for an unusual project. This pair blends freedom and responsibility in only the best of ways. Enjoy!

Tricky Transits
It might be tough to get your point across around February 27, when Mercury, in your sign, will form an uneasy inconjunct aspect with Jupiter, who can always be counted on to blow things out of proportion. If it's a work-related issue or the behavior of a colleague that's a problem, wait two days and all will be well. Honest.

Rewarding Days
3, 9, 14, 16, 25, 26, 29

Challenging Days
6, 7, 22, 27

Aquarius | March

Relaxation and Recreation
You'll have an opportunity to take off with an interesting friend on March 2, Aquarius, and since the culprits are Venus in your unpredictable sign and Uranus, your unpredictable ruling planet, one never knows where you two might end up, but it will most certainly be fun. You might also decide that being friends with this fascinating person just isn't enough.

Lovers and Friends
A Lunar Eclipse will arrive on March 23, Aquarius, all done up in partner-oriented Libra. This lunation will take place in your solar ninth house of long-lost lovers, so if you suddenly have the urge to see them again, no matter how far away they are from you, think before you hop on a plane and definitely call first.

Money and Success
Careful, Aquarius. The Solar Eclipse on March 8 will shake things up in your solar second house of money matters. The thing is, since the eclipse will fall in Pisces, a sign that's never been famous for being good with details, you might lose your wallet, your plastic, or even your cash. Don't agree to any financial obligations. Settle a nagging debt instead.

Tricky Transits
On March 20, Venus will conjoin Neptune, both of them all done up in woozy, dreamy Pisces. Now, this could add up to love at first sight, but it might also mean that someone is sending you mixed signals and you're none too pleased about it. Your mission is to stay calm, ask pointed questions, and let them know you expect pointed answers.

Rewarding Days
2, 7, 15, 19, 24, 26

Challenging Days
4, 5, 8, 14, 23, 30, 31

Aquarius | April

Relaxation and Recreation

Venus will set off for your solar third house on April 5, Aquarius, all done up in impulsive Aries. Now, this house refers to the way we talk—and who we're talking with—so with this charming energy in assertive Aries, you'll be chatting up just about everybody who crosses your path. You'll also be quite persuasive. Smile pretty and sell your cause.

Lovers and Friends

The Moon will make contact with passionate, impulsive Mars on April 24, Aquarius, right smack dab in the middle of your solar eleventh house of friendships and group affiliations. If you're single, a friend of a friend could pique your interest, and since these two planets will be in fiery Sagittarius—well, let's just say things could move along rather quickly.

Money and Success

Mercury will set off for Taurus on April 5, Aquarius, which will put this thoughtful energy in your solar fourth house of home and family matters. If you've been thinking about buying your own home, take a peek around April 14, when a tip from a neighbor might bring you right to the front door of your new home.

Tricky Transits

If one of your kids has misbehaved—in a very big way—much as you dislike it, you might need to punish them. Mete out their punishment on April 30, when the Moon in your sign will get together with Saturn in an easy sextile and you'll find a fair and reasonable way to make the penalty fit the crime.

Rewarding Days

2, 3, 5, 12, 29

Challenging Days

4, 6, 10, 15, 16, 17

Aquarius | May

Relaxation and Recreation

A sky full of easygoing Taurus planets will make it easy for you to relax, Aquarius. This earthy sign just loves physical comforts, and with Venus set to remain on duty there until May 24, it's not hard to imagine you kicking back with a beverage in your hand. Do yourself a favor and try to stay away from the computer and the phone. Just for a little while.

Lovers and Friends

If you're unattached at the moment, Aquarius, look to May 24 for the chance to connect with a like-minded soul who'll appeal to you on a variety of levels, but most especially on the intellectual plane—which, of course, has to come first in your book. Venus will take off for chatty Gemini and your solar fifth house, bringing along new playmates with actual opinions.

Money and Success

Venus is quite powerful in Taurus, where she'll stay until May 24. Now, this lady knows quality when she sees it, and since she'll spend her time in your solar fourth house of home and family matters, you might need to raid your piggy bank for a domestic matter—but I'll bet you won't mind a bit.

Tricky Transits

Jupiter and Saturn will square off on May 26, Aquarius, creating tension between your solar eighth and eleventh houses. Now, the eighth house is where joint finances are handled, along with loans, so if you're after a mortgage or other installment loan, this might not be the best time to apply. May 30, however, is an entirely different story.

Rewarding Days

1, 2, 10, 13, 16, 20, 24

Challenging Days

4, 5, 25, 26, 27

Aquarius | June

Relaxation and Recreation

Oh, boy, Aquarius. You might not get much sleep this month, but you'll certainly have a great time. It seems that your solar fifth house of playmates and fun will play host to a bevy of quick-witted, fast-moving Gemini planets, all of which will be determined to keep your brain amused and your body active. Enjoy!

Lovers and Friends

The Universe is about to send a parade of Gemini planets through your solar fifth house of lovers, so you'll have your pick. Now, Gemini is a cerebral air sign like your own that just loves to chat, discuss, and learn, so chances are excellent that at least one someone will touch your brain just the right way—a prerequisite for anything more, in your book.

Money and Success

The New Moon on June 4 will team up with two action-oriented squares to bring along an unexpected expense, Aquarius, possibly related to your children. If they're in a bad spot, you might need to bail them out. On the other hand, if this isn't the first time and you've had this conversation before, it might be time for some tough love.

Tricky Transits

Assertive Mars will stop in his tracks on June 29 to turn direct, Aquarius, right in the middle of your solar tenth house of career and professional matters. Now, he's wearing intense Scorpio, so this could mean that there's a power struggle of some kind going on at work—but there are other far more appealing options. A sexy authority figure who's noticed you too? A long-overdue raise?

Rewarding Days
8, 12, 13, 19, 27

Challenging Days
1, 2, 3, 4, 24, 25

Aquarius | July

Relaxation and Recreation

The Sun, Venus, and Mercury will pass through Cancer this month, a family-oriented sign that just loves to be home with the kids. If you have some of your own, it's time for some quality time. The weekend of July 8 will be delightful fun with them—and you might even get some exciting news about a brand-new family member.

Lovers and Friends

If you've been seeing someone for a while now and your friends are curious, don't tease them anymore. Take advantage of the nice, peaceful trine Venus will form with Saturn on July 20, linking your solar seventh house of relationships with your solar eleventh house of groups. This is the stuff that long-lasting friendships are made of.

Money and Success

Venus will be in the mood to make some money this month, Aquarius. She'll get into an energizing sextile with generous Jupiter on July 1, who just so happens to be in your solar eighth house of shared resources— which bodes quite well for your financial situation. Now, when Mr. Extravagance meets Ms. Feelgood, it's easy to overspend, too. Take it easy with the plastic.

Tricky Transits

Venus and chatty Mercury will get together to form uneasy aspects with woozy Neptune and controlling Pluto on July 21, Aquarius. Now, they'll be in your solar seventh house of relationships at the time, so someone you adore may be going through a tough time. Talk it over and help them get to the real root of the issue.

Rewarding Days

18, 20, 26, 31

Challenging Days

2, 7, 10, 21, 24, 29

Aquarius | August

Relaxation and Recreation

Mars will set off for Sagittarius on August 2, Aquarius, putting this fiery fellow in the mood for adventure. Traveling with a group will be great fun, and you'll have some exciting new experiences. You might even run across someone delightful along the way who'll turn out to be more than just a friend—around August 16, in particular.

Lovers and Friends

It's a great month to be you, Aquarius. The Sun will spend his time in your solar seventh house of one-to-one relationships, all done up in fiery, playful Leo, guaranteeing you lively, entertaining companions. Plus Mars in equally fun-loving Sagittarius will spend his time in your solar eleventh house of friendships. Yes, indeed. It's time to socialize, mingle, and play with kindred spirits.

Money and Success

A pack of planets in hardworking, detail-oriented Virgo will pass through your solar eighth house this month, Aquarius, where matters concerning joint finances, loans, and inheritances are handled. If you're in the market for a mortgage, this is the time to explore your options. Look to August 27 or 28 to sign papers. Be sure to get it done before Mercury turns retrograde on August 30.

Tricky Transits

Mars will collide with Saturn on August 24, Aquarius, right smack dab in the middle of your solar eleventh house of friendships and group associations. This powerful team is perfect for working together with a team to get some work done, provided you have a clear goal in mind and the personnel you need to accomplish it. Otherwise, it could be quite the frustrating experience.

Rewarding Days
1, 2, 10, 11, 16, 18

Challenging Days
3, 7, 13, 14, 24, 25, 30

Aquarius | September

Relaxation and Recreation

The big astrological news this month is Jupiter's sign change, from Virgo to Libra. He'll move into this partner-oriented sign on September 9, which will place him in your solar ninth house of travel and new experiences. If you're off for a vacation with a partner, it's going to be absolutely unforgettable. Choose a place neither of you have ever visited and go exploring.

Lovers and Friends

Well! With loving Venus and generous, benevolent Jupiter in partner-loving Libra, it's not hard to imagine you spending an awful lot of time with someone delightful this month. This team is extremely good at creating camaraderie, by the way, so group experiences will also go quite well. If there's any way you can fit in some travel, this is the time to hit the road.

Money and Success

Your solar money axis will be triggered twice this month, Aquarius, by the Solar Eclipse on September 1 and the Lunar Eclipse on September 16. Now, eclipses bring about change of the sudden variety, so prepare yourself, but don't worry. First of all, you're always up for change. You find it invigorating. But remember, sudden windfalls also fall in the category of big money-related changes.

Tricky Transits

Mercury will be retrograde as the month begins, Aquarius, and he'll stay in that tricky condition until September 21. That said, September 1 and 21 could be challenging for travel, and since it looks like that's going to be on your agenda, try to plan around these dates. If you can't, do some serious troubleshooting before you go.

Rewarding Days
7, 8, 9, 19, 25, 30

Challenging Days
1, 11, 12, 13, 16, 21

Aquarius | October

Relaxation and Recreation

If you haven't yet taken that vacation we talked about last month, you really should try to arrange it during October. On October 6, curious, fast-moving Mercury will join Jupiter and the Sun in your solar ninth house of travel, the perfect team for exploring and adventuring. Of course, they're all wearing partner-loving Libra, so traveling in tandem would be especially enjoyable.

Lovers and Friends

Venus will take off for fun-loving, easygoing Sagittarius on October 17, Aquarius, which will put her in your solar eleventh house of group adventures and gatherings of kindred spirits. Now, this house just so happens to be your favorite—and you're probably going to love it even more on October 26, when Venus might direct your attention to that lovely stranger across the room.

Money and Success

Bright and early on October 1, Venus and Mercury will get together with Neptune, activating your solar eighth house of shared resources and joint finances, Aquarius. Now, Neptune has never been very good with details, so if you're about to negotiate a loan or mediate a money matter, get right on it.

Tricky Transits

October 2, 12, and 23 will play host to some uneasy energies, Aquarius, and in your case, it might be your personal finances that become quite challenging to handle. Dreamy Neptune will be involved, and she's been known to be in the neighborhood when misunderstandings occur. Be sure you've read and understood the fine print, and have someone else check for errors.

Rewarding Days

1, 4, 11, 14, 17, 26

Challenging Days

2, 7, 12, 13, 15, 19, 23

Aquarius | November

Relaxation and Recreation

Well, Aquarius, once again, it's travel, travel, and travel you'll most enjoy this month. Venus in Sagittarius will inspire you to make it a long-distance trip—say, to the other side of the country or even overseas, and on November 11 and 21, Mercury and the Sun will head off into that same sign. Got your passport? Good. Start packing.

Lovers and Friends

Mars will set off for your sign on November 8, Aquarius, and since you specialize in groups and friendships, he'll turn up the heat on your urge to mingle with like-minded others. Now, he's also quite the passionate fellow, so heaven help anyone who dares to disagree with your opinion on a cause that's near and dear to your heart.

Money and Success

On November 4, the lovely lady Venus will get into an easy trine with Uranus, your unpredictable ruling planet—and at the same time, she'll be forming a square with dreamy Neptune in your solar second house of money matters. Put those together and it's entirely possible that you'll win something that makes a dream come true. Lottery, anyone?

Tricky Transits

November 24 and 25 could be tricky to navigate, Aquarius, so listen up. Over that two-day period, Venus, Jupiter, and Pluto could cause you to get into a bit of an argument, most likely over money matters. If someone isn't pulling their weight, don't hesitate to call them on it. It's time to lay down the law and get the financial help you need.

Rewarding Days

1, 2, 4, 5, 15, 22, 23

Challenging Days

6, 18, 24, 25, 30

Aquarius | December

Relaxation and Recreation

Happy holidays, Aquarius! The Universe has arranged a wonderful month for you, full of warm gatherings that include long-distance friends and relatives you haven't seen in far too long. Mars in your sign will keep things exciting and give you the energy to keep up with a busy social life, and loving, affectionate Venus will help him out, as of December 7. Pass out some hugs!

Lovers and Friends

Once Venus enters your sign on December 7, the fun will really start, Aquarius. This charming energy will attract positive, optimistic people who share your core beliefs—and she might also introduce you to someone special through a friend of a friend or a family member who's been insisting you meet someone. Oh, go ahead. 'Tis the season for socializing.

Money and Success

Venus also rules money matters, Aquarius, and when she's in our sign, we all tend to do a bit more spending than usual. Of course, that's not surprising, given the season, but you really should at least try to rein in that urge just a tad. Gifts are nice, but your company is what matters most to others.

Tricky Transits

With the possible exception of Mercury's station to turn retrograde on December 19, there's really not going to be much to complain about in the heavens above this month. Now, New Year's Eve will be a different story. Impulsive Mars will collide with Neptune, and this is the stuff that misadventures are made of. Don't drive if you're indulging.

Rewarding Days

Just about all of them.

Challenging Days

19, 31

Aquarius Action Table

These dates reflect the best—but not the only—times for success and ease in these activities, according to your Sun sign.

	JAN	FEB	MAR	APR	MAY	JUN	JUL	AUG	SEP	OCT	NOV	DEC
Move	11, 12			13, 14, 15		5, 6, 7, 8		1, 28, 29, 30			18, 19	
Start a class	7, 8				22, 23			12, 13, 14		6, 7		4, 5
Join a club		8, 9, 10		11, 12			21, 22, 23		13, 14, 15		7, 8	
Ask for a raise		6, 7		27, 28			18, 19, 20				5, 6	
Look for work	9, 10		3, 4		25, 26			25, 26		19, 20		2, 3, 13, 14
Get pro advice			21, 22			21, 22			11, 12			
Get a loan	4, 5, 6		26, 27		19, 20, 21			10, 11			27, 28	
See a doctor		23, 24		17, 18		11, 12, 13			1, 28, 29			
Start a diet	24					20, 21				16, 17		29, 30
End relationship		1, 23, 24, 28, 29			21, 22		19, 20, 21				29, 30	
Buy clothes	18, 19			9, 10,			1, 27, 28			17, 18		
Get a makeover		14, 15			6, 7, 17, 18			23, 24				11, 12, 17, 18
New romance			8, 9			8, 9, 10			16, 17	1, 30	24, 25	
Vacation	7, 8		29, 30									

Pisces

The Fish
February 19 to March 20

♓

Element: Water

Quality: Mutable

Polarity: Yin/feminine

Planetary Ruler: Neptune

Meditation: I successfully navigate my emotions

Gemstone: Aquamarine

Power Stones: Amethyst, bloodstone, tourmaline

Key Phrase: I believe

Glyph: Two fish swimming in opposite directions

Anatomy: Feet, lymphatic system

Colors: Sea green, violet

Animals: Fish, sea mammals

Myths/Legends: Aphrodite, Buddha, Jesus of Nazareth

House: Twelfth

Opposite Sign: Virgo

Flower: Water lily

Keyword: Transcendence

The Pisces Personality

Your Strengths and Challenges

You're famous for those amazing antennae of yours, Pisces—and for good reason. They allow you to sense even the most subtle shift in your environment, connect intuitively with any living creature, and know right away whether or not someone is being honest with you. That's when you pay attention to them. When you don't, it's usually because you don't want to—because what you'd like to believe about someone is preferable to the reality of the situation. The thing is, reality and you don't always get along very well. You're an ultra-sensitive water creature—and that goes double now that Neptune, your ruler, is in your sign—so the harsh side of life on the planet can hurt. Really hurt. Loud noises, glaringly bright lights, angry, negative people…you can only handle them for so long, and then it's time to retreat, withdraw, and recharge your batteries. That's why you folks are so fond of escape hatches, and why they're absolutely necessary for you.

Now, on the positive side, you can find relief and comfort through spirituality, religion, or metaphysics, all of which allow you to make contact with The One—the very best way to soothe your tender little soul. Problems can arise, however, if you get into the habit of escaping through alcohol, drugs, or unhealthy fantasies. You're at your best when you're clear-headed and your antennae are operating without any baggage, so choose your getaways carefully. If all else fails, get thee to the water. The beach. The lake. Even a swimming pool will do in a pinch. You have so very much to offer to others—your kindness and compassion are legendary, as is your innate understanding of what makes others tick. You're particularly drawn to the helpless, the homeless, and strays of any species. There are plenty of positive, productive ways to extend yourself to them all, so make it your business to find them. Volunteer at a shelter. Attend spiritual gatherings. Your mission is to keep yourself away from negative vibes and unhealthy relationships. Surround yourself with kindred spirits who'll help you keep your faith in humanity alive and well. Your spirit will thank you for it.

Your Relationships

When it comes to love and kindness, Pisces, you have an endless supply, and you're always happy to pass some out to whoever needs it. That's a very, very good thing when you're with the right people. Relationships with kindred spirits will keep your heart happy and your attitude positive and upbeat. That said, once you find a like-minded soul and make a deep connection, you're in it for the long haul. That goes for friendships as well as romantic partners. You're a selfless, devoted lover and partner, and when you're with the right person, words are often unnecessary. You're also quite romantic. Candles, incense, bubble baths, and sweet, soft music are among the treats your lucky partner will enjoy. The sentimental, nostalgic side of you is also quite delightful. You often collect ticket stubs, pictures, and other mementos, and you love to bring them out and reminisce with your sweetheart by your side. Be very careful not to become involved with anyone shady or dishonest. If your gut tells you they're too good to be true, listen up and walk the other way.

Now, in friendships, the other water signs make fine choices. Home-loving Cancer will be only too happy to hang out at your place or theirs, listening to music and enjoying the company of family, pets, and other good friends. Scorpio's keen perceptive abilities will amaze and delight you, and the unending loyalty this sign is famous for is exactly what you need and will be happy to return. These signs are frequently who you'll choose when it comes to romantic partners, too. You might also find happiness in the arms of a stable earth sign, like practical Capricorn, whose love of structure and "just-the-facts-ma'am" attitude will balance nicely with your intuition, or solid Taurus, who'll consider it their mission to make you feel safe, secure, and confident.

Your Career and Money

Careers in the healing arts, such as massage, chiropractic, herbology, and feng shui, are often a natural fit for you, Pisces. More often than not, your amazing intuition will let you know exactly what needs healing in a person, as well as what to provide to heal it. And speaking of intuition, the metaphysical fields can offer you the opportunity to exercise your spiritual talents. Reading tarot, counseling with astrology, or becoming a psychic advisor would suit you just fine. You're the ultimate water sign, of course, so occupations that put you near water—or better still, in it—are great fun, and there are plenty to choose from, such as swimming instructor or underwater diver. Work that involves helping the underprivileged, the homeless, and the helpless is terrific for you, too. You'll find it endlessly rewarding—even if your tender heart does occasionally get broken. And speaking of your heart, you might want to consider a career that involves working with kids or adults with a disability, which will warm it up nicely. The care and comfort of animals should also be on your list. That goes double for strays, who'll bask in your much-needed love and compassion. Regardless of how you choose to earn your daily bread, you'll amaze coworkers and higher-ups with your ability to bond with others and your all-out willingness to tend to their needs.

Your Lighter Side

What's fun, Pisces? Well, anything involving water, of course. When you're walking on the beach, swimming in a pool, or enjoying watersports at the lake with your friends, you're a very happy camper. The side of you that adores fantasies will find a whole lot of pleasure in novels and films of that genre. Spiritual gatherings of any kind make your heart happy, and attending a séance or visiting with a psychic are endlessly fascinating. You also have a truly creative side, which is nicely fed by working with art or music, both of which come easily to you. Above all else, when you're out for rest or relaxation, be sure you're completely comfortable in your environment and in the company of kindred spirits.

Affirmation
My intuition guides me well.

The Year Ahead for Pisces

Jupiter is the heaven's answer to Santa Claus, Pisces, so wherever he travels, goodies, treats, and abundance follow—along with just a touch of excess and extravagance. Okay, more than a touch. At any rate, Jupiter will spend the entire year in your solar seventh house of one-to-one relationships, so it's not hard to imagine you making all kinds of new friends, most of whom will bring you luck, lollipops, and laughter. If you're happily attached, you two will have an absolutely terrific year, most of which you'll probably spend congratulating each other on your good taste in partners. Jupiter adores long-distance travel, so this would be the perfect time to take that cross-country or overseas trip you've been thinking of. Learning together is also a good idea, so take a look at a list of classes at an adult-education facility and find one that's to your liking. Now, Jupiter will be wearing precise, meticulous, detail-oriented Virgo, a combination that can certainly make mountains out of molehills. That means you'll have to be careful not to focus on the tiny habits or idiosyncrasies of others that tend to annoy you. You'll have to be even more careful not to pick at your partner when you're edgy or stressed. On the other hand, it might be others who seem to be pointing out your faults an awful lot or creating the kind of atmosphere that could have you walking on eggshells. For the most part, Jupiter's transits tend to be positive—but remember, he enlarges everything he touches, for better or worse. Your mission is to use the positive, optimistic, and generous side of this planet's energy in all your relationships, and to see to it that others do the same for you.

Now, let's talk about Mars, who'll spend an unusually long time in Sagittarius and your solar tenth house of career and professional matters. His trek through a sign is ordinarily about two months long, but this year, the grand total will be more like a bit less than five months. That said, you can count on being quite intently focused on the type of work you do. If it reflects your belief system and puts you in a positive atmosphere, Mars will heat things up and keep you extremely busy. If it doesn't, you'll want out, and you'll want out now. The thing is, if you're going to switch professions, much as it will be tough to stay put, stalking out and slamming the door behind you isn't a good idea if you don't have plan B in place and ready to go.

If that's the case, Mars's retrograde trip through Scorpio—from May 27 to June 29—will come in handy. He'll be in your solar ninth house of learning, giving you the energy and drive to get out there, explore your options, and even train for an entirely different occupation.

What This Year's Eclipses Mean for You

Well, to start with, two out of four of the upcoming eclipses will occur in your sign, Pisces, so you can expect some great big changes this year. There's no need to worry, though. Forewarned truly is forearmed when it comes to these tricky lunations. Now that you're aware they're coming, you can use their substantial energies wisely and productively.

Now, eclipses occur in pairs, two weeks apart, once every six months. In your case, they all seem to be set to influence your relationships during 2016, so get ready. The first Solar Eclipse of the year will take place in your sign on March 8, so if you were born close to that date, it will be a birthday to remember. Solar Eclipses bring the Sun and Moon together, a very powerful mix of energies. Your creative side will be running on high, so if you're into art, music, or performing, expect to be supercharged and ready to get your show on the road. Be careful not to begin any bad habits around this time, though, or they could become quite problematic in the fall.

The next eclipse will arrive on March 23, all done up in Libra, the most partner-oriented sign in the heavens. This will be a Lunar Eclipse—basically a high-octane Full Moon. Now, Full Moons are powerful in that they shed light on situations that might have previously been secret or hidden. Since this one will illuminate your solar eighth house of intimate encounters and joint resources, a debt could come to light or a loan might need to be repaid. If it's you who is owed, you'll have to be quite forceful to collect it. If not, it's time to take care of business. Someone near and dear to your heart may have a rather surprising announcement to make regarding a relationship matter, too.

The second Solar Eclipse of the year will take place on September 1, in your solar seventh house of one-to-one relationships. It will occur in detail-oriented Virgo, and since expansive Jupiter will also be on duty in that sign for another week or so, something insignificant could suddenly be blown out of proportion. It's your job to stay focused on what's important and rise above the petty. Virgo also rules work, so you might take on a partner, and if so, you'll be absolutely sure they're perfect for the job.

The final eclipse of 2016 will occur on September 16, once again in your sign. This time out, however, it will be a Lunar Eclipse, so the supercharged light of the Full Moon will illuminate your solar relationship axis. If you were born around March 15, this goes double. It's time to reassess what's working and what's not in this tender area of life. Your mission is to be totally honest with yourself and others, and to see that they return the favor.

Saturn

This strict taskmaster will spend the year in Sagittarius, a sign that makes him just a bit less strict. He'll be making his way through your solar tenth house of career matters, so a bonus, raise, or promotion is quite possible now. Chances are you've been working really hard for some time. The good news is that the powers that be have taken note of your efforts, and rewards will soon be coming your way. Saturn isn't easy, but he's fair. If you've earned it, you'll have it. If you're not happy with your current work, start investigating your options. Sagittarius planets love to travel, so you might consider taking a job that involves travel of the long-distance variety—and what fun that would be! This is the perfect time to learn a skill or go back to school to add to your resumé. Teaching is also a perfect use of this energy. Now, Saturn often brings along relationships with authority figures, so if you've had your eye on the boss, it might suddenly become clear that the boss has been returning the favor. In that case, as long as you're not jeopardizing your job, go for it. See what you've got there. Don't worry about age differences, either. Concentrate on what you two have in common.

Uranus

This unpredictable energy will be on duty in your solar second house of money matters and possessions once again this year, Pisces, and since he's all done up in impulsive Aries, you'll have to keep a careful eye on your finances. If you really want something, you'll be tempted to overspend or commit to monthly payments that aren't comfortable or reasonable. Don't do that. Remember, Uranus brings along major changes in the blink of an eye. In this house, he can make or break your financial situation, so don't get crazy. Shop around for the best deal. That goes double for electronics, computers, and other Uranian toys. This planet is a big fan of personal freedom, so you might also consider striking out on your own. Do your homework and have plan B ready to rock before you quit your day job. If you were born between March 6 and 17, you'll be enjoying a bit more specialized attention from this rebellious energy via a semisextile to your Sun. If anyone tells you that you can't, won't, or shouldn't—regardless of the subject—those words will have the opposite effect on you. If you need to stand up for yourself, you'll be well equipped to do it, but try not to rebel just for the sake of rebelling. This house also rules personal values, so be sure that whatever you choose to do supports your beliefs and ideals.

Neptune

If you were born between February 24 and March 4, Neptune has been or will soon be sitting right on top of your Sun—for quite some time. As you know, since she's your ruling planet, her visits are powerful, and remember, Neptune dissolves boundaries. This might mean that your psychic abilities have been keener than ever, or you may begin to feel them gradually strengthening. If your work doesn't have a spiritual or metaphysical aspect to it, you'll want that to be the case now. The good news is that you'll be able to sense the right path for you, so trust your intuition above all else and be totally honest with yourself. If you're not happy with habits you've begun or ended, it's time to change all that. Get back into a positive, productive state of mind and spirit, and get rid of whatever isn't doing you any favors. If it's a relationship that's having a negative influence on you, you'll do what comes naturally to end it: you'll disappear. Not all at once, of course, just a little bit at a time. You'll withdraw yourself gradually until the person finally realizes that you're no longer interested in sharing your life with them. You'll be especially sensitive to your environment, so stay away from bright lights, loud sounds, or angry people. Your mission is to avoid the urge to escape from it all by becoming addicted to drugs, alcohol, or anything else that muddies up your vision and shuts down your instincts.

Pluto

Pluto will continue to make his way through Capricorn and your solar eleventh house of groups, friendships, and social gatherings, Pisces. If you've suddenly discovered you're not at all satisfied with the choices you've made in that department, do the Pluto thing and ditch what's no longer working. You could feel betrayed or manipulated by someone, in which case, they need to leave your life. Period. It's okay, though. Your interests are changing, as well as your goals for the future, and you'll need to be around others who have already arrived or can at least put you on the right path toward having the life you want. It's time for a five-year plan. Just be sure it's reasonable, and stick to it. If you were born between March 5 and 9, your Sun will be enjoying a sextile from this powerful planet during 2016—and this is the type of transit people would pay big bucks for. Pluto regenerates and rejuvenates, so regardless of what you've been through recently, you'll be able to let it go and move forward, if you haven't already. He's also the kind of planet that inspires us to take charge of our lives, and provides us with the willpower and determination to stick to our guns. Think of it as being temporarily endowed with superpowers. You can make anything happen now, so figure out what you want and set some major life changes in motion.

Pisces | January

Relaxation and Recreation

With Jupiter set to spend the month in Virgo and your solar seventh house of one-to-one relationships, Pisces, one thing is for sure: you will have far more fun this month if you share it with just one special person. Jupiter loves long-distance travel, so if you two have been planning a trip, stop putting it off and go!

Lovers and Friends

Loving Venus will spend her time in Sagittarius and your solar tenth house of career matters and dealings with authority figures, Pisces, straight through until January 23. That gives you three good weeks to use her charms to promote yourself on the job—and with lucky Sagittarius energy on board, that won't be hard. Promotions, bonuses, and raises are all possible now.

Money and Success

Venus will march off into efficient, no-nonsense Capricorn on January 23, and together with a Full Moon, will shed some much-needed light on a financial situation that's been rather problematic lately. You might also be asked to assume leadership of a group you're involved with. Think about it, but don't worry. With Venus on duty, all will very likely go well.

Tricky Transits

Mercury will turn retrograde on January 5, Pisces, and thanks to his presence in Aquarius, he'll spend the first few days of it inspiring you to think about a friendship that's been a bit disappointing lately. If you've got to finally cut ties with someone, this is the time to do it. Afterward, Mercury will be in authoritative Capricorn and your solar eleventh house, also related to groups. Grab the steering wheel and drive.

Rewarding Days

12, 13, 14, 23, 27, 30

Challenging Days

3, 5, 7, 20, 22, 29

Pisces | February

Relaxation and Recreation

Jupiter will continue on his merry way through your solar seventh house of one-to-one relationships, Pisces, urging you to expand your horizons with your significant other. Take a trip, take a class, or have an adventure together. If you're single, remember: Jupiter arrives with an entourage, so expect a veritable buffet of new admirers.

Lovers and Friends

Passionate Mars in sexy Scorpio will get together with the lovely lady Venus on February 7, Pisces, urging you to throw caution to the wind and allow yourself the luxury of getting up close and personally involved with that certain someone you're madly attracted to. Get to know them well, and by the Full Moon on February 22, you two might be quite the item.

Money and Success

Venus will get together with intense Pluto on February 5, Pisces, and a financial issue related to loans, inheritances, or joint resources could be tough to navigate. If someone else has been managing your money, your best bet is to take charge of the situation. That includes the checkbook, the plastic, and all dealings with the authority figures involved.

Tricky Transits

Communicating with your sweetheart could be challenging around February 27, thanks to an uncomfortable inconjunct between chatty Mercury and Jupiter, in your solar seventh house of one-to-one relationships. If you need to put some distance between the two of you until you figure out how to say what's on your mind, do it. Everything will be better by the next day.

Rewarding Days

3, 4, 7, 8, 14, 22, 29

Challenging Days

6, 10, 27

Pisces | March

Relaxation and Recreation

With a pack of planets making their way through your sign and your solar first house of personality and appearance, you probably won't get much sleep this month, but you'll definitely have the chance to relax with friends, family, and your significant other. In the long run, of course, recharging your batteries by surrounding yourself with warm, happy people is just as good as eight solid hours of sleep.

Lovers and Friends

The lovely lady Venus, the Goddess of Love herself, will tiptoe delicately into your sign on March 12, Pisces. Now, this will be just a few days after a Solar Eclipse, also in your sign, so if you're single, someone quite romantic this way comes. Just be sure you're seeing them clearly. If you're attached, you can count on your partner to be sympathetic, understanding, and helpful.

Money and Success

If you're after a loan and looking for quick approval, Pisces, set up your appointment on March 16 or 17. Lucky, generous Jupiter in your solar seventh house of one-to-one relationships will provide you with someone benevolent and helpful to give you a hand with the details, and thorough, practical Pluto in Capricorn will see to it that the authorities in charge are quite cooperative.

Tricky Transits

A Lunar Eclipse in partner-oriented Libra will arrive on March 23, Pisces, and along with a testy square between no-nonsense Saturn and expansive Jupiter—who, you'll remember, is in your solar seventh house of one-to-one relationships—this eclipse might bring along some fireworks in the relationship department. Try to keep a cool head.

Rewarding Days

2, 6, 7, 10, 12, 16, 26

Challenging Days

5, 14, 22, 23, 25

Pisces | April

Relaxation and Recreation

A break in the action will be exactly what you need to recharge your batteries around April 13, 14, and 15, Pisces, so be sure to plan ahead and give yourself some time alone or with someone you trust implicitly. As per usual, your spirit will do best if you also allow yourself some quality time near a large body of water.

Lovers and Friends

Venus will spend her time in fiery, impulsive, and pretty darn assertive Aries from April 5 through April 29, Pisces, so if you're taken with someone or they with you, one of you will take the initiative, march over boldly, and ask—quite passionately—for the pleasure of your company. Resistance will be futile, so don't even try.

Money and Success

Once Venus settles into quality-conscious Taurus on April 29, financial matters will be far easier to navigate. Before that, however, and from April 5 on, you'll have to watch for a tendency to spend what you don't have on impulse or to make financial commitments that will be tough to accommodate in your present situation.

Tricky Transits

Mars will turn retrograde on April 17, Pisces, and may open up an old wound. If that's the case, you'll need to keep reminding yourself that the past is the past, which might not be easy. Of course, since Mars will be all done up in travel-loving Sagittarius, it might also be that you'll take a last-minute trip back home, or to a far-off place you haven't visited in a very long time.

Rewarding Days
5, 12, 13, 14, 18

Challenging Days
4, 10, 15, 16, 17, 19, 28

Pisces | May

Relaxation and Recreation

The Sun, Venus, and Mercury will take turns this month forming fun, stimulating sextiles with Neptune, your ruling planet, so get thee to the water. A vacation by the ocean or a week up at the cabin, lakeside, would be ideal, but a pool will do in a pinch. If you're feeling extravagant, a cruise might also be in order.

Lovers and Friends

The parade is about to begin, Pisces, so get yourself a good seat and prepare to be presented with all kinds of choices in this tender department. Loving Venus has been on duty in your solar third house, so you've been meeting a whole lot of new folks lately, and it seems that many of them are interested in getting to know you better. What fun!

Money and Success

Venus will be in Taurus until May 24, Pisces, which just so happens to be the sign more often thought of as a money magnet. Investments you make between May 10 and 13 will be quite profitable. Oh, and get yourself a lottery ticket—just one, now, not a hundred. It only takes one to win.

Tricky Transits

On May 26, Jupiter will square off with Saturn, possibly putting some stress on your relationship with your partner. If it's your work that's the issue—too much of it for your partner's taste, that is—remind them that you can't play if you don't have the means. Authority figures could be problematic around that time. Don't feel pressured by someone who expects more than you can reasonably deliver.

Rewarding Days

1, 2, 6, 7, 9, 10, 12, 13, 30

Challenging Days

4, 5, 21, 22, 23, 26

Pisces | June

Relaxation and Recreation

Several planets will dash through lighthearted Gemini this month, a restless sign that's never been able to tolerate boredom. These planets will pump up the pace of your family life and bring visitors to your home, many of whom you probably haven't seen in a while. A cookout or family reunion is definitely in order. Yes, at your place. Delegate the cleanup and enjoy yourself.

Lovers and Friends

Venus will take off for your solar fifth house of lovers and playmates on June 17, Pisces, all done up in home-loving Cancer. Entertaining at your place will be great fun, and it might be time to introduce a certain someone to your family. Shoot for June 27. If you're attached, expect terrific news from your partner around that same time.

Money and Success

The opportunity to work from your home could come along around June 12 or 13, so if you've pretty much perfected a craft or hobby, it might be time to show your work around. What starts out as a part-time source of added income could soon turn into your full-time work. People have been telling you to do this for years. Make it happen.

Tricky Transits

Saturn will square off with Neptune on June 17, forcing us all to wake up and smell the coffee. In your case, a rather rude awakening with regard to a higher-up or an authority figure might be on the astrological agenda. If you're presented with some disturbing information about someone you thought you knew, be sure it's true, then take steps to get them out of your life.

Rewarding Days
12, 13, 24, 25, 26, 27

Challenging Days
1, 2, 4, 16, 17, 18, 20, 22

Pisces | July

Relaxation and Recreation

This is your kind of month, Pisces. The Sun, Venus, Mercury, Mars, and Neptune will be in water signs, for starters, so you'll be comfortable expressing your feelings. They'll all take turns forming happy trines and sextiles with Jupiter in your solar seventh house of one-to-one encounters, too. Talk about a good time! Lots of warm hugs are on your agenda. Enjoy!

Lovers and Friends

What a terrific month to be you! The lovely lady Venus will spend her time in your solar fifth house of lovers and playmates, and Jupiter will continue on his path through your solar seventh house of one-to-one relationships. Yes, indeed. Whether you're single or attached, expect lots of sweet romance. The New Moon on July 4 could bring along the announcement of a new arrival, too.

Money and Success

If you're after a high-ticket item, try to hang on until July 20, when Venus and Saturn will get together to see to it that you find what you need at the perfect price. Likewise, if you're planning a trip, you can put down your deposits now and rest assured that a good time will be had by all.

Tricky Transits

A long-distance call or email could hold some rather stressful news around July 16, 28, or 29, and you might need to travel quite suddenly to be with a loved one who's going through a tough time. Fortunately, you'll be able to count on your family and your partner for support. Try not to get too stressed. Remember, this too shall pass.

Rewarding Days

1, 3, 5, 6, 8, 9, 19, 20, 21

Challenging Days

7, 10, 11, 16, 29

Pisces | August

Relaxation and Recreation

The Sun will spend the first three weeks of August in playful Leo and your solar sixth house of work, Pisces, so if you haven't taken a vacation yet, it's prime time. You won't feel like doing anything that even remotely resembles work, so why force yourself if you don't have to? If you do have to, however, make sure your evenings are free for fun.

Lovers and Friends

Venus will be in Virgo and your solar seventh house from August 5 through August 29, Pisces—which certainly sounds like someone's going to be busy in the department of romance. If you're happily attached, you two should warn your friends that they might not see much of you. If you're single, it's time to mingle.

Money and Success

The opportunity to add to your income through a part-time job could arrive around August 16, and chances are good it will involve doing something you just love. Might be a hobby, might be a craft, might be working with kids. On August 27, luck will be with you. Expect happy financial news from your partner.

Tricky Transits

Mercury and Venus will get into an astrological shouting match with Saturn and Mars on August 6, Pisces, and since the subject will probably be money, you might expect an argument over who's responsible for what. If it's not a major problem, try not to make too much out of it. If it is, lay down the law in no uncertain terms.

Rewarding Days
1, 8, 9, 10, 16, 22, 27, 28

Challenging Days
5, 6, 7, 13, 14, 19

Pisces | September

Relaxation and Recreation

Everything will be more fun with a companion this month, Pisces, since Jupiter is off for partner-loving Libra on September 9. The Sun and Venus will also make their way through that sign, so compromise will be easy to come by. Making amends will go smoothly, too. Your mission is to resist the urge to do anything that might cause the need for it.

Lovers and Friends

There will be two eclipses this month, Pisces, on September 1 and 16. Both will affect your solar seventh house of one-to-one relationships, so buckle up and prepare for some major changes. Someone new will be along to rock your world, for better or worse. Take your time getting to know them. If you're involved and tempted to stray, think it over carefully.

Money and Success

Stability will be on the agenda in this department on September 6 and 7, Pisces, thanks to a lovely sextile between Venus and solid Saturn. If you've earned a raise or bonus, it will either arrive soon or be set in the works that day. Finding something practical and affordable will be easy, so if you need to shop, get thee to the mall.

Tricky Transits

Mercury will be retrograde in your solar seventh house of relationships until September 21, so getting in touch with someone could be problematic, especially if they don't live nearby. If you're attached, be very careful to choose your words with an eye toward keeping things clear between you and your partner. Honest, open communication is the key.

Rewarding Days

5, 6, 7, 19, 20, 23, 24, 25

Challenging Days

9, 10, 12, 13, 18, 21

Pisces | October

Relaxation and Recreation

If you're in the mood to travel, make your plans around October 26. Book your lodgings, make your reservations, and put down your deposits. If you're already on the road and you happen to be single, someone delightful will be along to serve as tour guide and a whole lot more. It's playtime. Enjoy!

Lovers and Friends

Venus will spend her time in your solar fifth house of lovers straight through October 17, Pisces, which is always a good thing—but she'll also be wearing her sexy Scorpio outfit. Yes, indeed. Sounds like someone's going to be quite preoccupied with dimly lit places in the company of someone delicious. Better not forget your vitamins.

Money and Success

The Full Moon of October 15 will shine a bright light directly into your solar second house of money matters and personal finances, helping to clear up an issue that's been rather murky lately. If you're not working, a job opportunity could arrive that day, and if so, it will get you back on your feet in no time flat.

Tricky Transits

Fiery Mars will square off with unpredictable Uranus on October 28, making it absolutely vital that you keep yourself safe. When these two irritate each other, events are fast and furious. If you feel as if a situation is about to turn volatile, get away, right away. Don't get in a vehicle with anyone who's not in any condition to drive.

Rewarding Days

1, 2, 3, 4, 14

Challenging Days

5, 7, 13, 15, 16, 28

Pisces | November

Relaxation and Recreation
Mercury, Venus, and the Sun will take turns passing through Sagittarius this month, Pisces, making this prime time to expand your horizons. Take a trip to somewhere you've never visited, or sign up for classes on a subject that has always fascinated you. If you've ever wanted to learn another language, it will come easily to you now.

Lovers and Friends
Venus will take off for sturdy, reliable Capricorn on November 11, putting you in the mood to settle down. The thing is, it might be a former friends-only relationship that appeals to you, and if so, the feeling will be mutual. Just be sure you can go back to being friends if things don't work out between you romantically.

Money and Success
Careful now, Pisces. Venus will be in Sagittarius until November 11, plenty of time for her to convince you to go overboard in money matters. It's easy to forget that a piece of plastic will turn into a debt within a month, but lest you choose to ignore that fact, it might be best to entrust your credit cards to a friend with a lot of willpower.

Tricky Transits
Jupiter and Pluto will square off on November 24, Pisces, putting these two astrological superpowers in the mood to do battle. Their dispute will activate your solar eighth house and your solar eleventh house, so financial matters involving groups could be tricky to negotiate and might not end well. If someone asks for a loan, be sure they know when it will need to be paid back.

Rewarding Days
1, 2, 5, 11, 19

Challenging Days
4, 6, 18, 23, 24, 25

Pisces | December

Relaxation and Recreation

Just in time to make the holidays delightful, Saturn and Uranus will get into an easy trine, bringing well-deserved surprises your way in the department of career and professional matters. You may be starting the new year with a new job or an increase in your paycheck. With financial worries eased up, you can relax and enjoy your time with family and friends.

Lovers and Friends

Mercury will set off for your solar eleventh house of friendships on December 2, Pisces, all done up in sturdy, reliable Capricorn. Someone—at least one someone—will go out of their way to make sure you know how much your stable presence in their life has meant. If you need help of any kind, you won't have to look far to find it. You may not even have to ask.

Money and Success

A happy change in your financial situation is due this month, Pisces, but it may not kick in until after the first of the year. Expect the news to arrive between December 9 and 11, and prepare to celebrate. That said, do your best not to spend what you don't yet have. Your loved ones will always prefer your company to a gift anyway.

Tricky Transits

Behaving yourself this New Year's Eve won't be easy, Pisces, but you really should give it a shot. Fiery Mars will collide with Neptune, your ruling planet, both of them in your very own sign. If you must indulge, be sure you're not driving and don't accept a ride from anyone who's been drinking. Matter of fact, grab their keys and hide them.

Rewarding Days
9, 10, 11, 24, 25, 26

Challenging Days
18, 19, 31

Pisces Action Table

These dates reflect the best—but not the only—times for success and ease in these activities, according to your Sun sign.

	JAN	FEB	MAR	APR	MAY	JUN	JUL	AUG	SEP	OCT	NOV	DEC
Move			16, 17, 18		10, 11		4, 5					15, 16
Start a class	11, 12		23, 24	25, 26		26		12, 13			7, 8	
Join a club		8, 9, 10			1, 27, 28					11, 12, 13		
Ask for a raise	13, 14		26, 27				21, 22		1, 2, 7, 8			29, 30, 31
Look for work		6, 7, 8		1, 2, 27, 28		3, 4	14, 15		8, 9		5, 6	
Get pro advice			21, 22			23, 24	18, 19			8, 9		19, 20
Get a loan	4, 5, 6				20, 21			10, 11			1, 27, 28	
See a doctor		7	22			11, 12				26, 27		19, 20, 21
Start a diet		24, 25		22, 23			19, 20		16, 17, 18		29, 30	
End relationship	24, 25				18, 19			18, 19				29, 30
Buy clothes			12, 13				11, 12, 27, 28			3, 4	14, 15	
Get a makeover		14, 15, 16	8, 9		6, 7				21, 22	17, 18		11, 12
New romance				5, 6, 7, 8, 9		20, 24		2, 3	3, 4, 5			
Vacation		3, 4, 5			22, 23						1, 2, 3	

Notes

Notes

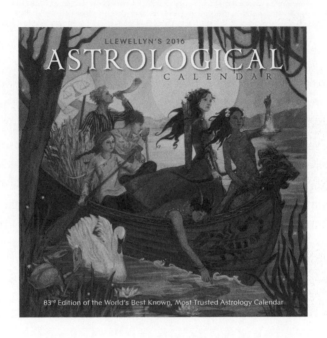

Llewellyn's 2016 Astrological Calendar
Horoscopes for You Plus an Introduction to Astrology

Llewellyn's Astrological Calendar is the best-known, most trusted astrological calendar sold today. Everyone, even beginners, can use this beautiful and practical calendar to plan the year wisely.

There are monthly horoscopes, best days for planting and fishing, rewarding and challenging days, travel forecasts, and an astrology primer. Advanced astrologers will find major daily aspects and a wealth of other essential astrological information.

This edition features Kim Kincaid's gorgeous artwork, inspired by the signs and symbols of astrology.

978-0-7387-3409-5, 40 pp., 12 x 12   **U.S. $14.99**

Complete Astrology
At-A-Glance

LLEWELLYN'S 2016
Daily
Planetary
Guide

Your Best Opportunity Periods
from Jim Shawvan and
Forecasts by Pam Ciampi

Llewellyn's 2016 Daily Planetary Guide
Complete Astrology At-A-Glance

Empower your life with the most trusted and detailed astrological guide available. Take advantage of cosmic forces on a daily, weekly, or monthly basis with *Llewellyn's Daily Planetary Guide*.

With exact times down to the minute, this astrological planner lists ideal times to do anything. Before setting up a job interview, signing a contract, or scheduling anything important, consult the weekly forecasts and Opportunity Periods—times when the positive flow of energy is at its peak.

Even beginners can use this powerful planner, which includes a primer on the planets, signs, houses, and how to use this guide.

978-0-7387-3407-1, 208 pp., 5 x 8¼ $12.99

Llewellyn's
2016
ASTROLOGICAL
POCKET PLANNER

DAILY EPHEMERIS & ASPECTARIAN
2015–2017

Llewellyn's 2016 Astrological Pocket Planner
Daily Ephemeris & Aspectarian 2015–2017

Empower your future—plan important events, set goals, and organize your life—with *Llewellyn's Astrological Pocket Planner*. Both beginners and advanced astrologers can use this award-winning datebook, the only one to offer three years of ephemeris and aspectarian data.

Choose optimal dates for job interviews, weddings, business meetings, and other important occasions. Pinpoint ideal times to plant a garden, begin new projects, conduct self-reflection, go fishing, and more. Avoid planetary pitfalls by following the easy-to-read retrograde and Moon void-of-course tables.

Comprehensive and compact, *Llewellyn's 2016 Astrological Pocket Planner* also contains time zone information and space to jot down your daily appointments.

978-0-7387-3408-8, 192 pp., 4¼ x 6⁵⁄₁₆   **$8.99**

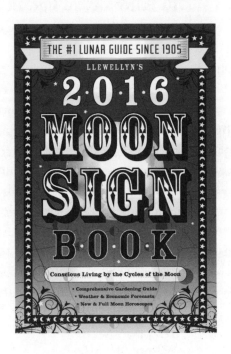

THE #1 LUNAR GUIDE SINCE 1905

LLEWELLYN'S

2·0·1·6

MOON SIGN BOOK

Conscious Living by the Cycles of the Moon

• Comprehensive Gardening Guide
• Weather & Economic Forecasts
• New & Full Moon Horoscopes

Llewellyn's 2016 Moon Sign Book
Conscious Living by the Cycles of the Moon

Since 1905, *Llewellyn's Moon Sign Book* has helped millions take advantage of the Moon's dynamic energies. Use this essential life-planning tool to choose the best dates for almost anything: getting married, buying or selling your home, requesting a promotion, applying for a loan, traveling, having surgery, seeing the dentist, picking mushrooms, and much more. With lunar timing tips on planting and harvesting and a guide to companion plants, this popular guide is also a gardener's best friend. In addition to New and Full Moon forecasts for the year, you'll find insightful articles on growing a tea garden, cultivating roses, organic and natural food labeling, the Moon and earthquakes, outer planets in water signs, and Greek lunar folklore.

978-0-7387-3404-0, 312 pp., 5¼ x 8 $11.99

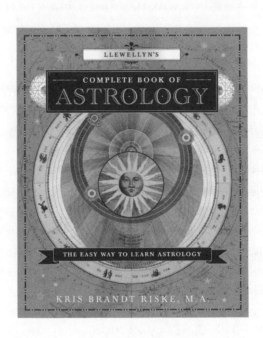

LLEWELLYN'S

COMPLETE BOOK OF

ASTROLOGY

THE EASY WAY TO LEARN ASTROLOGY

KRIS BRANDT RISKE, M.A.

Llewellyn's Complete Book of Astrology
The Easy Way to Learn Astrology
KRIS BRANDT RISKE, M.A.

The horoscope is filled with insights into personal traits, talents, and life possibilities. With *Llewellyn's Complete Book of Astrology*, you can learn to read and understand this amazing cosmic road map for yourself and others.

Professional astrologer Kris Brandt Riske introduces the many mysterious parts that make up the horoscope, devoting special attention to three popular areas of interest: relationships, career, and money. Friendly and easy to follow, this comprehensive book guides you to explore the zodiac signs, planets, houses, and aspects, and teaches how to synthesize this valuable information.

Once you learn the language of astrology, you'll be able to read birth charts for yourself and others, determine compatibility between two people, track your earning potential, uncover areas of opportunity or challenge, and analyze your career path.

978-0-7387-1071-6, 336 pp., 8 x 10 $19.99

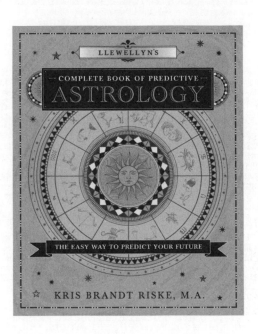

LLEWELLYN'S

COMPLETE BOOK OF PREDICTIVE

ASTROLOGY

THE EASY WAY TO PREDICT YOUR FUTURE

KRIS BRANDT RISKE, M.A.

Llewellyn's Complete Book
of Predictive Astrology
The Easy Way to Predict Your Future
KRIS BRANDT RISKE, M.A.

Find out what potential the future holds and use those insights to create the life you desire with this definitive guide to predictive astrology.

In her signature easy-to-understand style, popular astrologer Kris Brandt Riske offers step-by-step instructions for performing each major predictive technique—solar arcs, progressions, transits, lunar cycles, and planetary returns—along with an introduction to horary astrology. Discover how to read all elements of a predictive chart and pinpoint when changes in your career, relationships, finances, and other important areas of life are on the horizon.

Also included are several example charts based on the lives of the author's clients and celebrities such as Marilyn Monroe, Martha Stewart, and Pamela Anderson.

978-0-7387-2755-4, 288 pp., 8 x 10 $18.95

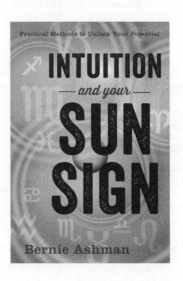

Practical Methods to Unlock Your Potential

INTUITION
—and your—
SUN
SIGN

Bernie Ashman

Intuition and Your Sun Sign
Practical Methods to Unlock Your Potential
BERNIE ASHMAN

Your hidden spiritual and practical gifts come alive when you make the most of your intuitive potential. Astrologer Bernie Ashman reveals how to use a basic understanding of astrology to instantly tap into and use your varied intuitive gifts to overcome blocks and find the mental clarity you seek.

You'll need no astrological background to make use of this information in practical situations. Even more excitingly, you'll develop your own insights and intuition about others, letting you make better choices quickly and more easily and raising your self-confidence. Looking at someone else's Sun sign will allow you to communicate with them better, bringing improved harmony and understanding to your relationships. You'll master challenges, improve your imagination, achieve goals, and find personal empowerment.

978-0-7387-3894-9, 360 pp., 6 x 9   **$18.99**

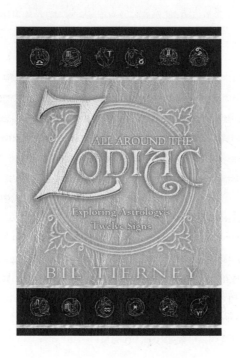

ALL AROUND THE

Zodiac

Exploring Astrology's
Twelve Signs

BIL TIERNEY

All Around the Zodiac
Exploring Astrology's Twelve Signs
BIL TIERNEY

Here is a fresh, in-depth perspective on the zodiac you thought you knew. This book provides a revealing new look at the astrological signs, from Aries to Pisces. Gain a deeper understanding of how each sign motivates you to grow and evolve in consciousness. How does Aries work with Pisces? What does Gemini have in common with Scorpio? *All Around the Zodiac* is the only book on the market to explore these sign combinations to such a degree.

Not your typical Sun sign guide, this book is broken into three parts. Part 1 defines the signs, part 2 analyzes the expression of sixty-six pairs of signs, and part 3 designates the expression of the planets and houses in the signs.

978-0-7387-0111-0, 480 pp., 6 x 9   **$22.99**

Bernie Ashman

SUN SIGNS

&

PAST LIVES

Your Soul's Evolutionary Path

Sun Signs & Past Lives
Your Soul's Evolutionary Path
BERNIE ASHMAN

Discover how to break free from destructive past-life patterns and reach your full potential.

Sun Signs & Past Lives offers an easy, foolproof way to pinpoint behaviors that may be holding you back from a rewarding life of peace and fulfillment. All you need to know is your birthday. Bernie Ashman divides each Sun sign into three energy zones, allowing easy access to innate strengths and the spiritual lessons for this lifetime. With his guidance, you'll discover how to transform these precious insights into action—reverse negative past-life tendencies, find healing, discover your life purpose, and get back on the road to empowerment.

978-0-7387-2107-1, 264 pp., 6 x 9   **$16.95**